# The Oxford Introductions to U.S. Law

# Intellectual Property

The Oxford Introductions to U.S. Law

# Intellectual Property

DAN HUNTER

Dennis Patterson, Series Editor
The Oxford Introductions to U.S. Law

OXFORD
UNIVERSITY PRESS

# OXFORD
UNIVERSITY PRESS

*Oxford University Press, Inc., publishes works that further Oxford University's objective of excellence in research, scholarship, and education.*

Oxford  New York
Auckland  Cape Town  Dar es Salaam  Hong Kong  Karachi  Kuala Lumpur
Madrid  Melbourne  Mexico City  Nairobi  New Delhi  Shanghai  Taipei  Toronto

With offices in
Argentina  Austria  Brazil  Chile  Czech Republic  France  Greece  Guatemala
Hungary  Italy  Japan  Poland  Portugal  Singapore  South Korea  Switzerland
Thailand  Turkey  Ukraine  Vietnam

Copyright © 2012 by Dan Hunter

Published by Oxford University Press, Inc.
198 Madison Avenue, New York, New York 10016

Oxford is a registered trademark of Oxford University Press
Oxford University Press is a registered trademark of Oxford University Press, Inc.

Library of Congress Cataloging-in-Publication Data
Hunter, Dan, Prof.
  The Oxford introductions to U.S. Law : intellectual property / Dan Hunter.
    p. cm. — (Oxford introductions to US law)
  Includes index.
  ISBN 978-0-19-534060-0 ((pbk.) : alk. paper)
  1.  Intellectual property—United States. I. Title.
  KF2979.H86      2011
  346.7304'8—dc23                                                    2011028493

1 2 3 4 5 6 7 8 9

Printed in the United States of America on acid-free paper

**Note to Readers**
This publication is designed to provide accurate and authoritative information in regard to the subject matter covered. It is based upon sources believed to be accurate and reliable and is intended to be current as of the time it was written. It is sold with the understanding that the publisher is not engaged in rendering legal, accounting, or other professional services. If legal advice or other expert assistance is required, the services of a competent professional person should be sought. Also, to confirm that the information has not been affected or changed by recent developments, traditional legal research techniques should be used, including checking primary sources where appropriate.

*(Based on the Declaration of Principles jointly adopted by a Committee of the American Bar Association and a Committee of Publishers and Associations.)*

You may order this or any other Oxford University Press publication by visiting the Oxford University Press website at www.oup.com

For Elena and Nate

"[Congress may make laws]...To promote the Progress of Science and the useful Arts, by securing for limited Times to Authors and Inventors the exclusive Right to their respective Writings and Discoveries."—U.S. Constitution, Article I, Section 8, Clause 8

"Overprotecting intellectual property is as harmful as under-protecting it. Creativity is impossible without a rich public domain. Nothing today, likely nothing since we tamed fire, is genuinely new: Culture, like science and technology, grows by accretion, each new creator building on the works of those who came before. Overprotection stifles the very creative forces it's supposed to nurture." — Judge Kozinski[1]

"I am aware that copyright must have a limit, because that is required by the Constitution of the United States ... When I appeared before ... [a] committee of the House of Lords the chairman asked me what limit I would propose. I said, 'Perpetuity.'" —Mark Twain[2]

---

1. White v. Samsung Elecs, Am., Inc., 989 F.2d 1512, 1513 (9th Cir. 1993) (Kozinski C.J. dissenting).

2. Mark Twain, December 6, 1906, appearing before the Congressional Committee deciding on the proposed Copyright Bill.

# Contents

# Acknowledgments

Many people helped enormously in creating this book. Rather than try to list everyone's contribution, let me just thank all of the following for all of their work, their editorial help, their citation checking, their corrections of my legal errors and English grammar, their editorial suggestions, and, most of all, their kindness. I owe a great deal more than thanks to Derek Bambauer, Megan Carpenter, Katherine Cooper, Shana Don, James Grimmelmann, Nyasha Foy, Tim Hunter, Steve Kahn, Greg Lastowka, Joe Miller, Raphael Majma, James Major, Beth Noveck, Kaydi Osowski, Jessica Picone, Jillian Raines, and Courtney Thorpe.

# Preface

This book provides an overview of the laws of intellectual property, and does so by focusing on the battles that are fought over these laws.

Any number of texts provide basic introductions to intellectual property law and practice, and they all explain the basics of copyright, patent, trademark, trade secret, and related laws. Like this book, those introductory texts all detail, for example, how fair use operates as a defense to copyright infringement, they all discuss the requirements of misappropriation in trade secret protection, they all walk the reader through the way that file wrapper estoppel operates in patent law, and they all note the significance of secondary meaning in trademark law. And they all make the assertion, explicitly or implicitly, that intellectual property is a boon for society because it encourages the production of such vital products as AIDS drugs, the Coca-Cola logo, or books such as this one. Few of these other texts explain why intellectual property is a legal area where the people who teach the subject are often its strident critics. Few if any of those introductory primers note the presence of strong activist movements against patent, copyright, and trademark laws. And none of them spend much, if any, time exploring the political economy of intellectual property—the influence of money, the tireless efforts of lobbyists, and the failings of legislators and judges—or the psychology and rhetoric of possession and control that operate within this hotly contested arena of law.

This book is intended to provide you with a basic overview of intellectual property, but more importantly, it is intended to explain how and why battles about intellectual property are fought, and to provide a way to understand how these battles might and should be resolved. I wanted to call this book *A Dyspeptic Introduction to Intellectual Property*, but the publishers understandably said "Um, no." But even if the modifying adjective is not in the title, the description is accurate because it conveys the sense that intellectual property may well be a good thing in society, but it's not a *wholly* good thing. Any worthwhile introduction to intellectual property should give you, the reader, some indication of the queasiness and uncertainty of its field of study. Innovation is a fundamentally wonderful thing, and intellectual property has contributed greatly to the myriad innovations that we enjoy, love, and need in our modern lives. But there is evidence that the expansion of intellectual property has reduced innovation by stopping others from implementing their great ideas or producing their new work. Any serious introduction of intellectual property should be a little suspect of the laws it describes. So this work will endeavor to explain intellectual property by seeking to sail between the Scylla of Joyous Embrace and the Charybdis of Despairing Rejection. Little is gained by uncritical acceptance of the current regime of intellectual property law, but then equally little is gained by its wholesale snubbing.

This book will therefore provide a guide to the current laws of the various regimes of intellectual property, and will explain how we got here. One of the characteristic features of intellectual property over the last fifty to a hundred years has been its relentless expansion, and so this book will explain the process of expansion and the territorial wars that have emerged from it. As the empire of intellectual property has grown, various tribes have fought battles over the expansion. At times the battle has been between two competing interests, such as those over the point at which competitors can begin to reproduce the idea in a patent to make a cheaper, generic competing drug. At other times the battle is a contest between private property interests and those who represent the public interest, or the interests of those in developing countries, or those who are just not crazy about the dominance of property systems. Like most wars, no side is completely virtuous or completely evil, and no side can claim always to have acted wholly honorably. There is the danger that in using the metaphor of territory and war that I'll simplify nuanced and sophisticated positions into a banal Manichaean struggle. So I will try to provide as neutral an account as I can, even though I am as partisan as any commentator in the intellectual property arena.

But in thinking about modern intellectual property in this way, as we discuss the details of the current laws I hope you will be able to see how innovation and progress is linked to intellectual property law. I also hope that you will be able to see how numerous small changes in intellectual property law have had significant consequences for our society. And, I hope that, as you learn the law, you will discover for yourself your political orientation in relation to intellectual property.

# ONE

# Introduction

*INTELLECTUAL PROPERTY* IS THE expression used to denote a series of legal principles and domains that create exclusive rights in intangible "property of the mind." Thus, the federal statutes that establish and regulate copyrights, patents, and trademarks are commonly referred to as intellectual property laws, as are various state statutes and common laws dealing with issues such as trade secrets, rights of publicity, celebrity rights, and even some types of unfair competition. Although they differ dramatically in their historical development, their subject matter, their reasons for existence, and their specifics, these laws share certain characteristics that mean that they can be treated as a distinct category of law. Most important, they all confer in one shape or another state-sanctioned exclusive rights of use for the specific types of intangible things. In other words, they create a monopoly right for certain types of imaginary property.

Intellectual property rights are fundamental to social progress and innovation, and they have become central to the sorts of businesses that characterize modern economies. Newspapers, book publishers, television broadcasters, software developers, music labels, movie studios, web studios, graphic designers, fashion houses, and all manner of media companies assert copyrights over various types of content, in all its myriad forms. Drug companies, semiconductor chip fabricators, financiers, and inventors of all stripes claim patent and/or trade secret protection for their commercially valuable innovations. Celebrities assert rights over the use of pictures of them. And the significance of trademarks is obvious to anyone who has been confronted by the serried ranks of brands in the supermarket, or who has walked down the street and tried to count the number of trademarks arrayed on storefronts or stamped on products as diverse as banking services, candy bars, and cars. And what of anyone who has watched an hour of network television and noted the advertisements and brand placement at every level? If it can be said that the Industrial Age was built out of legal and social control of land, plant, and heavy equipment, then the post-Industrial Age is built around control over intangibles such as brands, information, celebrity, and ideas. And these are the province of intellectual property.

So it's not far-fetched to claim that intellectual property is one of the most important legal subjects for modern society: it is like the air around us, invisible and unseen, but vital to our functioning. But intellectual property is more interesting than this, because much of it is founded on a strange, inconsistent premise. We create the monopolies of intellectual property in order to increase the amount and types of valuable innovation and information in our society. Thus, the main justification for the grant of intellectual property is to increase knowledge. But in order to increase knowledge, we have to restrict it. For that is what property rights confer: an exclusive right for me, the property owner, to stop you and the world at large from using my property without my permission. And while this *may* make sense when it comes to physical property such as my car or my computer where your use of it deprives me of it— what the economists call a "rivalrous" good—it makes less sense when we consider the non-rival nature of the sorts of things that intellectual property laws protect. My creation of a generic "knock-off" of the chemical structure of Viagra does not deprive the patent owner of the use of its drug; my listening to an illegal recording of Katy Perry's latest masterpiece does not stop others from listening to it; my use of the likeness of Arnold Schwarzenegger on a bobble-head doll does not deprive him of using his likeness.

Thus, the core of intellectual property does not operate in the same way as regular property. But more than this, the increasing significance of intellectual property in society has led to the emergence of two distinct groups: those who see intellectual property as wholly important and socially beneficial, and those who argue that intellectual property cuts down on expression and makes felons of ordinary citizens. This is a strange development. It wasn't long ago—probably not more than twenty years—when intellectual property law was seen as a wholly positive force in society. In those simpler times, intellectual property was thought to guarantee social progress, promote innovation, and (no doubt one day) cure baldness. But within the blink of an eye, the golden period faded, and intellectual property became a mare's nest. In the field of copyright, scholars and civil society groups led a series of attacks on term extensions. They claimed that by extending rights to private owners, we were diminishing the "public domain" (whatever that might mean). Within patent law we witnessed increasing concerns about the extension of patent scope and the grant of wildly overbroad patents, and recently a number of civil society groups announced plans to challenge the grant of those patents that they see as the worst offenders. Internationally, criticism was leveled at the role of Western intellectual property policy on developing nations in areas such as plant and seed protection, access to essential medicines, and development of indigenous high-technology industries. At the same time, intellectual property owners such as music labels and movie studios became terrified of the internet and peer-to-peer file sharing, and daily foretold the deaths of their industries at the hands of billions upon billions of "intellectual property thieves and pirates." Where once intellectual property was seen as good for everyone, we now survey a modern day Hobbesean battlefield that pits all against all.

This book provides an explanation of the laws of intellectual property, as well as one of the ideology and politics that shape these laws. This chapter will introduce the history of intellectual property as a whole and provide some basic discussion of the theories and justifications that underlie intellectual property. Subsequent chapters will explore the main regimes that make up the collection of laws that we call intellectual property. Chapter 2 will discuss copyright, Chapter 3 will deal with patent, Chapter 4 trademark, and Chapter 5 trade secrets. The final chapter will cover the remaining mixed bag of state and federal laws that fit, untidily, into the intellectual property domain. Within each chapter on the substantive areas of law, the basic format will be the same: each will begin by looking at the history and theory of the applicable law, and then focus on the creation of the rights within that regime and the way in which those rights are infringed, then survey the available defenses. Finally, each chapter reviews the current fault lines in that law by examining the main criticisms that have been leveled at it. The idea behind adopting this structure for each chapter is to provide a balance between the theory and the principles that you need to know in order to be able to understand intellectual property law. This common structure will also demonstrate that each area of law comes from a specific historical milieu, with specific sorts of justifications for its existence, but that all types of intellectual property law create a type of property right that the plaintiff has to establish, and upon which the defendant may or may not be infringing.

In the chapters that follow we will examine the theory and principles of the main types of intellectual property in some detail, but it's worth spending a moment to consider the basic scope of the laws that we will soon study in more detail. Copyright protects works of authorship—things such as books, magazine articles, computer programs, drawings, movies, and so on. Anything that is created by an author is probably protected by copyright, and it's protected for a really long time: typically the life of the author plus seventy years. Patent law, on the other hand, only protects creations for twenty years, but it protects ideas and inventions, and that protection—for reasons we'll see later—is much broader than copyright allows. Trade secret law, similar to patent law, generally protects commercially valuable ideas—such as the recipe for KFC chicken or customer lists—and does so for an even longer period, potentially forever. But trade secrets are very fragile, and once the secret leaks out, there is little that the law will do for the wronged plaintiff. Celebrity rights—also called rights of publicity—are created under state laws, and generally protect the commercial persona of well-known singers, actors, and athletes. And, finally, trademarks don't try to protect ideas, creations, or personas, but rather brands that indicate where a product comes from.

In the subsequent chapters we'll spend a lot of time fleshing out the details underlying this sketch. But before we do so, we need to understand the "how" and "why" of intellectual property; that is, we need to understand the historical development and the theories underlying intellectual property law. And so it's these two topics that we consider in the remainder of this chapter.

## ⚅ History

For much of human history there has not been a concept called "intellectual property," although there have, of course, been various laws and concepts that were precursors to the myriad laws that make up that category in modern times. To understand many features of our current systems, it's useful to look at how we got to where we are today.

The first stage in the development of intellectual property is what we might call the Premodern Period. Prior to the Enlightenment, there were various actions and laws that are often denoted as the beginning of the intellectual property system. Since historical records are sparse prior to the Classical Period, the earliest examples of intellectual property rights usually come from Ancient Greek and Roman times, including the efforts of Roman courts to forbid third parties from corrupting slaves so that they will disclose information about their owners' business secrets, and examples of Greek pottery with trademarks impressed in the clay. However after this, and during the medieval era, we find few examples of intellectual property law, in large part it seems because the political institutions of the period were attuned to different needs. The feudal system did not recognize private property except through the system of estates that derived from the Crown. Protection of ideas during this period seems to have been relatively unimportant because of the nature of feudalism, which emphasized control over land and over people rather than over ideas. And of course trade was relatively small-scale and local. Thus, during this time there was little in the way of precursors to patent or trade secret protection. And, until the invention of the printing press, there was little need for a set of laws to protect expression; thus copyright didn't exist.

The second stage in the development of intellectual property can be called the Early Modern Period, which began in the period after the Enlightenment with the rise of the Westphalian state and the emergence of large-scale trading between states. Numerous features contributed to the development of intellectual property as a significant artifact of this era, principally the appearance of mercantilism (the first time that merchants were granted autonomy to produce and trade goods), the emergence of trade guilds (which policed the knowledge of their members), and the new interest of rulers in gaining competitive advantage within their new geographic boundaries.

It's reasonable to identify the birth of modern intellectual property as the patent system that emerged in Venice during the fifteenth century. With the rise of the modern state, European rulers came to issue *letters patent*, a term derived from the Latin *litterae patentes* or "open letters." These were letters from the sovereign to everyone, stating that a group or an individual now had the monopoly to produce an identified product (or the monopoly to ply a given trade) within the sovereign's realm. These monopolies covered a huge range of industries and products and were *not* issued for the reasons that underlie modern intellectual property. They were as likely to be issued to court favorites in order to control the production of gunpowder, or certain types of clothing, as they were to inventors conferring a benefit on society. But in 1474 the senate in the Republic of Venice passed an act that began intellectual property as we know it:

> Be it enacted that, by the authority of this Council, every person who shall build any new and ingenious device in this City, not previously made in this Commonwealth, shall give notice of it to the office of our General Welfare Board when it has been reduced to perfection so that it can be used and operated. It being forbidden to every other person in any of our territories and towns to make any further device conforming with and similar to said one, without the consent and license of the author, for the term of 10 years. And if anybody builds it in violation hereof, the aforesaid author and inventor shall be entitled to have him summoned before any Magistrate of this City, by which Magistrate the said infringer shall be constrained to pay him one hundred ducats; and the device shall be destroyed at once.[1]

These types of intellectual monopolies spread outward within Europe. From the late fifteenth century until the late seventeenth century, the development of intellectual property occurred through the intertwined development of guilds and the advancement of the autonomous nation-state. Guilds such as those controlling the glassblowers of Murano sought to advance their interests and consolidate their power by protecting the secret processes of their trade, and by ensuring there were no lateral entrants into their business. The state was happy to use the guilds and the rise of mercantilism generally as part of its competitive advantage, at first militarily and then for the benefits conferred by international trade and domestic taxation of the industry. Thus European states enacted the modern precursors of trade secret laws protecting the

---

1. Giuli Madlich, Venetian Patents (1450–1550), 30 J. PAT. & TRADEMARK OFF. SOC'Y 166, 177 (1948).

secrets of the guilds while modern precursors to the patent system granting monopolies to the guild emerged throughout the city-states and nation-states of Europe.

Copyright emerged in a similar way. Johannes Gutenberg developed the printing press around 1440, and worked on perfecting it for the next twelve years. The year 1452 saw the first printed edition of the Bible, an event that profoundly changed the world. Venice was again notable for its speed in adopting the new printing technology and for encouraging its use within the city by granting monopolies. It granted its first print-related patent in 1469 to Johann Speyer, giving him the monopoly over all book printing in the territories for the subsequent five years. Printing spread throughout Europe during the next hundred years, and, like other trades, was carefully overseen by the sovereign and the guilds.

The U.S. tradition of copyright stems from the English copyright system, one that emerged from the response of the English Crown to the revolution of printing. William Caxton brought the printing press from the Continent to England in 1476, setting up in Westminster and changing forever the relationship between sovereign and subject. The opportunity for widespread dissemination of printed documents—including seditious material—was suddenly a pressing political concern. Unsurprisingly, the response of the Crown was to try to police printing and printing presses as completely and efficiently as possible. Initially the approach was to control the presses directly, but during the period 1486 to 1557 there was great experimentation with printing privileges and letters patent, and a better system emerged. The Crown delegated control of the presses to a guild of printers who were given enormous trade advantages as a result, and whose self-interest in maintaining their monopoly transformed them into literary enforcers for the Crown. This guild was called the Stationers' Company, and the publication rights granted to the guild during this period were not similar in any meaningful sense to the copyright we know today. The "copy" right was a right to print, and it was granted to the authorized printer—or "stationer" as the printer was then called—rather than the author. It was the stationer's copy right that was infringed when an unauthorized copy was made by a rival printer. Authors didn't feature much, if at all, in this system of copy right, and certainly there was no conception that authorship of the work was the significant event: printing was all. Royalties for authors were essentially unknown, and if payment to an author was made at all—many works were simply printed without the author's approval or even involvement—it was usually the case that the stationer would commission a book from an author for a lump sum, at which point the author's economic, legal, and practical interests in the work were extinguished.

This system went on for the better part of 159 years, during which societal attitudes to the Crown and censorship changed, and the first intimations of democracy emerged within the British state. Censorship by the Crown became more unpalatable and with this, the power of the Stationers' Company declined. This brought competition from other printers and, in response, the Stationers sought newer and greater protections against piracy. Eventually these protections were enacted in the Statute of Anne 1709, the world's first modern copyright act and one that ushered in a series of profound changes. We will examine this act in the next chapter, but the important difference to understand here is that it was the first act that provided protection to the author, rather than to the state, the church, or the printer. As a practical and commercial matter, the author would transfer his or her interest to the publisher in order to make enough money to live; but, for the first time, there was a law that created the starting position that authors had rights over their intellectual product. This marked the beginning of what we can think of as the third stage in the development of intellectual property, the Modern Period, in which the laws developed their recognizable current form.

In each of the chapters below we will examine how the fundamental change of the Statute of Anne—granting the creator the initial rights—worked its way through the different intellectual property regimes, and how over time it came to be expressed in U.S. law.

The basic story of intellectual property protection in the Modern Period from the early 1700s to the beginning of the twentieth century was an initial recognition, and then slow expansion, of the rights of authors, inventors, and creators. The three fundamental grants of intellectual property interests—patent, copyright, and trademark—were relatively both narrow and unimportant. There was the understanding that certain types of businesses deserved some special protections as otherwise they could not flourish. So patent law developed to provide monopolies in certain industries, for example those dealing with mechanical or chemical processes, and copyright developed to deal with the interests of book authors, newspapers, and publishers. Few other businesses cared much about either regime. During this period, trade secrets and trademarks were important (but not central) to the operation of many businesses. On the whole, industries during the Modern Period didn't care that much about intellectual property. Rather, they cared about the factory, the production line, and the land on which these were sited: this was the property that mattered.

As the Modern Period advanced, the importance of industrial production waned. No longer were heavy machinery and physical plant the predominant means of production, and physical inventory wasn't the most important asset. In the developed world, control over intangibles came to dominate the business agenda, and thereby the political agenda. In the latter part of the twentieth century the importance of property interests in these intangibles—information, brands, pharmaceuticals, and so on—became obvious to business and government, and so the intellectual property system grew. This stage we'll call the Late Modern Period, and we're living in it now.

The Late Modern Period of intellectual property law is defined by two trends: the extensive expansion of intellectual property protection, and the eventual opposition against this expansion by various publicly oriented groups. The expansion during the latter half of the twentieth century was profound. Copyright had been limited in its infancy to protecting maps, charts, and books. During the Late

Modern Period it broadened to encompass musical and dramatic works, photographs, movies, sound recordings, software, architectural drawings, and the like. As we'll see in the next chapter, the term of protection was extended from a modest period—initially a slim fourteen years, with the chance of one extension of fourteen years—to increasingly extended periods each time Congress considered the matter, eventually reaching a period of life-plus-seventy-years. Patent law followed the same path: its scope widened, over time annexing new inventive territories such as plants, surgical procedures, computer algorithms, and business methods. Eventually even life-forms became patentable, including gene sequences of the human genome. The strict early patent requirement that only the specific claims could be infringed was loosened with the introduction of the doctrine of equivalents, giving judges the flexibility to determine that nonidentical-but-equivalent methods were infringing. Trademarks too were set loose from their historical moorings. The trademark term was extended, and the prototypical application of a physical brand to a physical product no longer marked the limit of trademark's dominion. Not only could the hourglass shape of the Coke bottle be a trademark in itself, but sounds such as the Harley-Davidson exhaust note for motorcycles, the fragrance on sewing thread, or the distinctive color of dry cleaning pads were protected by trademarks.

At first these manifold expansions were ignored, not only by socially progressive commentators but by the public. The growth of intellectual property didn't seem to involve a reduction of any interests in the common wealth. Of course, the grant of a patent over a new class of inventions, a new form of trademark, or the extension of a copyright might affect a direct competitor—but after all, that's just business. Society at large just didn't care much, and the expansion of private interests didn't awaken any public concern. However, there has long been the sense that the public does have some stake here. The concept of the *public domain* was first advanced in 1896, in a Supreme Court case involving the Singer sewing machine. The court noted that upon the expiration of a patent, the public gained the right to exploit the technology: in the court's words, the invention fell into the public domain. However, over the following eighty or ninety years, as intellectual property rose in importance, the concept of the public domain was either ignored, or defined in negative terms: the public domain was what remained after all the private interests had been allocated. It was the carcass left after the intellectual property system had eaten its fill.

In the late 1970s David Lange, then a young Duke law professor, attended an entertainment law symposium to present a paper on the right of publicity, in light of two cases before the California courts asking whether the heirs of Bela Lugosi and Rudolph Valentino could control the representation of these famous actors after their deaths. Lange thought this was a technical question that might be of narrow interest to estate lawyers and those lucky few who are strangely excited by the law of succession. He was surprised at the distress of a group of screenwriters who attended his presentation and peppered him with fearful questions. Rather than rejoicing in greater protection, they saw the recognition of celebrity publicity rights as taking something away from them: they said that if the courts expanded publicity rights, writers would have a harder time adapting, using, or re-imagining the histories of famous people. As Lange described it years later, "the law of publicity was dispossessing individual creators in order to benefit the interests of celebrities." From this epiphany, Lange recast the public domain: rather than being the negative leftovers, it was a vital, affirmative entity, the publicly accessible collection of knowledge, ideas, history, and expression on which creators draw in order to make new works. It was, in short, the repository of public culture. The concern that motivated Lange—and the issue that made his paper more than a doctrinally interesting law article—was the recognition that if private interests were to continue to expand, they would eventually overrun the public domain altogether, and thereby choke off all creativity.

From this beginning, the movement in defense of the public domain grew slowly. It was another ten years before law professors began systematically to analyze the importance of the public domain to the intellectual property system and to society, but eventually they did. Scholars voiced concern about the expansion of intellectual property in various arenas, and began to react against the one-way ratchet of intellectual property expansion. However, their concerns were mostly ignored. Perhaps the public indifference can best be explained by an absence of compelling examples where creators were obviously disenfranchised as a result of the diminution of the public domain. It wasn't until the introduction in 1998 of two pieces of legislation that these examples became clear, and at this point activists and theorists were galvanized.

Two acts in 1998, the Sonny Bono Copyright Term Extension Act and the Digital Millennium Copyright Act, did a number of things: they extended copyright terms, renewed copyrights on some works that had already fallen into the public domain, and made illegal the circumvention of digital locks on copyright works (the so-called "anti-circumvention provisions"). But more importantly, perhaps, these statutes motivated public-interest groups in a way that had never occurred before. Up until the passing of this legislation, corporate interests lobbied for intellectual property expansion without much (if any) public comment. These two statutes changed that. Not only were they widely recognized as driven entirely by corporate interests—the copyright term extension was (not unfairly) seen as motivated by the Disney Corporation's fear that Mickey Mouse's first film, *Steamboat Willie*, would soon fall into the hands of the public—but the unanticipated uses of the statutes, and of the DMCA in particular, drew widespread attention. Computer scientists were appalled when a Princeton computer science professor was threatened with prosecution under the anti-circumvention provisions of the DMCA if he disclosed research that he and his lab had performed in breaking the preferred encryption system of the music industry. A Russian computer science student was arrested by the FBI while presenting a paper at a conference that demonstrated how his software made it possible to read Adobe's digitally encrypted electronic books. As a result, computer scientists boycotted U.S.

computer security conferences, while others were warned to stay away for fear of being jailed for discussing computer security. By the time that students at Swarthmore College were threatened with an injunction against posting details of a potential election scandal involving electronic voting machines, the message was clear to many civil society groups. The restrictions on speech, the threat to research and enquiry, the quashing of dissent, the jailing of researchers: all of Lange's worst fears and then some were now realized. Intellectual property was choking the public domain and public discourse. But unlike previous times when this had happened, the public started to notice, and activists began attacking the intellectual property system.

The challenge to intellectual property is most evident in copyright; indeed copyright reform is the only part of the movement that is publicly recognizable outside the specialist legal literature. Most of the credit for this can be attributed to Larry Lessig's popularizing works *The Future of Ideas* and *Free Culture*. In these he argued that we need to wind back intellectual property expansion in order to protect the public domain and the commons environments that allow for creative activity. Though he is widely considered the leader of the copyright reform movement, many others have joined the battle on the side of the reformers. Yochai Benkler, Siva Vaidhyanathan, and others make the case for a significantly more circumscribed copyright system than we currently enjoy.

Outside of copyright, intellectual property reform is less well-known, but no less important for its obscurity. Patent law has been the subject of ever-increasing scrutiny. Domestically, there has emerged a concern with overbroad patent grants as a result of new patent categories and a perception that patents were not being appropriately scrutinized. This is most evident in the flurry of commentary over the grant of business-method patents that seem as though they should never have been granted in the first place. (How could it be that Amazon could obtain a patent for "inventing" one-click shopping?) The vast increase in the number of filings of patent applications, and the sense that the system had failed to weed out unmeritorious claims, has led to civil society responses. In trademark law also we have seen numerous scholarly concerns raised about changes allowing for new types of infringements that don't rely on consumer confusion, and for extensions to the law that apply trademarks to domain names.

We will look in more detail at each of these concerns in the chapters that follow. But it's important to understand the way the Late Modern Period of intellectual property is defined by expansion and opposition. There is a culture war being waged at the moment, but unlike the conflict between the left and right in U.S. politics (which is often called the "culture war"), this isn't a war *between* cultures, but a war *over* our culture. Who owns it, who controls it, who can use it in the future, and how much it will cost? This is where the history of intellectual property has brought us, and this is the battlefield that we will explore in the subsequent chapters.

In order to make some sense of how to resolve these battles, it will be important to understand our current theoretical approach to intellectual property. Once we understand why we have intellectual property in our society, it will be easier to make some decisions about its appropriate limits, and who should win in the war over the appropriate boundaries of intellectual property.

## Theory

Any law needs some reason for being, of course, otherwise why bother to enact it? But more than this general observation, any type of law relating to property entitlements requires a set of very clear justifications, because property laws involve the transfer of the means of production from one entity to another. The laws of intellectual property are particularly troublesome in this regard because they also involve ownership of ideas, control over elements of our culture, and rights over speech itself. We should therefore be fairly clear about why we are granting private interests over these high-value and high-stakes elements of our society.

In the sections below we examine the three basic normative justifications for the existence of various intellectual property laws. These justifications are based (1) in economic or utilitarian theory, (2) on the labor-desert theory of John Locke, and (3) in the personality theory derived from Hegel and Kant. We'll briefly examine these three different approaches and talk in broad terms about how they are applied to the different regimes of intellectual property. Then in the later chapters we'll come back to these theories in more detail, and examine how they affect the specifics of the law that we are studying at that stage.

### Economic and Utilitarian Theory

Jeremy Bentham's philosophy of utilitarianism has become the dominant justification for the creation of private property, and intellectual property is no different. Bentham suggested that the appropriate basis for making important social decisions is to ask what will provide the greatest good for the greatest number—what he called the "felicific calculus"—and this philosophy provides the basis for the modern application of economics to almost every field of human endeavor and for the ascendancy of justifications that are predicated on conceptions of utility, rather than immanent or deontological precepts of the good. Utilitarianism as the basis for decisions about social policy has been formalized in the law and economics movement, and its precepts can be found in almost every justification given for the introduction of new laws in federal and state legislatures. Within the subset of law that concerns itself with property, utilitarianism is invoked to give a warrant to private property generally, and to provide a relatively simple bright-line policy. Thus, according to utilitarianism, we should grant private property interests if to do so would increase overall utility. And as a corollary, numerous accounts suggest that we are all better off if we initially grant private interests, because it increases investment, avoids the tragedy of the commons, or otherwise generates some other similar useful outcome.

Intellectual property is no different. There are two main uses of utilitarianism as justifications for intellectual property. The first is in relation to patent and copyright (and to a lesser extent trade secrets and publicity rights), whereas the second is within trademark.

## Copyright, Patent, and Related Rights

Within copyright and patent law, utilitarianism is applied to the problem of underproduction. The argument is that copyrights and patents suffer from what is called the "public goods" problem: everybody gets the benefit once they are produced, but no one wants to pay to create them. This is because once they are produced, they are free to everyone to use, so the creator can't charge a price for the use that recovers the cost of creation. Consider lighthouses. Let's say that I notice that there are a lot of ships foundering off the coast, and that I happen to be able to build and operate a lighthouse that will stop this from happening. (I have access to the land and materials with which to build, and am happy to become a lighthouse keeper). Presumably the owners of the ships that sink, and of the cargoes that are lost, would be delighted about the existence of my lighthouse, and so I should be able to charge a price to them to create and operate it. But of course, I realize that I can't charge them a price, because once I build the lighthouse, every ship's master can avoid the shore by using the light of my lighthouse. I can ask them to pay for the light, but I can't force them to pay in a market exchange. The light from my lighthouse is thus a public good, because I can't insist on a private transaction for its use. And thus when I consider whether I should build and operate the lighthouse, I'm going to realize that it's a bad idea, and so I'll take my resources somewhere else—investing them in a hedge fund or a plastic surgery clinic. And so the social benefit of my lighthouse is lost to society.

So too with copyright and patents. I have the Great American Novel inside me, or the formula for the newest erectile dysfunction drug. I know that I can invest the time and money necessary to bring these creations to market, but I also know that they are public goods and so—the very second that I produce the first one—some free rider will swoop in and copy, reproduce, or otherwise set up in competition to me. Thus, in the absence of any way to ensure that this doesn't happen, I will decide that I'm going to invest my talents and resources elsewhere, and become a private equity trader or a plastic surgeon. And thus the latest wonderful work or invention will be lost to the world.

Many intellectual property laws can be justified based on this concern, and indeed the utilitarian justification is the one that is usually the starting point when people ask why we have copyright, patent, or even trade secret law. These laws provide for an exclusive right or a monopoly over some part of the intangible idea or product to ensure that production occurs in the first place. Without copyright (it is said), I won't produce the next Great American Novel because I know I will be ripped off; but with copyright, I will produce it, because I can get a return on the investment of the years writing it, since no one else is legally entitled to copy it. The same is true for an expensive-to-produce drug, or the secret formula to Coke that without protection would otherwise be lost to the world.

The incentive justification, based on utilitarianism and economics, is the primary justification given for much of intellectual property. The Progress Clause of the Constitution specifically provides for this incentive justification: it says that Congress may make laws for patents and copyright "[t]o promote the Progress of Science and useful Arts." The Progress Clause is explicitly utilitarian; it allows for a limited monopoly in order to provide an incentive for the production of otherwise underproduced inventions and works. The Supreme Court also has adopted this utilitarian justification in deciding intellectual property cases dealing with copyright[2] and patent,[3] and it is clear that the Court these days considers this to be the main reason for these types of laws.

The main problem with this justification—and it is a problem that we will see emerge time and again in later chapters—is that there is conflicting evidence as to whether there would be an underproduction of works and ideas if we didn't have the utilitarian incentive for intellectual property laws. The recent rise of the open source movement, Wikipedia, blogs, and numerous other internet-enabled content has demonstrated that people produce creative works and ideas in situations where they have no economic reason for doing so. Further, numerous industries have pointed to the way that the grant of rights disincentivizes certain types of activities and makes some types of innovation impossible, because it either crowds out altruistic behavior or creates barriers to the production of these sorts of innovation (due to thickets, high costs, or whatever). As we'll see in the discussion in subsequent chapters, numerous commentaries have emerged critiquing the descriptive basis of the incentive justification within copyright, patent, and trade secret law.

### Trademark

Trademark is also dependent on utilitarianism and economics for its main justification. It is important to recognize that trademarks are completely different than copyrights and patents: there is absolutely no danger that there will be an underproduction of trademarks—take a look at a NASCAR race if you want proof—and, unlike copyright works and patented inventions, a trademark is not

---

2. *See e.g.* Mazer v. Stein, 347 U.S. 201, 219 (1954); New York Times Co. v. Tasini, 533 U.S. 483, 495 (2001).

3. Precision Instrument Mfg. Co. v. Auto. Maint. Mach. Co., 324 U.S. 806, 816 (1945).

a worthwhile social object in itself (i.e., not like a novel, or a newspaper, or the design for a better mousetrap).

At its core, a trademark is a way for consumers to identify the source of a product so that they can make better purchasing decisions. Say that today you buy a soda at lunch that you happen to like: it's delicious, it's fizzy, it has an excellent balance between sugar and cola flavors. Tomorrow you want to purchase the same product. How are you going to be able to do this? Well, if today you buy a drink that is labeled "Coke" or "Coca-Cola," which comes in a bright red can with a white ribbon, or an hourglass-shaped bottle, you are likely to recall these features. So tomorrow you can walk into the bodega and buy the same drink, just by asking for a Coke or picking out the distinctive can or bottle from the refrigerator.

In this view of trademark law, the main theoretical justification from utilitarianism stems from the benefit conferred by marks to the costs that the consumer faces in his or her search for products. Trademarks lower the search costs of the consumer because, having once bought and liked Coke, or having been recommended a Coke by their friends, consumers are able to rely on the stability of the trademark to be able, time after time, to buy a drink that meets their preferences. The payoff to the firm is the flip side of this: it gets a reputational benefit from the stability in the trademark because competitors can't use it. It is therefore motivated to invest in the stable quality of the trademarked product since no one can free ride on its mark. The search costs justification in trademark relies on lowering costs and improving quality, and is explicitly an economic argument derived from utilitarianism.

The other main reason that is posited for trademarks is an unfair competition justification that suggests it is unfair to allow competitors to free ride on the positive reputation that a mark owner has created in its mark. This too is a kind of economic/utilitarian justification, since it seems to assume, implicitly, that if we allow this kind of unfair free riding, the firm will eventually stop marking its products with a stable trademark, or it will stop investing in quality control. This will create an environment where no marks exist, and consumers will be forced to find other higher-cost ways of identifying the products they want. This is expensive, wasteful, and inefficient: all of which, utilitarianism suggests, is a socially retrograde way of regulating. Thus we should provide for a trademark system that resembles our own—one that allows consumers to rely on a stable identifier of the source of the product or service.

In Chapter 4 we will investigate this justification for the existence of trademark law, and will discover some unusual features of trademark that can't easily be reconciled with this account.

## Labor-Desert Theory

The second type of justification is the labor-desert theory, and its genesis is usually attributed to John Locke. It begins with the proposition that resources of all sorts are initially held in common for all to use. Locke captured this idea in an arresting image: he said "in the beginning all the world was America."[4] He meant that America, at the time he was writing, was a seemingly boundless resource, the benefits of which everyone shared in. If, in the state of nature that we find the resource, everyone shares in it, then how can we justify the grant of private property to one individual? Well, if people take the common resource and mix their labor with it, then they deserve to reap the benefits of that admixture of initial resource and their labor. Or, in Locke's own words: "[w]hatsoever [man] removes out of the state that nature hath provided and left it in, he hath mixed his labour with, and joined to it something that is his own, and thereby makes it his property."[5]

This is why Locke's property theory is called a labor-desert or desert-from-labor theory: the person who expended labor to render

---

4. John Locke, Treatise of Civil Government and a Letter Concerning Toleration 32 (Charles L. Sherman ed., 1937) (1689).

5. John Locke, Second Treatise of Government § 27, at 19 (1980) (1690).

the "thing in nature" into valuable form deserves to reap the value of it.[6] This theory is commonly pressed into service to justify the existence of private property in land and chattels, but it applies—perhaps more strongly—in relation to intellectual property. Unlike property in land, much of intellectual property is almost totally dependent on the work of the individual: the idea simply wouldn't exist were it not for the mental exertions of the inventor; the copyrighted work—the book, movie, or musical recording—is brought forth almost entirely by intellectual efforts, and its value is dependent on the quality of the intellectual effort, not the quality of the paper or disk on which it's coded.

Moreover, intellectual property doesn't suffer from the so-called Lockean proviso: Locke placed a limit on the justification of granting private property rights from the commons where the grant of private rights would not leave "enough and as good" in common for others. The idea is that enough must be left for those coming along afterward to be able to mix their labor with the common resources, and if the earlier grant of private property denies that, then there is a fundamental unfairness that destroys the initial justification. The Lockean proviso is hard to meet when it comes to physical property—the only way it would be possible is if there were such a thing as infinite land, or, as Locke might put it, if all the world were America. (That is the America of the 1700s). But intellectual property rights generally don't suffer from this problem, because the grant of a copyright or a patent (it is said) does not deny others from independently coming up with their own ideas or works. (Although, as we'll see, this is not quite true, since patents, for example, forbid later independent inventors from using the idea. Furthermore, critics charge that the grant of private intellectual

---

6. *See* STEPHEN MUNZER, A THEORY OF PROPERTY (1990) (explaining Locke in terms of desert from labor); MARGARET JANE RADIN, REINTERPRETING PROPERTY 105–06 (1993) (calling the theory the "Lockean labor-desert theory").

property rights take away from the public domain in important ways—something we shall study in later chapters.)

Locke's labor-desert theory is usually not relied on very much when new intellectual property laws are introduced, since utilitarian justifications are more often used in determining policy these days. However, the desert theory is often found in court decisions, in pleadings, and in journalistic accounts of intellectual property. It is routine to hear plaintiffs mount moral claims about their ownership, or about their need for more protection: "I made this! It's mine! I deserve to be protected!" We hear this, for example, in the claims by intellectual property owners that they are discriminated against because, unlike real property owners, their property grant expires eventually.[7] We will hear many echoes of the labor-desert theory in the chapters that follow.[8]

## Personality Theory

Finally, the "personality" philosophies of Hegel and Kant have been applied to justify the existence of private property. Both of these philosophers were concerned about the ability of individuals to express their wills within the material world. Hegel, for example, suggested that property was an extension of personality, and ownership over private property allowed the individual to expand his or her natural sphere of freedom beyond the body. In essence, the theories of Kant

---

7. "Sonny [Bono] wanted the term of copyright protection to last forever. I am informed by staff that such a change would violate the Constitution. I invite all of you to work with me to strengthen our copyright laws in all of the ways available to us. As you know, there is also Jack Valenti's proposal for term to last forever less one day. Perhaps the Committee may look at that next Congress." 144 Cong. Rec. H9952 (1998) (statement of Congresswoman Mary Bono).

8. For the first of many, consider the quotation from the Supreme Court: "The rights conferred by copyright are designed to assure contributors to the store of knowledge a fair return for their labors." Harper & Row v. Nation Enters., 471 U.S. 539, 546 (1985).

and Hegel advance the thesis that property rights are related (either as necessary conditions for, or as connected to) the ability of a person to be in the world, and are thus connected to human rights such as liberty, identity, and privacy. A simple example is the property interest that one has in a wedding ring or a house: these objects and rights are deeply connected to one's sense of self, and thus the laws providing exclusive rights over them can be justified by the need of people to control these objects. One can then take this insight in relation to emotionally significant property and extend it to other forms of property that people feel strongly about. As a result, even absent any other justification for having property rights in these objects, the theory of personality would argue that we should grant property rights in them in order for the possessor's self to be realized.

This justification is sometimes found in our intellectual property system. It certainly makes sense in relation to publicity rights, which forbid the commercial appropriation of the persona—face, image, recognizable voice, etc.—of celebrities. We can justify stopping others from using these facets of persona on the basis of personality theory since these facets are features or representations of the individual within the material world. Other types of intellectual property invoke personality-based justifications: notably the German and French copyright systems, together with some small parts of the U.S. copyright system, provide for "moral rights" to authors, providing, for example, that their work cannot be denigrated or defaced. These kinds of "human rights of authors" stem directly from Hegelian and Kantian personality theories. Furthermore, one can use these theories to justify the grant of copyright more generally, since a copyright work of authorship is, arguably, highly expressive and highly constitutive of the author's sense of self. To deny the authors ownership would be to reduce their abilities to express their wills within the material world.

There are, however, many difficulties with applying personality theory to modern day intellectual property, which may explain why it's rarely used as a basic justification. It doesn't seem to provide much traction for our understanding of rights created in industrial settings, whether we're talking about patents over agricultural chemicals produced by a multinational corporation or the latest album by Eminem that is produced by numerous people within the record label. Neither does it explain why copyright law has no overall right of attribution: in general I am free to describe your work as mine, as long as I don't copy it. Further, most intellectual property laws are silent on applicable considerations of personhood, such as privacy or autonomy. And finally, personality theory has essentially nothing to say to trademark law at all. As a result, it tends to be the last justification deployed by courts or legislatures, and tends to be of limited application in most arenas.

## ℳ Conclusion

Apart from these justifications, a range of approaches are used both to justify and criticize intellectual property. Terry Fisher calls these "social-planning" theories of intellectual property.[9] These theories typically include elements drawn from theories of social welfare, theories of the good life, theories relating to creating an engaged democracy and a vibrant environment for ideas, or theories of distributive justice. There are probably as many theories of this sort as there are theorists, and we will encounter some of these as we examine the criticisms made of the intellectual property system. None of these approaches has gained acceptance as widespread as the approaches discussed above, and it is relatively rare for legislatures or judges to invoke them. They are not fundamental to an understanding of the standard reasons for intellectual property laws.

---

9. William W. Fisher, *Theories of Intellectual Property*, *in* NEW ESSAYS IN LEGAL AND POLITICAL THEORY OF PROPERTY (2001).

# Copyright

THE BEST BOOK EVER written about copyright, Benjamin Kaplan's *An Unhurried View of Copyright,* begins with an account of how he became interested in the subject. He had read the opinion of Judge Learned Hand in the celebrated case of *Sheldon v. Metro-Goldwyn Pictures Corp,*[1] in which a movie studio's picture was held to have infringed the plaintiff's play. Kaplan noted that there was no literal infringement of the dialogue of the play, and, at most, the movie had taken various features of the play's plot and some characterizations. Yet Judge Hand ruled in favor of the playwright.

Kaplan mused on this intriguing result:

> I could see why copying a work word-for-word might be a legal wrong; and no doubt one must go further and punish copying with merely colorable variation. That liability should extend to so indefinite a use or appropriation as seemed to me involved in the *Sheldon* case, however, was not at all obvious or self-proving. I reflected that if man has any "natural" rights, not the least must be a right to imitate his fellows, and thus to reap where he has not sown. Education, after all, proceeds from a kind of mimicry, and "progress" if it is not entirely an illusion, depends on generous indulgence of copying.

---

1. 81 F.2d 49 (2d Cir 1936), *cert. denied,* 298 U.S. 669 (1936).

This quotation captures the fundamental tension at the heart of copyright. We can't allow defendants to get away with colorable imitations, but we must allow a generous indulgence of copying. Thus, in much of intellectual property we must find the appropriate balance between public and private rights. If we grant and enforce overbroad rights to private interests, there will be—as Kaplan observes—no mimicry, and bad education; as well as fewer if any new songs and the end of a vibrant creative culture. Grant overly expansive interests to the public and we might end up with no novels, no movies, and no songs. How are we to balance the interests of creators and society?

Kaplan's discussion of *Sheldon* demonstrates two important and related features of the balancing act inherent in copyright. First, the issue isn't some abstract, philosophical one, but a profound and difficult consideration for judges in actual cases. In *Sheldon* the issue at bar was whether "non-literal" elements such as the plot and characterizations of a play could be infringed by a film that took only certain parts. Whatever the decision of the court,[2] the nature of the analysis is not self-evident from the terms of the Copyright Act, and a decision either way expresses to some extent the judge's view of whose interests to prefer, the public or the private. If the judge concludes for the plaintiff, she is making a judgment about what an author needs to ensure that he continues to create works, rather than do something else. In concluding for the defendant, the judge is expressing a view about the need for others to be able to appropriate certain types of material without the copyright holder's permission.

The second feature of Kaplan's quotation is that we need to understand that the balancing act is found in every part of the copyright system. Each of copyright's doctrinal areas that we will examine below—creation, infringement, defenses, and so on— involves the balancing act. We will see that courts and legislative

---

2. The defendant was held to have infringed in the case.

bodies have grappled with numerous questions over copyright's evolution in considering the appropriate place to draw the line between public and private interests. Should we extend copyright to new forms of authorship as they emerge? What is the appropriate length of copyright's protection: fourteen years, twenty-eight, a lifetime, or longer? What sorts of features of a copyright work are protected: only the literal words or brushstrokes, or the characters, the sounds, and the general gestalt of the work? Each of these questions, and many more besides, concern how judges, legislators, and members of society strike the appropriate balance between the public and the private.

In the following sections of this chapter we will try to answer these questions. We begin by tracing the historical development of the copyright system, and then look at what is necessary for authors to gain copyright protection of their intellectual product. Here we focus on issues such as: What can be a copyrighted work? Why are ideas not protected? What is the length of copyright protection? We then examine the nature of the rights granted to the author and how they can be infringed. Then, in the penultimate part, we will examine the defenses available to a defendant before we turn in the final part to a discussion of how copyright has become such a battlefield of conflicting views.

## ⅏ History

As we saw in the last chapter, the modern period of copyright law began around three hundred years ago, with the passing of the Statute of Anne in 1709.

That act asserted three principles that we find in all modern copyright systems: a limited term of exclusive rights, the recognition of the author as the initial possessor of the property rights granted by the law, and the articulation of the types of rights that the system encompasses. Except for those books already published prior to the promulgation of that act—which were given an exceptional twenty-one-year term of protection—books were granted an initial fourteen-year term of protection, with the possibility of an additional fourteen-year extension. The nature of the "copy right" was, by current standards, also remarkably circumscribed: it was limited to the right to "print, reprint, or import." Although the author initially was granted a copyright, his assigns[3] also retained the copyright for the duration of the term, and had the same set of rights. The assumption—certainly the assumption of the Stationers' Company, which lobbied for the act—was that very quickly the copyright would end up in the hands of the printers who, unlike the impoverished author, had the capital to exploit the work. This economic reality persists to this day: just think about why "The Artist Formerly Known As Prince" renounced his music-label-created name and performed with "Slave" written on his cheek in protest of an early recording contract that transferred rights in his later-produced works. The changes of the Statute of Anne spelled the end of the monopoly of the Stationers' Company, leading to its eventual dissolution[4] and the emergence of myriad forms of publication and dissemination.

Our Constitution was written with an expectation that federal laws on copyright would be enacted, notwithstanding that twelve colonies already had some form of copyright at the time of the creation of the union. In 1790 the first federal Copyright Act was duly passed. This act followed the Statute of Anne closely, granting copyright protection for two fourteen-year terms post-publication, to the author (and his assigns), and limiting protection to books, maps, and charts. It has since been significantly revised four times (in 1831, 1870, 1909 and 1976), with minor amendments at regular intervals in between. Of these, it is the 1909 and 1976 acts that are

---

3. At the time it was always "his" assigns.

4. The company didn't go down without a fight, however, successfully claiming for fifty years that the Statute of Anne did not apply to works published by its members and that its common law copy right was perpetual. This position was eventually overturned by Donaldson v. Beckett, (1774) 98 Eng. Rep. 257 (H.L.).

most significant in this section for our understanding of the development of copyright.

The 1909 Copyright Act is important because it was the last copyright statute that maintained a meaningful distinction between published and unpublished works. Briefly (and not altogether accurately), federal copyright under the 1909 act only applied to published works, and the initial twenty-eight-year term only began on publication. Unpublished works were not covered by the federal law, and were governed by multiple, often-inconsistent state acts. The 1909 act also required compliance with a number of very seriously mandated formalities, notably registration of the work and the inclusion of a copyright notice, in order for a work to enjoy the protection of copyright. Failure to comply with the formalities often meant complete denial of copyright in the work. These features, inter alia, meant that U.S. law was inconsistent with the main international copyright treaty, the Berne Convention for the Protection of Literary and Artistic Works, and this, together with a series of other problems with the 1909 act generated continuous calls for amendment.

The 1976 Copyright Act—which in amended form applies today—remedied most of the problems with the 1909 act and made a series of changes to update the copyright law for the end of the twentieth century. Gone was the distinction between published and unpublished works, with the salient issue becoming instead whether a work was appropriately fixed in a material form. Gone also was the bifurcated term, as the act provided now for one period of continuous protection with no option of renewal. The other significant change of the 1976 act was to remove, more or less completely, the involvement of state-based law from the copyright system. Prior to the amendment, state and federal copyrights existed side-by-side, but section 301 of the 1976 act preempts all legal and equitable rights within the general scope of copyright as provided in the federal act. A very few copyright-like rights still exist outside this act—generally limited to those rights outside the general scope of the rights granted in the federal system such as state rights and remedies related to sound recordings made before February 15, 1972 that will exist until February 15, 2067—but these are minor and very unimportant.

The final major changes in the copyright regime came in 1989 and then through the 1990s. In 1989 the United States acceded to the Berne Convention, the major international multilateral treaty in this arena. This significantly reduced the U.S. emphasis on formalities, since most other countries had no formality requirements within copyright. Thus the U.S. formalities requirement was amended so that there was no need for registration, notice, or deposit within the Library of Congress in order for protection to be granted. As we'll see when examining the requirements of the current law, we still hear echoes of these older requirements—there are, for example, some good reasons authors and publishers register their works with the Copyright Office and why they might include a copyright notice—but the echoes get fainter with time. A number of other protections were added in the 1989 amendments, including the introduction of a new type of right—so-called moral rights— and protection for architectural works.[5]

During the 1990s the copyright act experienced a number of changes associated with the increasing significance of computer systems and the later rise of the internet as a distribution mechanism. During this period Congress introduced various amendments, targeted mostly at protecting the music industry. These culminated in the No Electronic Theft Act of 1996, which increased criminal sanctions and enforcement for digital piracy, and the Digital Millennium

---

5. Now that we've briefly introduced the differences that have come with the changes to the Copyright Act, it is worth noting that for the remainder of this chapter we will just focus on the current law. The primary benefit of this is simplicity, but it does mean that the statements made here may not apply to all works. Largely as a result of the remarkable length of the copyright term, there are still works that were produced under older copyright acts, which give rise to some difficulties in relation to copyright term especially. Thus the law explained in this chapter applies to works produced today.

Copyright Act of 1998, which introduced the "anti-circumvention" provisions that were aimed at stopping those who broke or bypassed digital copy protection schemes. These latter changes politicized copyright in a way that really hadn't been seen before, which we'll discuss in the last section of this chapter.

In the following sections we'll see how the history has affected our copyright system. We begin by looking at how copyright comes into being in the first place.

## ▨ Subsistence

Copyright "subsists" in original works of authorship that are fixed in material form, and which are appropriate expression. No one seems to be able to explain just why we say that copyright "subsists" rather than "exists" in the appropriate sorts of works. Nothing much rides on the term, but it is worthwhile noting that copyright isn't granted by anyone: as long as the work fulfills the necessary preconditions, copyright automatically subsists in the work. The trick, of course, is to work out what are the necessary conditions, and it is to these conditions that this section turns. We shall study what amounts to appropriate subject matter before moving to the issue of ideas versus expressions, then conclude with a discussion about ownership, duration, and the like.

### Subject Matter

Copyright only protects (1) works of authorship of certain types, (2) that are original to the author, (3) that are fixed in certain forms, and (4) that are expressions of ideas, and not the ideas themselves. We'll discuss the first three of these issues in this subsection. The issue of how we distinguish between ideas and expression is so important that it deserves its own subsection.

## Originality

Copyright protects "original works of authorship fixed in any tangible medium of expression."[6] The requirement of originality is a very low bar for the author to hurdle, and "original" here can best be understood in the sense that the work "originates" with the author rather than being "original" in the sense of being exceptionally creative or innovative. Thus, the most prosaic of works will generally enjoy protection: copyright subsists in grocery lists and children's sketches, in blog postings and Twitter tweets. The two requirements of originality are that the work be the independent creation of the author—as opposed to being copied from another work—and that the work satisfies some minimally creative standard. The latter element is almost always present in any work, as the courts are very reluctant to impose any standard of artistic merit.

The notable exception where creativity does matter is the case of factual works. Generally copyright's originality requirement will preclude protection for purely factual material because the claimed material wasn't created by the "author" but rather discovered by him or her. This issue is especially significant where an author has collated and compiled factual information, such as phone directories or databases. For a long time there was an exception for this type of work, and copyright was said to subsist under the "sweat of the brow" test: that is, the collector of factual information gained copyright protection for the compilation based on the effort expended in collecting the information, rather than on any requirement of creativity. The Supreme Court killed this doctrine in *Feist,*[7] concluding that for copyright to subsist in works of this type, there needed to be some creativity demonstrated in the selection, coordination, and arrangement of the factual material. Correspondingly, the Court denied copyright protection for the plaintiff's telephone

---

6. 17 U.S.C. § 102(a).

7. Feist Publ'ns Inc. v. Rural Tel. Serv. Co., 499 U.S. 340 (1991).

directory that was arranged alphabetically because it failed to demonstrate the necessary creativity under this new test of originality. It's not really clear why the court introduced this approach, and it is a plain departure from the general principle that originality should not be a proxy for creativity.[8] But while this remains the law, relatively few works will be denied copyright's protection on the basis of originality.

## Works of Authorship

Works of authorship are defined by section 102(a) of the Copyright Act to include literary works; musical works, including accompanying words; dramatic works, including accompanying music; pantomimes and choreographic works; pictorial, graphic, and sculptural works; motion pictures and other audiovisual works; sound recordings; and architectural works. Although the definition is not intended to be exclusive, and it is said that *any* work of authorship is eligible for copyright protection, the practical reality is that works must fit within these enumerated categories. When new forms of authorship emerge, they inevitably are pushed into one of the existing categories either by case law or congressional action. So, for example, when confronted with computer software in the 1970s and 1980s, the courts held that they were literary works, and the Copyright Act was duly changed to accommodate this understanding. The categories of works are meaningful in that slightly different rights and limitations attach to the different works; for example, architectural works cannot be infringed by taking a photograph of

---

8. It's instructive to compare this test with the approach of courts in England and Australia, which usually have almost exactly the same approach as the U.S. copyright system. In those jurisdictions the courts still follow the sweat-of-the-brow test—an approach arguably more consistent with copyright theory in general—and have expressly declined to follow the approach of the U.S. Supreme Court in *Feist*.

the building if it's in a public location,[9] and the "useful article" doctrine (that we will discuss in a moment) denies protection to utilitarian features of pictorial, graphic, and sculptural works, but not to any other type of work.

### Fixation

Fixation was a requirement that was introduced in the 1976 act, arising in part as a consequence of doing away with publication and registration as preconditions for copyright protection. Absent any need for registration or publication, there is an evidential issue about how to prove that a work has attracted the interest of the copyright system. There are also a number of other benefits to requiring fixation: it generates certainty about the work that is actually being claimed (rather than allowing expansionist claims by the plaintiff), it encourages the author to produce the work in a form that can be used by society, and it creates jurisdictional certainty that allows a clear demarcation between works that are covered by the federal system and those that might be protected by state-based systems.

The Copyright Act demands that works be "fixed in any tangible medium of expression, now known or later developed, from which they can be perceived, reproduced, or otherwise communicated, either directly or with the aid of a machine or device."[10] The emphasis upon function (i.e., that the work can be perceived or retrieved) rather than on form (e.g., in writing, on canvas, etc.) was to ensure that the rights of authors were not frustrated by technological advances that were not contemplated by the framers of the 1976 act. The development of digital technology has borne out this insight, and courts have had no difficulty concluding that a computer program and other sorts of works satisfy the fixation requirement upon

---

9.  17 U.S.C. § 120(a)

10. 17 U.S.C. § 102(a).

their being stored in ROM, on hard disks, or on magnetic tape. A special definition defines fixation for live broadcasts—of sporting events, music concerts, and the like—provided the event is being simultaneously recorded.

## The Idea/Expression Dichotomy

While originality and fixation are necessary for copyright to subsist in an appropriate type of work, a more fundamental limitation is given in section 102(b), which codifies the so-called "idea/expression" dichotomy. Copyright protects only the expression of the idea, and not the underlying idea, method, or process. This limitation is central to the innovation policy expressed in the copyright and patent laws: patents protect ideas with an extremely strong monopoly right that forbids independent invention, but does so only after a difficult examination process and only for a relatively short duration (i.e., twenty years from filing). Copyright protects the author's actual expression and not the ideas, and it does not forbid independent creation; but these limited exclusive rights are conferred with no examination or registration requirements, and protection is granted for a very long period, typically the "life of the author plus 70 years."

As central as the idea/expression dichotomy might be, and as simple as the principle is to state, it is often remarkably difficult to distinguish between protectable expression and unprotectable ideas. Judge Learned Hand confronted this question in *Nichols v. Universal Pictures*, and his formulation of the problem has become a classic:

> Upon any work . . . a great number of patterns of increasing generality will fit equally well, as more and more of the incident is left out. The last may perhaps be no more than the most general statement of what the [work] . . . is about, and at times might consist only of its title; but there is a point in this series of

abstractions where they are no longer protected, since otherwise the [author] . . . could prevent the use of his "ideas," to
which, apart from their expression, his property is never
extended. Nobody has ever been able to fix that boundary, and
nobody ever can.[11]

This is called the "levels of abstraction" test and it is a simple—
perhaps overly simplistic—test for determining what elements of
a work are protected by copyright, and consequently what a defendant is not entitled to copy. Take, as an example, Shakespeare's
*Romeo and Juliet*. At the lowest level, it is clear that the actual words
he wrote are protected—say, "O Romeo, Romeo! wherefore art thou
Romeo?/ Deny thy father and refuse thy name./ Or if thou wilt
not, be but sworn my love/ And I'll no longer be a Capulet"—and
a word-for-word copy of this text would be an infringement.
One level up would be the sentences, and above that would be the
stanzas (i.e., the paragraphs) of the text. Above that are the structural features and plotline, and the names and features of the characters. Then there is the overall narrative drive underlying the work,
that of the two warring families, the beloved children of whom fall
in love and are fated to die. And above all of that there would be the
concept of a play, rendered in the form of a romantic tragedy.

Although *Romeo and Juliet* was created before copyright law
existed, let's imagine that copyright applied to it. (It's a useful example because everyone knows the play.) The central question is
at what level of abstraction is any use of *Romeo and Juliet* actionable? A literal word-for-word taking of the text would be an infringement of Shakespeare's expression. We are equally clear at the other
end of the spectrum: merely writing any play is not an infringement
of Shakespeare's work, and neither is writing a tragedy involving
two "star-cross'd" lovers. But what of the reproduction of the
characters and basic plotline of *Romeo and Juliet* in works such as

11.  Nichols v. Universal Picture Corp., 45 F.2d 119, 121 (2d Cir. 1930).

*West Side Story*, or *High School Musical*? Do these works, which feature very similar protagonists, similar love stories, and similarly warring families or groups, involve the appropriation of William Shakespeare's copyrightable work?[12] (Even if, in the case of *High School Musical*, slightly fewer people die in the end?)

As a pragmatic matter, where a court is confronted with material that sits somewhere between literal expression and abstract idea, it's often the case that the plaintiff's and defendant's behavior will influence the outcome, no matter what theory might say. And in general, the idea/expression dichotomy is the legal basis for courts to apply the highest level reasoning about the purposes of copyright law. An influential treatise writer suggests that ideas can be split into three general categories—concepts, solutions, and building blocks—and that courts seek to avoid giving exclusive rights in any of these categories because this will grant an overbroad monopoly and preclude other usages. But, with all due respect to the treatise, this is mostly nonsense. "Expression" and "idea" are meaningless concepts that are virtually worthless as meaningful categories to direct courts to appropriate results. They are in fact little more than *ex post* explanations of what courts decide to do: if a court wants to protect the nonliteral elements it will label them "expression," and if it doesn't it will call them "ideas."

However, a number of specific doctrines are marginally useful in helping resolve the idea/expression issue. First is the merger doctrine, which states that copyright will not protect the expression

---

12. Judge Learned Hand explains his example with Shakespeare's *Twelfth Night*: "If *Twelfth Night* were copyrighted, it is quite possible that a second comer might so closely imitate Sir Toby Belch or Malvolio as to infringe, but it would not be enough that for one of his characters he cast a riotous knight who kept wassail to the discomfort of the household, or a vain and foppish steward who became amorous of his mistress. These would be no more than Shakespeare's 'ideas' in the play, as little capable of monopoly as Einstein's *Doctrine of Relativity*, or Darwin's theory of the *Origin of Species*. It follows that the less developed the characters, the less they can be copyrighted; that is the penalty an author must bear for marking them too indistinctly." *Nichols*, 45 F.2d at 121.

where there is only one way, or a very small number of ways, to express an idea. In this case, the expression and idea are said to have merged and, thus, protecting the expression necessarily will give a monopoly over the idea. Often-cited examples include a jewel-encrusted bee-shaped brooch[13] and the rules in a sweepstakes competition.[14] In each case courts held that there were so few ways of representing the idea of the pin or the rules that granting copyright would exhaust all possible ways of using the idea—an outcome that copyright law could not sanction.[15]

A related approach is found in the common law doctrine of *scènes à faire*, which denies copyright protection for elements of a work that are dictated by commonplace ideas or clichés. The main types of works where courts have applied this doctrine have been plays and movies where the relevant elements have constituted stock scenes, character traits, or images that are necessary for that type of narrative: think of uniformed Nazis goose-stepping in a World War II movie, the heroine tied to the railroad tracks by the moustache-twirling villain in a *Perils of Pauline*-type adventure, or the steely-eyed hero in an action movie flying through the air as glass flies all around him. Outside movies and plays, the *scènes à faire* doctrine has been applied to hackneyed elements in other types of works such as photographs, images, and computer software to deny protection for features such as the depiction of wreaths on Christmas cards or typical formatting features in spreadsheets.[16]

---

13. Herbert Rosenthal Jewelry Corp. v. Kalpakian, 446 F.2d 738 (9th Cir. 1971).

14. Morrisey v. Proctor & Gamble Co., 379 F.2d 675 (1st Cir. 1967).

15. One can always disagree with the conclusion of the court on whether these cases involve merger of idea and expression. For example, if you do a Google image search for "bee brooch" you'll find innumerable different ways to express that idea, and so the court in *Rosenthal v. Kalpakian* probably applied the merger doctrine incorrectly. But it's pretty hard to imagine how to express the idea of a sweepstakes competition—or a bingo board, or the like—in a way that doesn't implicate the merger doctrine.

16. Taylor Corp. v. Seasons Greetings, LLC, 315 F.3d 1039 (8th Cir. 2003).

There are also a number of specific statutory provisions that are related to the idea/expression dichotomy. For example, section 101 of the Copyright Act explicitly limits protection for pictorial, graphic, or sculptural works to those features that can be identified separately from, and are capable of existing independently of, the utilitarian aspects of the article. The "useful article" limitation was included to distinguish between copyrightable works of applied art and uncopyrightable industrial designs. The intention was to grant copyright protection for aesthetic elements of a piece of applied art, but not to the functional or mechanical features that properly are the subject matter of patent law, especially design patent law. Drawing this distinction has been remarkably difficult, and it is often hard to find much to distinguish cases where courts have concluded the works are protected by copyright and those that are denied protection under the useful article doctrine. So statuettes of Balinese dancers used as table lamp bases have been held protected,[17] as have the shape of a telephone used for a pencil sharpener,[18] the elaborate sculptural designs of belt buckles,[19] and a coin bank shaped like a dog.[20] But courts have refused to apply copyright to the undulating shape of a bike rack[21] or the shape of outdoor light fixtures.[22] The test that can be derived from these cases is as follows: if the claimed design elements can be identified as reflecting the designer's artistic judgment exercised independently of functional influences, then copyright will protect the work. Trying to work out when this applies is why they pay judges the big bucks.

---

17. Mazer v. Stein, 347 U.S. 201 (1954).

18. Ted Arnold Ltd. v. Silvercraft Co., 259 F. Supp. 733 (S.D.N.Y. 1966).

19. Kieselstein-Cord v. Accessories by Pearl, Inc., 632 F.2d 989 (2d Cir. 1980).

20. Royalty Designs, Inc. v. Thrifticheck Serv. Corp., 204 F. Supp. 702 (S.D.N.Y. 1962).

21. Brandir Int'l, Inc. v. Cascade Pac. Lumber Co., 834 F.2d 1142 (2d Cir. 1987).

22. Esquire, Inc. v. Ringer, 591 F.2d 796 (D.C. Cir. 1978).

(In truth, judges mostly make it up as they go along, and cases in this area are a mess.)

## Consequences of Subsistence

As long as the work of authorship satisfies all the elements discussed above, then its author automatically gains the protection of copyright. Certain issues emerge once copyright comes into being, and here we need to look at those of ownership, duration, and effect of formalities.

### Ownership

Generally speaking, the author of a copyright work is the initial owner of the property interest conferred by copyright.[23] The ownership of the copyright is independent of the ownership of the physical medium in which the work is expressed, and so it is perfectly possible for one person to own copyright in an object physically owned by another. This can create some puzzling situations, such as when a famous author's letters are sold at auction, but he insists that the contents not be reproduced and published by the new owner of the physical manifestation of the letters.[24]

Ownership is usually only problematic in two situations: where the work is produced by two or more people, or where it is produced in the context of employment. In the former situation, multiple authorship may result in either a number of separate works, or one joint work. A joint work is a work prepared by two or more authors with the intention that their contributions be merged into inseparable or interdependent parts of a unitary whole.[25] The intention to

---

23. 17 U.S.C. § 201.

24. Salinger v. Random House, Inc., 811 F.2d 90 (2d Cir. 1987).

25. 17 U.S.C. § 101.

form the work into one indivisible whole must be made at the time the work was created. Furthermore, courts will examine the nature of the contributions made by the authors, and for a joint work to arise each author must have contributed some original expression that is itself copyrightable, although the amount and significance of each author's contribution is not important. Thus, if author A contributes the majority of the expression, there will still be a joint work as long as author B contributes some expression, and both parties will be considered to be tenants-in-common of the work.[26] However, if A merely supplies the ideas for a work that B expresses, then B holds the sole copyright in the work because copyright only subsists in the expression, not the idea.

The other problematic ownership situation is where the work is produced in the course of some kind of employment relationship. The basic question is whether the work was "made for hire," that is made as part of the creator's job responsibilities. If so, then the normal ownership principle is overridden and the work is owned by the employer of the creator. The Copyright Act has a two-part definition of work "made for hire": it's either prepared by an employee within the scope of her employment or it involves one of nine special types of works. The Supreme Court in *CCNV v. Reid* examined the test for the "made in the course of employment" part of the "work for hire" definition. It adopted the common law test for assessing the master-servant relationship, which looks at a range of factual considerations such as whether the hiring party has a right to control the manner and means by which the work is produced,

---

26. One circuit, the Ninth, has a special rule for highly collaborative works such as movies: even where there are two authors who express ideas, a joint work will only come about if the other elements are satisfied and both authors had artistic control over the work, Aalmmuhamed v. Lee, 202 F.3d 1227 (9th Cir. 2000). This test can only be seen as a response to the difficulties of assessing authorship in situations where there are large numbers of people working on a single copyrighted work, such as in films, television programs, or music recordings. It makes little sense in other contexts, and is broadly inconsistent with most of copyright doctrine.

the level of skill required by the hired party, whether the hiring party has the right to tell the hired party to perform additional work, and so on. As with all multifactor approaches, this test trades certainty in favor of flexibility, and so naturally gives rise to all manner of litigation in marginal (and high-value) cases. And as with all open-ended tests, it tends to favor the party with the largest war chest (which in this case means the employer).

The second part of the definition of work for hire specifies nine specific situations, based around commissioned works that are often highly collaborative. They include works specially ordered as a contribution to a collective work (such as a literary anthology), as part of a motion picture, as a translation, as an atlas, etc. Apart from fitting into one of the nine categories, the parties must also sign a written agreement to the effect that the work is made for hire.

### Duration

Copyright subsists in ordinarily authored works for the life of the author plus seventy years. But of course works made for hire have no uniquely referable human author, and so, they enjoy copyright protection for ninety-five years from the date of publication or 120 years from the date of creation, whichever is shorter.

More important than this, however, works made for hire are immune from the termination provisions that were incorporated into the 1976 act. Ordinarily, authored works are often the subject of transfers of ownership by way of the assignment of all of the author's rights or the licensing of some of them. Since the beginning of copyright, authors have complained about the way that publishers have exploited them, abusing their unequal bargaining power, and generally gotten rich at the authors' expense. As a result of this concern, the Copyright Act includes provisions allowing for authors to claw back rights from assignees and transferees under certain conditions: the basic proposition is that an author may terminate the transfer between thirty-five and forty years from the date of the transfer. A couple of different sections apply to this termination right, one that deals with copyrights granted under the act preceding the 1976 act, and one relating to copyrights under the 1976 act. Because the systems are so different, and because the mechanics of the termination right are so arcane, we won't be examining those provisions here. But this right continues to be one that vexes large content companies: Disney's $4B purchase of Marvel Comics was not enough to protect them from suit by the widow of Jack Kirby (one of Marvel's early comic book illustrators and the creator of "The Hulk") seeking termination of the transfer of the rights granted to Marvel and the return of those rights to her, his heir.[27] Since the first of the termination provisions kick into operation in 2013—thirty-five years after January 1, 1978 when the 1976 act came into effect—over the coming years we will likely see lots of litigation about termination.

### Formalities

Formalities comprise the final issue stemming from subsistence. There are three formalities: (1) registering the work with the Register of Copyrights, (2) depositing some requisite numbers of copies with the Library of Congress, and (3) affixing the appropriate copyright notice to the work.[28] It used to be under the old copyright laws that failing to meet all the requirements of the formalities sections meant surrendering the protections of copyright altogether.

---

27. Brook Barnes & Michael Cieply, *A Supersized Custody Battle over Marvel Superheroes*, N.Y. TIMES, Mar. 19, 2010, at BU1.

28. Some schools of thought suggest that publication of the work is one of the Copyright Act's formalities. It used to be the case that federal copyright only applied to published works, with unpublished works being the preserve of the states. Since 1976 this hasn't been the case, and unpublished and published works are now part of the federal system. While it's true that published works are treated a little differently from unpublished works—they have requirements of deposit for example, and duration is calculated slightly differently— the distinction is irrelevant to our discussion, and treating publication as a formality is a confusing way of understanding copyright law.

This isn't so under the 1976 act, but there are some benefits conferred by formalities, and some issues if the author doesn't abide by the formalities.

The first formality is registration. This means registration of the copyright work with the Copyright Office, which may take place at any time during the work's copyright term; it involves filling out a form detailing some features of the work such as authorship and type of work, paying a small fee, and depositing one or two copies of the work. Unlike patents or even trademarks, there is a very limited examination for copyright registrations: essentially the examiner will grant registration unless it is clear that the work is not an appropriate work or there is some other glaring problem. This makes sense when one considers that the Copyright Office isn't *granting* the copyright: the copyright in the work subsisted from the moment of fixation in material form as long as the elements discussed above are met. So the Copyright Office is merely noting the copyright that has already come into existence. This also explains the relatively limited benefits conferred by copyright registration. Registration is a precondition to filing suit for copyright infringement—although there are exceptions for foreign works—and it provides a presumption of validity of copyright in the event of suit. It is also generally a precondition to recover statutory damages (which we will examine in the next section). As a result, all commercial content producers will register the copyright upon publication. Few others do.

The second formality is the deposit of two copies of the published work with the Library of Congress. This requirement grew out of an initial need of the young republic to stock its library, but remains to this day. However, the failure to deposit with the Library of Congress carries only minor penalties: if the work is not deposited within three months of publication, then the Register of Copyrights can demand that it be done, and can levy small fines of up to a couple of thousand dollars if the deposit doesn't occur. As mentioned in the prior paragraph, the registration formality requires deposit also, but this is technically a different requirement  of deposit. However, deposit with the Library of Congress will satisfy the requirement to deposit copies for the purposes of registration, thereby killing two birds with one stone.

The final formality, that of notice, refers to the display of the name of the copyright holder, the date of first publication of the work, and the familiar copyright symbol or the word "Copyright" or "Copr." So for example, I might put "© Dan Hunter 2011" at the beginning of this work. This requirement was removed by the 1988 amendments, and nowadays placing a copyright notice on a work is at the election of the owner. Nonetheless, if the work comes with an effective notice, a defendant will be unable to claim innocent infringement. As a practical matter then, all content industries continue to place prominent notice of their copyright on their published works in order to enjoy as expansive rights as possible.

## ⁂ Rights

When I take your book and copy it rather than buy a version from you, then I have engaged in a copyright infringement. This was the historical starting point for the entire copyright system: so much so that it's found in the name of the law itself: that is, the law grants a series of *copy rights*. But from this modest beginning the system of rights has extended and the nature of the wrongs against those rights has also expanded. So these days the rights of a copyright owner might extend to the right to display the work, or to perform it in public, or to translate it into a different language. And the activities that amount to infringement of these rights are no longer confined to a direct copy, but also include appropriating some elements of the work, encouraging others to copy the work, and so on. This interlocking system of rights and infringements is the subject of this section, and what follows is divided into an examination of these two core features. It is also true to say that this is where the difficult issues emerge in most copyright cases.

In this section and the one that follows, we examine the intertwined issues of the rights granted by copyright law and how these rights are infringed. We start with the five basic economic rights that the author gains upon creation and fixation of the work. We'll take a short detour into moral rights—an oddity within our system because they are not primarily economic in nature—before we examine the way that these rights are infringed. We will conclude the section with a discussion of the way that the digital era has changed some of the doctrinal realities of the rights granted by copyright, and of their infringement.

## Exclusive Rights

Section 106 grants a bundle of five basic rights to the author, or the licensees or assigns who take from the author: reproduction, adaptation, distribution, performance, and display.[29] They are "exclusive rights" in two senses. They are exclusive to the author, and thus, without permission of the author, no one else may perform the actions—copying, performing, etc—that are exclusively given to the author. But these rights are also exclusive in the sense that they are the sum total of the rights granted to the author, and if a third party does anything that doesn't fall within these rights—wallpaper their house with the pages of a book, for example—then there is no infringement.

The five basic exclusive rights are complicated in practice, and don't apply in the same way to each type of work because it doesn't make sense to give the work that right. For example, graphic, pictorial, and sculptural works don't enjoy the public performance right because granting this right would, essentially, forbid people from displaying the physical object. A similar limitation applies to architectural works, which cannot be infringed by

---

29. Section 106 actually nominates six rights, the unmentioned one being the transmission right granted to sound recordings. This right amounts to a slight variation of the performance right, tailored specifically to the requirements of sound recordings. We'll consider it as part of the performance right.

photographing them (which would ordinarily be an infringement of the adaptation right).

The rights that are granted overlap to some degree, and so it's often the case that multiple infringements lie against the one work: an online magazine article that uses an unauthorized photograph may infringe the photographer's reproduction right (because it's a copy), the adaptation right (if the photograph is digitally manipulated), the distribution right (because it's disseminated on the web), and so on.

So, let's look a little more closely at the rights that *are* granted.

### Reproduction

The first—and still the core—right that is granted by section 106 is the reproduction or "copy" right. The owner of the copyright has the exclusive right to reproduce the copyrighted work in copies, and "copies" are defined as "material objects . . . in which a work is fixed by any method now known or later perceived, reproduced, or otherwise communicated, either directly or with the aid of a machine or device." The Copyright Act was changed to include this definition at the advent of the digital era when new forms of media—the silicon chip, the magnetic disk, etc.—gave rise to hard cases over whether a computer program burned into a chip was a copy of the same program that was visible only as the printed version of the code. Nowadays there is no question that it is.

The reproduction right is fundamental because it captures the majority of infringements: most things that amount to an infringing work copy some part of the original work. This is particularly so in the digital era when to do anything with a work essentially involves making a copy: a computer has to copy a work from hard disk into memory in order to display it, and it's been held that these kinds of transitory copies are infringements of the reproduction right. If we take the principle seriously then almost everything that a consumer does to manipulate a digital file will amount to an infringement of the reproduction right. This makes most other types of infringements unnecessary, and dramatically restricts the ability of people to use the works they've paid for. As a result, this type of interpretation is very controversial. Also, unlike many of the other rights, infringing the reproduction right can be done in private, and for no commercial benefit. It therefore remains the starting point for most aggrieved plaintiffs.

### Adaptation/Derivative Works

The inclusion of the adaptation right came about because of concerns about the production of derivative works that used the original copyright work, but that didn't directly reproduce it. Essentially this right applies to any translation, rearrangement, recasting or re-versioning of a copyright work and simple examples include translations between languages, turning a book into a movie or a movie into a book, or creating an audiobook sound recording of a novel. It isn't hard to agree with the sentiment that a plaintiff should be protected from ripoffs of her work that happen to be rendered in a different guise, but derivative works cause all manner of difficult issues that are often poorly handled by courts. For example, what of a defendant who mixes his significant creative work with a relatively small amount of the plaintiff's work? Should the court recognize the defendant's copyright in this newly created work, and is it appropriate to enjoin the defendant from using the work at all? (Courts differ on both questions in ways that are inconsistent and often unfair).

Even more problematic are cases where the defendant has enhanced the copyrighted work, or merely used it in a different form—situations that courts regularly find infringe the adaptation right. Consider the case of *Mirage Editions, Inc. v. Albuquerque A.R.T. Co.*,[30] where a defendant was found liable for mounting photographs

---

30.  856 F.2d 1341 (9th Cir. 1988).

from the plaintiff's book onto tiles, on the basis that the tiles amounted to infringing derivative works.[31] Huh?

Although the standard limitations apply here—the idea/expression dichotomy we discussed earlier still applies, and as we will see in a moment, there must be substantial similarity between the allegedly infringing work and the plaintiff's work—the adaptation right is often the means by which judges overprotect copyright works. At times it seems that judges agree with the plaintiffs that *any* use of their work amounts to the production of an unauthorized derivative work, a conclusion that was never the intention of Congress and is certainly against the public interest.

### Distribution

The third exclusive right is the distribution right, which grants the copyright owner the right to distribute her work to the public, whether by sale, rental, leasing, or lending. In the internet age, this right is routinely infringed in conjunction with the reproduction right, such as when I copy your e-mail and forward it to a thousand of my closest Facebook friends. But it occurs as a separate infringement where, for example, I sell knockoff DVDs that you made: you have infringed the reproduction right because you made the copies, but I'm infringing the public distribution right because I am offering them for sale.

This right is subject to one major limitation: section 109 creates the "first sale doctrine," which says that, generally, the (physical) owners of authorized copies of a copyright work may distribute and display it as they see fit. So, if I purchase a book, the copyright holder cannot stop me from lending that book to a friend, or selling it,

---

31. This case is particularly problematic since the tiles cannot reasonably be considered to be works at all, and besides the defendant had bought legitimate copies of the book and so should have been covered by the first sale doctrine, an issue we examine in the next subsection. The opposite conclusion was reached in the similar case of Lee v. ART, 125 F.3d 580 (7th Cir. 1997).

or putting it on display in my library. The Copyright Act distinguishes between the physical ownership of the medium in which the copy of the work is published and the ownership of the copyright in the original work.

The first sale doctrine is an important example of how the Copyright Act balances public and private interests because without this doctrine, we could not have public libraries, flourishing secondary markets for casebooks, or even borrowing among friends.[32] I'm certain my publisher would much prefer for you to purchase this book new, rather than buy it secondhand from Amazon Marketplace or borrow it from the library or your friend, because it makes money on each sale of a new copy (and so do I), but not on any other type of exchange. Nonetheless, in the interests of a well-read public, our copyright system limits the distribution and display rights of the copyright owners once the copy has been legitimately sold. However, with the advent of digital content such as locked PDFs, or electronic books with digital rights management, the first sale doctrine has been effectively eviscerated. For these, there is no physical medium of dissemination, there is only the digital content that we download from the internet, and thus the public-oriented protections of the first sale doctrine are largely theoretical. Through mechanisms such as licensing use rather than selling a copy outright, digital content owners are correspondingly more able to limit the scope of the first sale doctrine, and the doctrine is likely to become increasingly irrelevant in future.

## Performance

The fourth exclusive right of section 106 is the public performance right. This right applies to all types of works except architectural

---

32. The first sale doctrine is the core protection for libraries, although there are specific defenses for public libraries and special restrictions on commercial lending of certain types of digital media, such as CDs and DVDs.

and pictorial, graphic or sculptural works. "Public" means the work is being performed at a place open to the public or where a substantial number of people gather (not counting family members and acquaintances), or it is being transmitted in a way that makes it public (e.g., radio, television, etc.). "Performing" a work includes the obvious examples, such as playing a musical work or showing a movie, but can also include reading a book out loud in a bookstore. For reasons too arcane to worry about here, sound recordings are granted a special variant of the performance right called the "transmission right": essentially this subsection grants an exclusive right of public performance by way of transmitting the sound recording using digital audio.

The public performance right is particularly important to the music industry, given that industry's historical reliance on radio as well as the cultural significance of listening to music in bars and restaurants and, these days, on the internet. Individual music and sound recording copyright holders do not have the means of finding and tolling every single use of their songs in every single tavern or bistro or on every single internet radio station. Hence, collecting societies or agencies have emerged over time to monitor these uses and extract royalties on behalf of the rights-holders; typically this is done by the sale of various types of licenses to those who wish to perform the work. The three main collecting agencies in the United States are the American Society of Composers, Authors and Publishers (ASCAP), Broadcast Music, Inc. (BMI), and SESAC. The Harry Fox Agency deals with mechanical licenses that are important for covers of recorded music, which we'll discuss shortly. Copyright owners strike deals with these agencies to enforce their rights on their behalf rather than having to go after every college radio station, karaoke club, or cover band themselves.

### Public Display

The final exclusive right is the public display right. This is closely related to the public performance right, except it doesn't apply to sound recordings or architectural works, but does apply to pictorial, graphic, or sculptural works. (This makes sense when you think about it: how exactly would you display a sound recording?) It uses the same definition of "public" as for public performance, which basically means that it is forbidden to display the work to a group of people who are not related to each other or are not social acquaintances. And like the public performance right, the public display right is limited by the first sale doctrine in section 109. It was once the case that the display right was among the least significant and least litigated of the exclusive rights: it was once confined to situations where a defendant put a copyright work on display without permission or showed an image of the work, for example, by putting a painting in a gallery or projecting parts of a movie. The advent of the internet has meant an increase in the importance of this right, and courts recently have concluded that placing pictures on a website amounts to a public display of those pictures. This has been of particular consequence for search engines that find and display photographs covered by the display right; some courts have, however, limited search engine liability by invoking fair use defenses, which we'll examine shortly.

## Moral Rights

The U.S. copyright system derives from the English Statute of Anne, and adopts the incentive theory as the main justification for copyright. That is, within the Anglo-American system the main motivation for copyright has been to encourage the production of socially beneficial expression that won't be produced unless we provide an economic incentive for it. The continental European system, however, began with a different premise: it saw copyright in terms more in keeping with the arguments of Hegel and Locke. So the rights that that system granted were more like natural rights or human rights, and were intended to protect the sanctity of the human creator. This tradition goes by many names—*droit d'auteur*, *droit moral, Urheberpersonlichkeitsrecht*—which are usually translated as "author's rights" or "moral rights." The rights granted under this tradition are not at all like the economic exclusive rights granted by section 106 that we have discussed above. Like other human rights—think of our Constitutional ones—these rights can't be bought, sold, or given up. They are fundamental to our integrity as human beings and so, just as I can't sell myself into slavery, under the purest version of the European continental moral rights system I can't sell my author's rights either.

The strength of protection and the nature of these rights differ somewhat in each European country, but they basically number three: the right to be identified as the author of the work (the right of attribution, or *droit de paternité*); the right to ensure that the work is not mutilated or distorted (the right of integrity, *droit au respect de l'oeuvre* or sometimes, *droit d'intégrité*); and the right to decide when and whether to have a work published (the right of disclosure, *droit de divulgation*). Some jurisdictions go further and provide for rights to reply to criticism, the right to correct or withdraw a work from the market, and even the right to resale royalties (*droit de suite*)—that is, where a work is resold, a percentage of the sale will go to the initial author and not to the owner of the work. This latter one is a right that is significant in situations where an artist sells a picture or a song early in his career, and then becomes noted later in his career or after his death.

When the United States decided to join the Berne Convention in the late 1980s, it was obliged to recognize some kind of moral rights system in its laws. The problem was that a U.S. system founded on economic exchange and the free alienation of rights was not well-suited to a set of rights based on inalienable authorial rights. Initially, the United States took the view that it was already in compliance with its obligations: it said that moral rights were already protected by the federal copyright system, supplemented by the federal trademark system and state systems that forbid defamation, passing off, and appropriation of publicity rights. However, it became clear that this interpretation was unlikely to be accepted, and thus, in 1990 Congress passed the Visual Artists Rights Act (VARA) to ensure that the United States was in compliance with Berne.

VARA implements a moral rights regime, but only in relation to "works of visual art," which are defined to include paintings, drawings, prints, signed photographs, and sculptures, as long as they are single or limited editions. The intention was to adopt the minimal protections consistent with U.S. Berne obligations, and apply the moral rights regime only to what we think of as the "fine art" market. There are only two rights granted by VARA: the right of attribution (which amounts to the right to be identified as the author of your work, as well as to preventing the use of your name in relation to works you didn't author), and the right of integrity (the right to prevent intentional distortion or mutilation of your work, or to prevent the destruction of your work if you are an author of "recognized stature"). These rights can't be transferred, but they can be waived by the author. Moral rights only last for the life of the author, unlike the other rights that endure for the period of copyright protection—which is, as we saw above, typically the life of the author plus seventy years.

As you can see, the U.S. moral rights are pale shadows of those granted to European authors: an outcome that reflects the deep suspicion of these sorts of protections within a system predicated on economic interests. These rights are often litigated, but the plaintiff is only sporadically successful. The outcomes in these cases might charitably be called "idiosyncratic," although a more accurate version might be that they're just strange.

## Infringement

"John David California" is the *nom-de-plume* of Frederik Colting, the author of *The Macho Man's Drinkbook—Because Nude Girls and Alcohol Go Great Together*, *The Pornstar Name Book*, and *60 Years Later—Coming Through the Rye*. This latter book involves a protagonist named "Mr. C" who wakes up one morning in his nursing home with a compulsion to leave. He gets onto a bus and flees to New York, where he visits a number of familiar places. His language and the characters he interacts with are also curiously familiar—he wonders about his sister Phoebe, and he uses a lot of 1940s' and 1950s' idioms—and it doesn't take a genius to recognize that Mr. C is an aged version of Holden Caulfield, J.D. Salinger's famous character from *The Catcher in the Rye*. For the tiny number of people who didn't read Salinger's book in middle school and who might have missed the connection, Colting helpfully dedicates *60 Years Later* to Salinger—"the most terrific liar you ever saw in your life"—and his European publisher notes on the blurb of the British edition that Colting's book is "a marvelous sequel to one of our most beloved classics." Notwithstanding the shout-out in the dedication and his appearance as a character later in the text itself, Salinger was not amused by this unauthorized "sequel." He brought suit to stop the publication of it in the United States.[33]

The *Salinger v. Colting* case focuses our attention on what copyright protects, and raises some questions about whether Colting has infringed Salinger's copyright by writing a book based on *Catcher*. Can you only infringe if you copy the exact words? Do you infringe if you use someone else's character? What about some of the scenarios, or plotlines? We mentioned these issues at the beginning of this chapter, and now we ask how we should go about deciding these questions.

To start, all plaintiffs in an infringement action must prove that the work at issue is copyrighted and that they own the relevant rights. This goes to the questions we discussed in the previous part; that is, the issue looks to the subsistence questions in copyright. Notably, the plaintiff must show that the work at issue does not fall afoul of the idea/expression dichotomy, that it is still within the copyright period, that it has been registered with the Copyright

---

33. See Salinger v. Colting, 607 F.3d 68 (2d Cir. 2010).

Office, and so on. And then there is the question of establishing ownership, an issue that can sometimes be problematic since the plaintiff must show that it holds the relevant rights.

Assuming that the plaintiff satisfies these requirements, the focus shifts to the actions of the defendant and whether it has infringed the plaintiff's rights. There are two different types of infringement that might be in issue here: primary infringement, where the defendant is accused of directly infringing one or more of the exclusive rights; and secondary infringement, where the defendant is alleged to have aided others in infringing. In the next section we examine the requirements for primary infringement, then take up the question of secondary infringement in the section after that.

## Primary Infringement

For primary infringement, the starting point is to consider whether the defendant has actually done that which is given to the plaintiff by the exclusive rights. Thus, has the defendant copied the work? Or made a derivative work from it? Or distributed it? And so on. It doesn't matter here if the infringement was undertaken for financial gain, although the penalties for commercial infringement are more serious. And again, except as far as penalties are concerned, it doesn't matter if the infringement was done unintentionally or accidentally. There is a very famous case of subconscious  infringement by George Harrison of *The Beatles* fame: his song "My Sweet Lord" has a remarkably similar melody to an earlier  song written by Ronald Mack and sung (with some success) by the Chiffons called "He's So Fine."[34] When the infringement suit was brought, Harrison testified that he had heard "He's So Fine" years before, but he noted that a songwriter of his ability and standing made it impossible to believe that he would bother to infringe

---

34. Bright Tunes Music Corp. v. Harrisongs Music, Ltd., 420 F. Supp. 177 (1976).

the copyright like this. The court accepted both propositions and concluded that Harrison had subconsciously copied the song, and, notwithstanding the absence of intention, found him liable for copyright infringement and accordingly awarded a large amount in damages against him.

The Harrison case demonstrates another fundamental requirement the plaintiff must establish: that the defendant actually copied the plaintiff's work. Copyright only forbids *actual* copying, and does not forbid independent creation of the same work.[35] So, for example, if George Harrison had been able to prove that he had never heard the Chiffons singing, then he could not have been found liable for copyright infringement. This gives rise to some amusing business practices: a number of Hollywood studios refuse to read unsolicited screenplays, and may return unopened any envelopes they receive that may contain screenplays. If the studio happens to make a hit movie that bears some similarity to one of the unsolicited scripts in the "slush pile," the producers are in an evidentiary bind in any copyright infringement action against them unless they can show that no one actually read the script and so could not have copied it.

Unless the defendant admits copying, the plaintiff will generally prove by circumstantial evidence that copying took place, and this requires a combination of access and probative similarity. For the first element the plaintiff must demonstrate that the defendant had some kind of access to the plaintiff's work: the defendant could have heard it on the radio, been sent a copy of the manuscript, received a copy from a business partner who had been given one, etc. If the plaintiff fails to show that the defendant had access, then there can be no infringement because the defendant could not have copied the plaintiff's work. In other words, the defendant establishes he or she independently created the work. The second element is whether the similarity between the works is such as to sustain the conclusion that the defendant actually copied the

---

35. Unlike patent law, which we will examine later.

plaintiff's work: that is, the similarity makes it more likely than not that the defendant copied the plaintiff's work. An example of the most probative evidence is evidence that mistakes in the plaintiff's work—typographical errors in books, coding mistakes for software, etc.—are also found in the defendant's work.[36] Both these issues are matters of factual determination, and the judge must rule on the credibility of the witnesses, the likelihood of the assertions, the scope and degree of similarity, and the like. And the two requirements are considered together in a kind of inverse relationship, so if the probative similarity is very high, then very slight evidence of access will often be sufficient to establish copying, and vice versa.

The final requirement for infringement is what is sometimes called "misappropriation." This is not a particularly useful way of phrasing the issue, but it is hard to find a better shorthand form for this third element. The question here is whether the defendant actually took enough of the plaintiff's copyright material as to warrant a finding of infringement. There are a number of considerations when considering misappropriation, notably whether the material that has been copied is actually subject to copyright, and whether the defendant's material is substantially similar to the plaintiff's work. Let's look at each in turn.

First, an example: let's say that you have written a book about a young boy, named Harry Potter, who attends a school for wizards. I am perfectly free to copy parts of your work as long as the parts I copy aren't subject to copyright, even if your work is copyrighted. So, the idea/expression dichotomy that we've discussed previously says that I am perfectly free to write a competing novel about a young wizard as long as I don't take elements of your expression.

---

36. As a schoolboy, I used to wonder why occasionally the answers in my math books were wrong. I mean, the people writing them are supposed to *have all the answers*! How could they get them wrong? It was only when I became an intellectual property lawyer that I realized that these errors were intentionally inserted, in case a rival textbook publisher used these problem-and-answer sets. Identical errors are the best evidence of copying.

But let's say that I have actually copied some part of your expression: then the question is whether my book is substantially similar to your copyrighted material.

There are a couple of salient points to note here. The first is that you shouldn't confuse probative similarity with substantial similarity. Oddly enough, courts often screw this up, but there is a simple distinction between them. Probative similarity is a factual question of *whether the defendant actually copied the plaintiff's work*. Substantial similarity is a legal question about *whether the defendant's work is sufficiently similar only to the copyright-protected elements* of the plaintiff's work to amount to an infringement. The first issue is about independent creation while the second is really a determination of whether the appropriation is de minimis. Go back to our wizard-book example. Both your book and my book involve wizards in school, and, let's say, both books have a scarred boy-wizard and feature magic mirrors. The fact that my book contains a scarred protagonist and has a magic mirror is very good evidence of probative similarity: as long as I had access to your work when I wrote mine, pretty much any court is going to conclude as a matter of fact that I copied your book. But the presence of a magic mirror is generally not going to be a copyright element—it's barely expression, and it is probably precluded based on the *scènes à faire* doctrine discussed above—and so it shouldn't feature in the question of whether my work is substantially similar to yours. On the other hand, the features of the main character are usually considered to be appropriate for the assessment of substantial similarity.

Courts wrestle with how best to assess the question of substantial similarity, and a number of tests have been formulated to assist the court in determining whether the defendant's work is infringing. First off, there is the general observation that courts will examine both quantitative and qualitative similarity, so it's as damaging for a defendant to have copied a large amount of relatively trivial material as it is to have copied a small amount of the gist of the copyright work. But beyond this, there often remains the fundamental question of whether the defendant has (impermissibly) infringed the plaintiff's expression rather than (permissibly) used the work's underlying idea. The Second Circuit created a test in *Computer Associates v. Altai*[37] that has become influential, and is instructive here. Its three-stage test has phases of abstraction, filtration, and comparison. *Abstraction* refers to the idea/expression dichotomy, and here the test winnows out any elements that are unprotected ideas, rather than protected expression. (Thus, the idea of a wizard in a book could not be protected). The filtration step removes any expressive elements that are unprotectable, such as familiar elements like a formal dining hall, or wizards having wands. These elements are subject to the merger doctrine, or amount to *scènes à faire*, and so aren't copyrightable. Only once these non-copyright features are removed does the court undertake the *comparison stage*: looking to see whether the defendant's material is substantially similar to the plaintiff's material that made it through the abstraction and filtration stages. Most courts undertake a version of this type of analysis even if they don't formally adopt the abstraction-then-filtration-then-comparison test of the *Altai* court.

## Secondary Liability

The statute provides only for primary infringement, as discussed in the previous section. However, courts have applied common law principles of secondary liability in order to find infringement for those who aid and abet others in their primary infringement. Over time the forms of secondary liability for copyright have stabilized into two types of infringement: contributory and vicarious. Contributory infringement occurs where a party intentionally induces or encourages primary infringement and declines to exercise a right to stop or limit the other's infringement, whereas vicarious infringement involves a greater degree of control—analogous to a principal or an

---

37.  Computer Assocs. Int'l v. Altai, Inc., 982 F.2d 693 (2d Cir. 1992).

employer—along with direct financial benefit to the secondary infringer. In both contributory and vicarious infringement there must be a primary infringement, so, if the plaintiff is unable to establish a direct infringement—say, for example that it can't demonstrate that it holds the copyright, or the defendant can establish that the direct infringer had a defense to the plaintiff's infringement claim—then there can be no secondary liability.

Vicarious infringement is derived from the tort principle of *respondeat superior*, which is the principle that a superior is responsible for the actions of those under the superior's control. It has two requirements: the "superior" party (i.e., the one made vicariously liable) must profit directly from the infringement of the direct infringer, and the superior must have the right and ability to supervise the direct infringer. The easiest example of this would be where an employee is infringing copyright for the benefit of an employer. If I were using pirated word processing software in the course of my work, my employer is responsible. The employer gains the direct financial benefit of not having to buy licensed copies of Microsoft Word while having the ability and right to tell me to stop infringing. Another well-known example from a few years ago was the proprietor of a flea market who leased space in the market to a seller of bootleg albums. The market operator gained the financial benefit of the rent from the bootlegger, and, although the operator may or may not have known directly of the infringement, it had the ability to shut down the bootlegger.

To be found liable for contributory infringement, a defendant generally must have directly induced infringement by others, or provided the means to infringe with the knowledge of infringement. The analysis tends to fall into a number of standard patterns. At the simple end of the spectrum are cases where the defendant has knowledge of the direct infringement and does everything possible to make the infringement happen, short of doing the copying itself. So there are cases of commercial "lending libraries" that provided the plaintiff's copyrighted work, blank media, copying facilities, and instructions on how their patrons could copy the plaintiff's material.[38] At the other end are cases where the defendant provides some significant step in the chain of infringement, but is not directly encouraging that infringement. These sorts include cases where credit card companies provide some billing function to the infringers.[39]

In between these two extremes lie many more-difficult cases, which these days usually revolve around various internet business models. It shouldn't come as a surprise that the law of secondary liability has been driven by internet file sharing. Since the emergence of Napster the recording and movie industries have faced numerous challenges to their control over the distribution of their content through various file-sharing applications and services. Although their strategy at one point was to sue large numbers of direct infringers, almost from the beginning the industries sought to impose secondary liability against the operators of Napster, and then against the innumerable replacements and improvements such as Aimster, Grokster, KaZaa, BitTorrent, etc. The analysis for these sorts of cases begins with the pre-internet Supreme Court case of *Sony v. Universal*[40]—a case involving Betamax videocassette machines—which established that selling a staple article of commerce that had a substantial noninfringing purpose did not amount to contributory infringement. Twenty years later the Supreme Court upheld this decision in the *Grokster* case, but held that the kinds of activity of file-sharing systems that encourage others to infringe were beyond the *Sony* test.[41] In short, the Grokster system encouraged active inducement, like the lending library cases.

---

38. *See, e.g.,* Elektra Records Co. v. Gem Elec. Distribs., Inc., 360 F. Supp. 821 (E.D.N.Y. 1973).

39. *See, e.g.,* Perfect 10, Inc. v. VISA Int'l Serv. Assoc., 494 F.3d. 788 (9th Cir. 2007); Perfect 10, Inc. v. Amazon.com, Inc., 508 F.3d 1146 (9th Cir. 2007); Perfect 10, Inc. v. CCBill LLC, 488 F.3d 1102 (9th Cir. 2007).

40. Sony Corp. of America v. Universal City Studios, 464 U.S. 417 (1984).

41. MGM Studios Inc. v. Grokster Ltd., 545 U.S. 945 (2005).

As each new file-sharing technology emerges, courts have to decide where along the contributory liability spectrum each new technology sits. The test is remarkably open-ended, and the outcome of each new case in this area is a crapshoot. Basically, the courts apply a smell test to the case and, if offended by the defendant's actions, will typically find contributory infringement. In this regard the *Grokster* decision was a profoundly unsatisfying one since it was a perfect opportunity for the Supreme Court to provide the modern interpretation of *Sony v. Universal* and create a balance between the content industries and the emerging internet businesses. The Court ducked that opportunity, and the uncertainty in this area can be traced back to this failing.

### Infringement in the Digital Age

The common law has responded to the development of digital technologies and the internet, but the statutory changes to these new technologies have probably been more significant. The introduction in 1998 of the Digital Millennium Copyright Act (DMCA) ushered in two profound changes to the copyright system.

The first is contained in section 1201, within what is called the *anti-circumvention* provisions. The new types of liability created in this section involve means of getting around (circumventing) digital rights management systems and related technological-protection measures. The sections forbid direct circumvention of these measures, as well as the sale and manufacture of devices that circumvent these measures. These are radical departures from the regular types of copyright liability discussed above, in part because they invoke criminal sanctions and in part because they don't actually require any copyright infringement at all. The reach of the anti-circumvention provisions have been narrowed somewhat by judicial interpretation, most notably in *Chamberlain*[42] and

---

42. Chamberlain Group, Inc. v. Skylink Techs., Inc., 381 F.3d 1178 (Fed. Cir. 2004).

*Lexmark*[43] where the courts denied the plaintiffs' attempts to use the anti-circumvention provisions to stop competing aftermarket products. In these cases the plaintiffs included encryption—a form of the technological protection measure mentioned in the section—in order to stop competitors from creating products that worked with their devices. So the plaintiff in *Chamberlain* made garage door openers and wanted to control all aftermarket add-ons, while the *Lexmark* plaintiff thought it could use the anti-circumvention provisions to control the market in toner cartridges for its printers. The courts in both those cases mercifully concluded that this kind of control was outside the purview of the section since there was no copyrighted work that the encryption was protecting.

This is not to say that all anti-circumvention cases turn out to be as nuanced. In a series of anti-circumvention cases, the motion picture industry brought suit under the anti-circumvention provisions to stop the circulation and use of DeCSS, a small piece of code that decrypted the content encoded on DVDs and allowed people to play DVDs on unauthorized devices. Notwithstanding that there are very good policy reasons to allow the circulation of DeCSS—for free speech reasons, to allow Linux-based computers to play DVDs—courts routinely concluded that circulation of the DeCSS code was contrary to the anti-circumvention provisions, and a number of defendants were enjoined and fined.

The second important change from the DMCA was the creation of limitations on Internet Service Provider (ISP) liability, including the notice-and-takedown provisions and the safe harbor provisions of section 512 of the act. Any transfer of data on the internet involves potential infringements of the reproduction right (backbone host computers on the network copy the data in order to hold it for sending on to the next part of the chain, and ISPs regularly store

---

43. Lexmark Int'l, Inc. v. Static Control Components, Inc., 387 F. 3d 522 (6th. Cir. 2004).

data locally to make it faster for their users to retrieve information from the edge of the network) and the public distribution right (as the providers transfer data on to their users, they may be unwittingly distributing the copyrighted content of some media conglomerate). Section 512 limits ISPs' liability for infringement of the distribution right to two situations: they will be liable where they are performing some function that is not part of the technical infrastructure of the internet, or where they had knowledge the data stored and passing through their system is infringing. Section 512 excuses ISPs for "technical" infringements that occur as a result of "transitory" communications involving passing content from one host to the other, and also for system "caching" (i.e., the local storage of content for the purposes of speeding retrieval by users). It also provides a mechanism for "notice and takedown" that insulates ISPs and other hosts as long as they remove allegedly infringing content upon notification of the infringement by the copyright owner. The limitations in section 512 have allowed ISPs to flourish without the fear of wholesale infringement actions against them, and the rise of the internet industry is in part due to this provision.

## Remedies

Copyright is typical of most intellectual property laws in that it has a broad combination of legal and equitable remedies, the most common of which are damages and injunctions. While there are special principles that can apply in relation to when, for example, a court will make an equity-based order for disgorgement of profits or how it accounts for actual damages, most copyright remedies are the same as any other area of law, and remedies need not detain us much. There are, however, two salient issues here.

First is the special nature of copyright statutory damages. Section 504 of the Copyright Act allows the plaintiff to elect to obtain "statutory damages" in an amount between $750 and "$150,000 for each act of infringement. The court has the discretion to work out the amount of damages. This section has become truly significant in the digital era where every transfer of an mp3 music track from a file-sharing site is an act of infringement, and so every now and again file-sharing cases hit the headlines because an infringer has been fined some unbelievably large amount as a result of the upload or download of a relatively small number of tracks. Statutory damages bear no relation to the actual damages suffered by the plaintiff, and are thus more in the nature of a fine or penalty. Although some argue against them, they remain an important weapon in the copyright owner's arsenal, and they are routinely used as a bargaining chip in file-sharing cases. ("Admit the file sharing, pay us a few thousand for the downloads, and we won't ask the judge for statutory damages.") The propriety or otherwise of doing this is debatable, but beyond our discussion here.

Second, there is the issue of how injunctions in copyright cases implicate prior restraint concerns from First Amendment law. For the longest time courts in copyright infringement cases would issue preliminary injunctions as a matter of course, rejecting the kinds of balancing that are typically used in other First Amendment arenas. The tide here seems to have turned, and in light of the Supreme Court decision in *eBay v MercEnchange*, lower courts are balancing the four factors used in assessing the grant of an injunction in a way that is more likely to favor First Amendment principles.[44]

### Defenses and Limitations of Rights

There are three basic categories of defenses to a copyright infringement. The most important is the fair use defense, which is codified

---

44.  See discussion of *eBay* in the Remedies section in Chapter 3: Patents.

in section 107. This is the defense that attracts all the public attention and which is the basis for many discussions about how we should strike the balance in copyright law between private and public interests. Because of its significance, fair use is the defense that we need to spend most of our time examining; but first we will spend a moment on the other two types of defenses, those grounded in equity and those that come from special statutory provisions.

### Equitable and Statutory Licenses and Defenses

The equitable defenses apply across the board to pretty much every type of intellectual property case, and cover situations where the plaintiff has engaged in unseemly delay—or *laches* as it's called in the old Law-French—or where the plaintiff comes to the court with unclean hands. In copyright there is one special variant of the equitable unclean hands defense called the "copyright misuse" doctrine. This defense is derived from the patent misuse doctrine, which is an application of equitable and antitrust principles. Both the patent and copyright forms of misuse rely on the same type of wrongdoing: the plaintiff uses its intellectual property to extend its rights beyond those granted in the statute, in ways that are anticompetitive. So, for example, in the *Lasercomb* case, the plaintiff licensed its software to the defendant and included a term in the contract that prohibited the defendant from implementing the software's (unprotectable) idea in a different form.[45] Although the defendant had engaged in a prima facie infringement, the plaintiff had sought to use the copyright in its software in a way inconsistent with the rationale for copyright—in short, to stifle innovation in ideas—and so was held to have engaged in a copyright misuse.

---

45. Lasercomb Am., Inc. v. Reynolds, 911 F.2d 970 (4th Cir. 1990).

Although it was accepted by the court in *Lasercomb*, the copyright misuse defense, like all equitable defenses, is rarely successful and requires very high levels of bad behavior by the plaintiff.

The statutory defenses and licenses are enshrined in sections 108 through 121 of the Copyright Act. These provide for a series of compulsory licenses and exceptions for specific sorts of uses. A compulsory license basically excuses a specific sort of infringement as long as the person using the work pays the copyright owner some statutory fee, or complies with some other requirement. These are called *statutory* or *compulsory* licenses because they create a regime where the use is licensed automatically and without permission of the copyright holder as long as the user pays a statutorily set royalty. A prime example is when a singer covers a song: under section 115 the copyright holder of a musical work cannot stop someone from singing and recording a version of that song as long as the song has been previously recorded and as long as the singer complies with certain requirements, notably by paying the *mechanical*, the statutorily set fee for singing the cover. The compulsory license sections are very different from the standard approach in copyright because normally we allow copyright holders to forbid any unauthorized use, and we rely on the market to set the reserve price for using the copyright work. Against this default, the compulsory license provisions and statutory defenses seek to change the balance between public and private interests in certain commercially important or socially significant arenas. Thus, in this set of provisions we also find defenses for the reproduction of works by libraries and archives, for the showing of films in class by teachers, for those who adapt works for people with disabilities, for the retransmission of satellite signals, and so on. The requirements of these sections are enormously detailed and complex and generate all manner of paid work for copyright attorneys. We don't need to cover them in more detail than this.

Important though these two categories of defenses may be, most of the interest and litigation in copyright defenses revolves around the concept of fair use, which we turn to now.

### Fair Use

The fair use defense originates from *Folsom v. Marsh*, a case involving the private letters of George Washington.[46] The defendant in that case produced a biography of Washington, copying a number of his letters in which the plaintiff held the copyright. In discussing the nature of the use permitted a defendant, Justice Story asked whether the defendant's use was such as to produce a substitute for the plaintiff's work. In doing so, Justice Story introduced some factors to help in the decision whether the defendant's work was a substitute, or whether it was a fair use: these factors included the nature, value, and extent of the taking; the objects of each work; and the degree to which the authors of each work had relied on the same common materials in producing their works. Over time these factors were expanded by the courts and then were eventually codified in section 107 of the 1976 Copyright Act. The codified section has two parts: the first provides some exemplars of fair use—criticism, comment, news reporting, teaching, scholarship, and research are the canonical examples given—and the second part provides four factors that are to be used in each case to assess fair use. The Supreme Court has said that the categories of fair use are never closed, and, although it's pretty rare for the court to find a new type of fair use, each new case, and even situations that fall into the enumerated examples are typically assessed using the four canonical factors.

So, to the factors. These are: (1) the purpose and character of the use, including whether it was of a commercial nature; (2) the nature of the copyrighted work; (3) the amount and substantiality of the portion used in relation to the copyrighted work as a whole; and (4) the effect of the use on the market or potential market for, or value of, the copyrighted work. As with any factor-based analysis, the court will usually assess each factor individually as

---

46. 9 F. Cas. 342 (C.C.D. Mass. 1841).

favoring the plaintiff or the defendant, and then combine them to come up with a view about the overall fairness of the use.

The first factor, then, is usually a question of whether the defendant made any money from his or her work—unsurprisingly, judges tend to be unimpressed if the defendant has any commercial interest—but it also regularly looks to see whether the defendant's use is one of the types mentioned in the preamble to the section. So, even if the use is commercial, if it's for the purpose of news reporting or scholarly examination, then the first factor will generally favor the defendant.

The second factor enshrines the policy distinction that we've already examined in relation to the *Feist* case: that fictional works are granted high levels of protection in copyright law while factual works get shorter shrift. Therefore, this factor will tend to favor the plaintiff if its work is a fictional or highly expressive work, but will favor the defendant if the work is factual or not highly expressive. However, we can't say that all fact-based works won't be protected: in the *Harper & Row* case that dealt with President Ford's about-to-be-published autobiography, the Supreme Court concluded that a magazine couldn't abstract the interesting parts of the president's forthcoming autobiography—specifically the bits about pardoning President Nixon—even though the information recounted was historical. In part this was because the magazine didn't just use the factual record but President Ford's actual language from the autobiography, and in part it was because the book hadn't then been published. This latter point shouldn't make much difference in copyright law since the amendments to the Copyright Act in 1976, but the shadow of the early distinction between published and unpublished work was still important back in the early 1970s in a way that it wouldn't be today.

The third factor examines the degree of taking, and as with the approach used in relation to infringement, qualitative assessments are as important as quantitative ones. Taking a small quantity of the plaintiff's work that is adjudged the "heart" or the "gist" of the plaintiff's work is often as problematic for the defendant as taking large quantities of other parts of the work. This approach is notoriously slippery, and is regularly used by courts as the basis for conclusory reasoning; that is, it's easy for a judge to say that a small taking of the copyright work is problematic simply by labeling the part taken—the quotations from President Ford's autobiography for example—as particularly salient to the work as a whole. Another way that courts can push the analysis in favor of the plaintiff, even in circumstances where this isn't warranted, is by focusing on how much of the *defendant's* work is made up of the plaintiff's work. The statute only asks what amount of the plaintiff's work is taken, but in *Harper & Row* the Supreme Court found that a taking that amounted to 1 percent of the Ford autobiography was significant because it represented 13 percent of the defendant's magazine article. It's hard to square this with the actual words of the statute, and numerous criticisms of this approach have been made. It seems often the case that judges apply the moral maxim that one must not reap where one has not sown, ignoring the purpose of the balancing act enshrined in section 107 as well as the purpose of the Copyright Act as a whole.

The final factor looks to whether the defendant's use destroys the value or supplants the potential market for the plaintiff's work. This factor is at once both the most important and the most problematic factor. An empirical study has shown that this factor is the one that most clearly predicts the outcome of any case, and a finding that the defendant's work might affect the market for the plaintiff's work is often dispositive of the case in favor of the plaintiff. And at first blush this makes a lot of sense. Justice Story in *Folsom* was rightly concerned about the situation where the defendant's work acts as a substitute for the plaintiff's work: we all agree that the fair use defense should not protect an unscrupulous defendant who abstracts large chunks of the plaintiff's work and puts out a cheaper competitor in the marketplace. This cuts directly against the incentive justification that we discussed earlier, and if fair use could be used to produce substitutes, we would presumably see fewer original works produced.

But the problem is that courts have interpreted the "potential market" language in a way that means that almost any use by the defendant will offend against the fourth factor. Consider *Castle Rock*, also known as the "Seinfeld Aptitude Test" case.[47] The studio that owned the copyright in the Seinfeld television series sued the publisher of a book called the *Seinfeld Aptitude Test*, which had a series of SAT-style questions drawn from events, quotations, and details from the *Seinfeld* series. The Second Circuit rejected the defendant's fair use defense, and its reasoning on the fourth factor was remarkable. Even though it was asserted that the studio then had no intention of producing a book of questions based on the series, the court concluded that the defendant's work usurped any potential market for such works that Castle Rock might possibly develop or license others to develop. Although this seems within the language and purpose of the fourth factor, the problem is that these days every single piece of intellectual property can be licensed to some merchandiser, or manufacturer, or packager of content. Novels beget movies, which beget television series, which beget game shows, which beget online quizzes, which beget e-mail discussion lists of favorite quotations, all of which amount to some kind of market. The approach of the Second Circuit—which has been followed in other courts—means that a large number of socially meritorious derivative works are lost to society. Why? Because copyright owners almost always overvalue their content. Copyright owners don't do a simple economic calculus of the value of their work; there is always an additional multiplier for the fact that they produced it.[48] Even commercially savvy authors resort to

---

47. Castle Rock Entm't, Inc. v. Carol Publ'g Group, 150 F.3d 132 (2d Cir. 1998).

48. This observation has been made in relation to personal effects and is called the endowment effect; *see* Christopher Curran, *The Endowment Effect*, *in* BIBLIOGRAPHY OF LAW AND ECONOMICS, VOLUME I 819, 819–20 (Boudewijn Bouckaert & Gerrit De Geest eds., 2000). It has only just begun to be studied by scholars in relation to intellectual property; *see* Christopher Buccafusco & Christopher Sprigman, *Valuing Intellectual Property: An Experiment*,

this type of magical thinking in conjunction with I'm-just-a-poor-struggling-author rhetoric. For example, the second richest woman in entertainment, J.K Rowling, sued the small publisher of *The Harry Potter Lexicon*, a crowdsource-generated reference work to her series of books. She said that the publication of it crushed her creativity, and, so great was her distress, after the print version of the Lexicon came out, she said that she no longer had the will nor the heart to publish her own reference work.[49] In the case of the *Seinfeld Aptitude Test*, Castle Rock persuaded the court that they might one day produce a quiz book based on *Seinfeld*, and the defendant was found to have usurped the potential market that Castle Rock had never even contemplated might exist.

To give it its due, fair use does work tolerably well in cases involving parodies of works, i.e., works that are reinterpretations of existing works. Indeed fair use works very well where the parodic derivative has some political message attached. These sorts of parodies are examples of highly transformative derivatives, and courts often emphasize the significance in transformation as highly valuable, and therefore determinative of fair use in favor of defendants. Thus, in the well-known *Wind Done Gone* case,[50] the court accepted the argument that a reinterpetation of Margaret Mitchell's *Gone With the Wind*—written from the perspective of Scarlett O'Hara's enslaved half-sister—warranted the fair use defense because of its

---

91 CORNELL L. REV 1 (2010), but a simple thought experiment should show you the power of the process in copyright. Think of something that you wrote or drew, that has no inherent economic value—a blog posting, a doodle, a letter—and ask whether you would be okay with people sending that work around to everyone without your permission and potentially making money (from subscription fees to the service they use, etc.). Most people would want to stop this sort of use of something which is theirs, which they created. In almost every case your reserve price—the price at which you would be happy to sell the right to use this work—is much higher than the market price.

49.  Warner Bros. Entm't Inc. v. RDR Books, 575 F. Supp. 2d 513 (S.D.N.Y. 2008).

50.  SunTrust Bank v. Houghton Mifflin Co., 268 F.3d 1257 (11th Cir. 2001).

highly valuable, highly transformative use of the original. But even here, courts are anything but generous with defendants, and routinely find against them even where their actions might usually be viewed as both culturally appropriate and meritorious.

We can conclude therefore that the fair use defense is a vital component in the balance between private and public interests in copyright, but it is not the savior of free expression and culture that we might wish. Even in the arena of art, where we might anticipate a generous shadow of protection, judicial interpretation of fair use gives little succor to the appropriation artist who reimagines existing works as a comment on society or on art itself. Appropriation art is, by now, a venerable tradition in modern art; stemming at least as far back as Marcel Duchamp's ready-mades of the early 1900s, we can trace a line through the Dadaists and Surrealists' found objects, Joseph Cornell's memory boxes, Andy Warhol's Campbell's soup cans, and Robert Rauschenburg's combines of the Pop era, culminating in the more recent work of appropriators such as Richard Prince, Jeff Koons, Damien Hirst, and Shephard Fairey. It's hardly surprising that these artists would attract copyright infringement suits—Warhol for example had to defend an action brought by a photographer whose photographs he used for some of his silk-screened paintings—but it is surprising how often courts have denied fair use protection even for established and famous artists such as Jeff Koons. Although Koons happened to win the latest suit against him, numerous cases before this found that his style of appropriation art was a copyright infringement and not covered by fair use, largely because judges concluded that in today's commercialized art world, Koons should have paid money to the people whose work he put to reuse. In an era where everyone with a computer and an artistic sensibility can become an appropriation artist—or as they are called these days, a remixer, a mashup artist, or whatever—this is a problematic result.

This discussion leads us neatly into the next section, where we examine some of the criticisms of copyright that have emerged in the last few years.

## 𝍷 Discontents

Of all the laws of intellectual property, copyright is probably the one that has attracted the greatest attention from reformers and critics. As a result, it is the area that probably faces the greatest range of criticisms, which makes it an impossibly challenging area to summarize. However, a number of common themes emerge that have had significant impact in the development of copyright and provide the basis for understanding criticisms of the law.

Probably the most important theme is the one that has animated the discussion in this chapter: how do we balance the interests of the public against those of the private rights-holders? Jessica Litman provided an early influential intellectual history on the way that copyright law was made, and showed that it was mostly a series of negotiations between private rights-holders. She documented how for the longest time the public was simply not involved in setting the agenda for copyright. From this, Jamie Boyle, David Lange, and others have been influential in identifying the scope of, and the need for, a robust public domain to provide an appropriate counterpoint to copyright industries and their interest in expanding the nature of copyright. As we saw in the first chapter, it's easy to ignore the public domain because its role in creativity is much less obvious than that of the private creator. But numerous scholars and activists have been vigorous in identifying where and how the public domain contributes to creativity. Probably the most influential and recognizable voice here has been Larry Lessig who, with his numerous books, his blog, and his public appearances, has demonstrated how private takings undermine the flourishing of some creative cultures.

The most significant impact of this work has been to challenge the seemingly inevitable expansion of copyright. We saw earlier that copyright's scope, term, and effect have never once decreased, and we've also seen how the rate of copyright's expansion has accelerated over the last forty or fifty years. The public domain theorists have provided a check on this expansion. Although the laws of

copyright have not decreased in their effect or scope, they no longer  seem to be expanding: the recognition of the public domain
seems to have brought copyright law to a point of equilibrium.
From time to time there are attempts to change or reduce the scope
of copyright; these efforts are always interesting but usually  fruitless. To take one example, a number of scholars have suggested that
we should institute a system that resembles the initial period of the
development of U.S. copyright law by reducing the copyright term
to some period—depending on the author, it might be as short as
five or as long as twenty years—and reinvigorate the importance of
formalities, notably the registration requirement. In return the
author would be allowed to renew the copyright multiple times.
The proponents of these reforms argue that this would mean that
low-value copyrights—which are most of them—would quickly
fall into the public domain to be used by anyone. However, commercially valuable copyrights could be renewed multiple times and
thus would be able to be exploited for an extended period.
The argument is that this would solve a number of problems,
including the so-called "orphan works" issue: works that are still
within the copyright period but where no one knows or can find
the current copyright-holder. As copyright law stands, those seeking to use orphan works are unable to do so because they don't
know who to ask for permission. As a result, the prospective user
of the orphan work will typically not use them for fear of an infringement action surfacing years later. Under the short-renewable-term-
plus-formalities reform, there would be no such thing as orphan
works, and we would presumably see more creative reuse of these
works and ideas.

Of course, there is exactly zero chance of this reform passing:
current rights-holders such as media and entertainment companies will never agree to it, and their lobbyists know exactly how
to influence Congress to get their way. And besides, it is contrary
to the international treaties in this area—treaties that are written
largely as a result of lobbying by trade representatives who have a
stake in the success of copyright-based industries—and so it is

extremely tricky to find a way to reconcile reforms with our international obligations.

It may be though, in this digital era that copyright laws and industries don't matter as much as we initially think. Another major theme of copyright changes has involved scholarship and actions that demonstrate that copyright is less central to authorship and creativity than we first thought. One strand of this work involves so-called "copy-norms" work, which has studied how people create in a number of different creative arenas, especially where they could, but do not, rely on copyright. So we have seen the emergence of studies on French chefs, stand-up comics, and magicians, and these studies have shown how these groups rely on norms of production and use that have little to do with the rights and incentives of copyright and more to do with entry into a group and the policing of common interests within these groups. Outside these unusual industries we have also witnessed a huge flowering of "user-generated content" as a consequence of digital technology and the internet. This content is produced largely without regard for the kinds of rights and incentives that are said to be so central to the need for copyright. The significance of Wikipedia, blogs, and open source software has been discussed by scholars such as Richard Stallman and Yochai Benkler,[51] and some have suggested that the rise of user-generated content demonstrates that the future of content is not one likely to have much to do with copyright.[52]

Aside from the scholarly work, perhaps the greatest challenge to copyright is found in the daily practice of millions. Two groups are notable. First is the group of creators who don't seem to care much for copyright. Millions of authors routinely give away some or all of their copyright-granted rights through the licensing system called

---

51. *See, e.g.,* Yochai Benkler, THE WEALTH OF NETWORKS: HOW SOCIAL PRODUCTION TRANSFORMS MARKETS AND FREEDOM (2007).

52. Dan Hunter & F. Gregory Lastowka, *Amateur-to-Amateur*, 46 WM & MARY L. REV. 951–1030 (2004).

Creative Commons. An initiative of a number of copyright professors and activists, Creative Commons licenses have been embraced by a huge number of authors as a way of getting their content out into the world without the restrictions of much of the copyright system.

The other group is comprised of the millions of people who digitally share files—usually music but these days also movies and other content—using peer-to-peer networks. Although it is clear that this type of file sharing is illegal, the scale is such that it amounts to a social practice of which we must take notice. Attempts by content owners to stop this have failed, and one of the most significant issues facing the framers of modern copyright law is: What now?

# Patent

UNITED STATES PATENT NUMBER 6,368,227 was granted to one Steven Olson of Otis Ave, St Paul, Minnesota, on April 9, 2002. It contains three elegant drawings demonstrating features of the invention, together with the text describing the background to the invention, a summary and a detailed description of the invention, and four claims that detail the actual features over which the monopoly is granted.[1] Like all modern patents, Patent No. 6,368,227 gives the inventor a twenty-year federally mandated monopoly on the novel, non-obvious, useful invention that is disclosed and claimed in the patent document. Which means that until 2020, Steven Olson—five years old when he was granted the patent[2]—was to have the exclusive right to practice the method of swinging sideways on a swing by pulling alternately on one chain and then the other.[3]

---

1. We'll use the term *monopoly* in this chapter as a synonym for the "exclusive negative rights" that a patent grants. Some might suggest that this is incorrect because they use the term *monopoly* in the sense of an economic monopoly i.e., power over a market; *see Schenck v. Nortron Corp.*, 713 F.2d 782 (Fed. Cir. 1983), per Markey J. Since "monopoly" is a perfectly good way of describing the effect of a patent grant and clearly explains the difference in the scope of rights between patents and copyright, we'll continue to use it here.

2. Jeff Hecht, *Boy Takes Swing at a Patent*, NEWSCIENTIST, Apr. 17, 2002, http://www.newscientist.com/article/dn2178-boy-takes-swing-at-us-patents.html.

3. The patent expired on May 10, 2006 for failure to pay a required maintenance fee, but had the patentee paid the fee at the time, tykes in the playground who discovered how to swing from side to side would (technically) have infringed Steve Olson's patent until the young inventor turned twenty-five: an age when, presumably, little Stevie no longer had much interest in swinging on a swing.

The "Method of Swinging on a Swing" patent was submitted by Steve's father—a patent attorney seemingly with too much time on his hands—as a lesson to his young son about what his dad did at work, and about inventions and the nature of the patent system. But it provides a useful waypoint for our navigation of the patent system and some of its problems. In a word, it's a stupid patent. And it is by no means alone in its foolishness: U.S. Patent No. 5,443,036 for a "Method of Exercising a Cat" granted a monopoly over the method of projecting a handheld laser onto the wall to send cats crazy as they chase it. U.S. Patent No. 6,329,919, is a business-method patent issued in December 2001 to four IBM developers for a system that issues reservations for using the toilet on an airplane. And so on. Endless numbers of these sorts of silly patents have been granted over the years, and by and large they are harmless. In reality Steve Olson isn't actually going to be able to stop kids from swinging side to side, and so the only potential harm is the waste of the patent examiner's time.[4] But consider U.S. Patent No. 6,004,596 issued to Smucker's for a patent over a sealed sandwich—like the one your mom used to make—which was litigated at ruinous expense, and eventually cancelled. Or consider Research In Motion, the Canadian company that makes Blackberrys, and that settled with a patent owner for an alleged patent infringement over essential communications technology, before that patent was eventually invalidated. The cost to Research In Motion? $621 million.

Poor quality patents, ones that never should have been issued in the first place, are rife and generate huge costs for businesses and society. At its core the problem is this: because an issued patent is presumed valid, and because patent litigation is ruinously expensive, most businesses confronted with a patent infringement suit will settle the matter rather than slug it out in court. It is a serious

---

4. And even this isn't really a harm, since the various patent fees are supposed to cover the administrative costs of examining and issuing the patent.

injustice and terribly wasteful inefficiency if legal threats and law-suits happen over patents that should never have been granted in the first place. This problem has led to all manner of criticisms of the patent system together with numerous calls for reform. We will come to these concerns and calls shortly, but before we do so, we need to examine how the patent system is supposed to work.

As a starting point, it's useful to recognize the differences between the copyright and patent systems. As you'll recall, copy-rights are simple to obtain and come into existence as soon as works are fixed in material form. Patents, on the other hand, are only granted after a rigorous examination process that typically takes two or more years and involves considerable expense. There are five requirements that an applicant must satisfy to obtain a patent: (1) she must show that the invention is over patentable sub-ject matter, that it is (2) novel, (3) non-obvious, (4) useful, and that (5) the patent adequately discloses and enables the invention. These demands are much more onerous than the requirements for copyright, but the term for which a utility patent is granted—twenty years from the time of filing—is much less than that for copyright. However, in return, the scope of protection that a patent grants is much broader than copyright: unlike copyright, which only protects expression and only forbids actual copying, patents protect the underlying idea of an invention and forbid independent invention by anyone else, even without copying.

Patent specifications are very specialized documents drafted by those qualified to practice before the patent bar, and the scope of the patent is defined by the claims. Each patent specification has three main parts: the written description, any necessary drawings, and the claims. The written description generally provides an abstract of the invention, a description of the field that the invention falls into, some background information describing the prior art (other similar inventions) and an adequate description of the invention and the way of practicing it. The drawings are important for the enablement requirement; that is, they are typically included because the patent applicant must ensure that others are able to make and practice the invention, and drawings are frequently the only, or the easiest, way to describe the invention adequately.[5]

The claims section is the most important part of the patent document; it comes at the end of the specification. Claims are a series of single-sentence statements that define the actual monopoly that the inventor is granted. Because the claims define the inventor's rights, significant attention is given to this part of the specification during drafting and examination, and much patent litigation revolves around the interpretation of the claims. To give you an idea of what claims look like, in the "Method of Swinging on a Swing" patent, the inventor claimed:

1. A method of swinging on a swing, the method comprising the steps of:

   a) suspending a seat for supporting a user between only two chains that are hung from a tree branch;
   b) positioning a user on the seat so that the user is facing a direction perpendicular to the tree branch;
   c) having the user pull alternately on one chain to induce movement of the user and the swing towards one side, and then on the other chain to induce movement of the user and the swing towards the other side; and
   d) repeating step c) to create side-to-side swinging motion, relative to the user, that is parallel to the tree branch.

In the sections that follow we will examine the history and theory behind the patent system before focusing on the requirements for obtaining a patent. Then we will investigate how one determines that a patent is infringed and the defenses available to defendants. We conclude by focusing on the calls for reform of the

---

5. Apparently, a picture is worth a thousand words.

patent system by returning to some of the problems that we first saw in this section.

## 𝘞 History and Theory

*Letters patent* were open grants of a monopoly right from the sovereign to a court favorite.[6] Arising during the medieval period in Europe, letters patent covered any type of monopoly—the sole right to produce playing cards, the monopoly over the weaving production of a certain types of cloth, and so on—and they became so numerous and widespread that, in time, they became a brake on the economy and the subject of political unhappiness.[7] The problem in England became so significant that in 1624 Parliament passed the Statute of Monopolies banning all royal grants of monopoly and privilege, except for

> . . . any letters patent and grants of privilege for the term of fourteen years or under, hereafter to be made, of the sole working or making of any manner of new manufactures within this realm, to the true and first inventor and inventors of such manufacture, which others at the time of making such letters patent shall not use, so as also they be not contrary to law, nor mischievous to the State, by raising prices of commodities at home, or hurt of trade, or generally inconvenient . . .[8]

This statute is usually seen as the birth of the modern patent system, because it represented a significant shift toward a modern type of

---

6. *Patent* comes from the Latin *patere*, "to be open." Letters patent were contrasted with letters couvert, which were secret or "closed" letters of grant.

7. As an example, a monopoly on the sale and importation of playing cards led to the first reported judicial condemnation of monopolies. *See The Case of Monopolies*, (1601) 77 Eng. Rep. 1260 (K.B.).

8. 21 Jac. I, ch.3 (1624).

innovation policy that assumes that free trade is preferable to tight governmental control of commerce. One of the few reasons for a nation-state to hand out monopolies is if they are demanded by the needs of innovation policy. Further, the act set the scene for current laws by demanding novelty for protection, by providing only a limited term for the monopoly, and by granting negative exclusive rights that forbade others from practicing the invention. Similar concerns and principles animate modern patent law, as we'll shortly see.

The patent system of England landed in America with the colonists—patents were granted in Massachusetts in 1641—and the Progress Clause of the U.S. Constitution included specific reference to patents as one of the appropriate areas of the federal congressional power. The first U.S. patent statute passed in 1790; it had similar requirements of novelty and invention as those in the English Statute of Monopolies. For a long period the grant of patents was controlled by a small number of officials—including, famously, Thomas Jefferson—but during the middle and latter part of the nineteenth century the system became significantly more bureaucratized, and here we saw the principle emerge of examination of the application by professional examiners. Various doctrinal additions occurred during this period, including the introduction of a requirement that the patented idea provide an "inventive lead," the precursor to the modern-day non-obviousness requirement.

Numerous changes occurred during the twentieth century but probably the most significant was the creation in 1982 of the Court of Appeals for the Federal Circuit, a specialized court that has the primary function of hearing patent appeals from cases in the U.S. district courts and from the internal decision-making tribunals of the U.S. Patent and Trademark Office (USPTO). The perceived effect of this has been the wholly positive feature of a more stable and consistent approach to patent doctrine, but it has come with a marked increase in the likelihood of patent validation on appeal as well as expansions in the doctrinal scope of patents. This has led to calls for some limitations on the court, and we'll discuss some of these issues in the final section of this chapter.

Although there have been many technical developments in the 350-plus years since the Statute of Monopolies, the underlying theories for the existence of patent law haven't changed much, as the same fundamental justifications that we discussed in the first chapter apply today. So, the natural rights justifications from Hegel or Locke that focus on the rights and needs of the individual apply neatly to the patent system: inventions are the unique creations of individual inventors, and so they should belong to the person inventing them. This may be justified either on the Hegelian basis that these inventions are a reflection of a person's self within the world, or on the Lockean basis that the property is deserved by virtue of the person's labor and effort. Of course, these justifications are perfectly explicable at the most general level but don't provide much explanation for most of the patent system: Why, if an invention is the unique creation of a person, would we limit its term to only twenty years, rather than for the life of the inventor (or even longer)? How do justifications that rely on the primacy of the individual explain the iterative, collaborative nature of most inventions? As the famous quote of Newton explains, even geniuses rely on the work of myriad inventors and scholars for their breakthroughs.[9] A reliance on Hegel or Locke doesn't get us far in apportioning proportionate interests in inventions that owe their existence to many creators. And these justifications are of little use in understanding the workings of modern industrialized systems of patenting in fields such as semiconductors, electronic commerce, drugs, or the financial black arts.

In part because of these difficulties, and in part because of the rise of economics as the preeminent means of determining policy outcomes, these days we find that the utilitarian justification is the most commonly accepted explanation for the patent system. This is true in the scholarly literature, in courts, and in Congress.

---

9. "If I have seen further it is only by standing on the shoulders of giants," Isaac Newton, http://www.bartleby.com/quotations/022002.html.

As we saw previously, this justification posits that a potential inventor is a rational actor and will only invest the time and effort necessary to invent if given an appropriate incentive to do so. This justification provides the basis for the system as a whole, as well as certain of its features. For example, a patentee gains a monopoly but at the cost of making the invention public, and utilitarian theory suggests why: we want to encourage the disclosure of secrets, since improved inventions are more likely once a secret invention is made public. Patents can thus be justified in utilitarian terms as solving the public goods problem, encouraging the production of otherwise underproduced inventions, and increasing the sum of human knowledge—in exchange for the grant of a twenty-year monopoly over exploiting the invention.

However, while utilitarian justifications provide some fundamental basis for patent law, they don't help much with the mechanics of the system, and their application turns out to be very messy in practice. Consider applying the incentive theory to explain and justify the choice of a twenty-year period of patent protection. For this to make sense, the term would have to be roughly appropriate as an incentive to encourage the maximal production of inventions and minimize the deadweight loss of people being unable to produce competing products or improvements. The evidence that twenty years is the right period of time to solve this particular differential equation is incredibly weak. Essentially there is *no evidence at all* that this is the right length of time, and there is good evidence that an overlong period of protection is causing losses in numerous industries, except perhaps in certain areas such as pharmaceuticals and biological sciences. In areas such as software and business methods, the evidence seems to suggest that drastically lowered periods of protection would produce more innovation, and some of the strongest proponents of reduced patent protection and improved patent quality are information technology companies. One way of resolving this problem would be to segment patent protection into different categories for different types of inventions, with increased protection and term limits for innovations that are very expensive to produce, and lessened protection for other sorts of inventions. There are many reasons this approach will never be implemented—notably, it's politically impossible to imagine amendments of this sort being passed—but a more nuanced patent system is certainly something that utilitarianism would favor.

Once we start to apply the lens of utilitarianism and economics, other parts of the patent system start to become worrisome. If we adopt a utilitarian calculus, we must weigh the social costs of the patent system against its benefits—and it's not clear that the patent system is justified on these terms. The costs of the system include administrative cost, the problem of improperly granted patents stopping competition, the costs of patent litigation clogging the courts, and the loss of innovation from foregone research and development caused by competitors avoiding the area covered by the patent grant, among many others. These costs must be balanced against the obvious and significant social benefits the patent system produces, such as the research and inventions created by the patent monopoly that would never be produced without the patent incentive, or the disclosure of secrets underlying the invention.

We'll discover that there is a dearth of evidence and a plethora of ideology in patents, as in every area of intellectual property. There is no clearly correct answer to the question of whether the patent system adequately manages this balancing act. In the final part of this chapter, we'll discuss some of the arguments made regarding this question. But as we progress through each one of the doctrinal features of the patent system, you might like to ask why this feature was included in the system, and whether it is justified based on the incentive argument, or any other.

## ⁋ Creation and Rights

Patent is entirely a creature of federal law, specifically Title 35 of the U.S. Code, and patent rights only come into existence upon the grant of a patent by the USPTO. The examination process, for all its flaws, is more rigorous than the process undertaken for any other type of intellectual property; there is, for example, no examination process at all for copyright, trade secrets, or celebrity rights, and trademarks have a registration process that is significantly less onerous than patent. Patent examiners are trained in the specific scientific or engineering disciplines that are the subject matter of the applications they are examining; thus, a trained chemist or chemical engineer will examine chemical and pharmaceutical patent applications, computer engineers will examine software patent applications, and so on.

There are five basic requirements that a (utility) patent application must satisfy: the invention claimed must be for (1) patentable subject matter that is (2) novel, (3) useful, and (4) non-obvious, and the patent description must be (5) such as to enable a person having ordinary skill in the art to practice the invention. But before we examine each of these five requirements, it's important to draw attention to one aspect of general usage. There are actually three different types of patents: utility, plant, and design. When people talk of "patents" they usually mean utility patents; these are the ones that grant twenty-year monopolies over new and useful inventions. Plant patents are a specific limited form of utility patent that, unsurprisingly, covers new plant forms. Design patents are a lesser type of patent that protects the ornamental features of a design. We will focus almost exclusively on utility patents in this chapter since they are the most significant type of patent, and when we say "patent" we'll generally mean "utility patent." At the end of this section we will briefly look at how one obtains a design patent or a plant patent and discuss the reasons for the differences among these three different forms of patent.

## Patentability Requirements

Five fundamental requirements must be met in order for an inventor to be granted a utility patent: the application must show that the invention is over patentable subject matter, that it is novel, non-obvious, and useful, and that the patent enables others to practice the invention. We'll look at each of these requirements in separate sections below.

### Subject Matter

The first requirement is that the claimed invention fall into an eligible category of inventions for which we grant utility patents; that is, that the application is for patentable subject matter. Section 101 of Title 35 allows for the grant of a patent for a "process, machine, manufacture, or composition of matter" provided that the other patentability requirements—novelty, non-obviousness, etc—are met. Thus, before a court or an examiner will consider the other elements, it will examine the fundamental question of whether the claimed matter is actually *invented*.

The legislative history to the 1952 Patent Act is clear that patents may be granted for "anything under the sun that is made by man,"[10] a formulation that would, on first glance, seem to include everything. But it doesn't. As a consequence of a number of judicially created policies, laws of nature, physical phenomena, and abstract ideas are not patentable subject matter. Natural laws and things found in nature are not patentable because they have always existed and therefore should not be monopolized by any one person. Einstein could not have patented the formula $E = mc^2$ because it is a law of nature, and Sir Humphry Davy, the first isolator of potassium, barium, and calcium, could not have obtained a patent over these elements because they are naturally occurring. However, it is possible to gain a patent over *invented* natural things and over *improvements* to naturally occurring things. Thus, a genetically engineered bacterium or mouse is patentable subject matter,[11] as is

---

10.  S. Rep. No. 82–1979 at 5 (1952); H.R. Rep. No. 82–1923 at 6 (1952).

11.  Diamond v. Chakrabaty, 447 U.S. 303 (1980).

a purified form of adrenaline,[12] because these things have taken human ingenuity to create, not merely uncover. Purely abstract ideas are not appropriate subject matter for slightly different reasons: depending on the nature of the application (and on the examiner and/or court considering it) this is forbidden protection because abstract ideas are neither a device nor an invention, and because they are often not "useful." That is, they are abstract and not tied to a useful implementation.

Recently, in the *Bilski* case, the Supreme Court addressed the issue of the patentability of processes that involve abstract ideas.[13] The claim in that case was for a procedure instructing buyers and sellers on how to protect against the risk of price fluctuations in the trading of energy through a well-known method called "hedging." The Supreme Court concluded that business methods were patentable subject matter, but the appropriate test for what processes can be patentable subject matter remains unclear. The Federal Circuit had previously concluded that the only way that a process satisfied the patentable subject matter requirement in section 101 was if the process is tied to a particular machine or apparatus, or if it transforms a particular article into a different state or thing. The Supreme Court concluded that the "machine-or-transformation" test was not the only way that a process patent could satisfy section 101, saying that it was a "useful clue" to patentability, but the Court indicated that there were some processes that would fail this test and yet still be patentable. Here the Court focused particularly on inventions in the information age that were useful and sufficiently concrete, but that might fail the machine-or-transformation test. Examples the Court mentioned included advanced diagnostic medicine techniques, inventions based on linear programming, data compression, and inventions involving the manipulation of digital signals. However, the Court provided very little guidance as to when it was appropriate

---

12. Parke-Davis & Co. v. H.K. Mulford Co., 189 F. 95 (C.C.S.D.N.Y. 1911).

13. Bilski v. Kappos, 130 S. Ct. 3218 (2010).

to step outside the machine-or-transformation test, and what test should then apply. Furthermore, the Court was remarkably split: Justice Kennedy wrote the opinion of the court, but there were three separate concurrences, with some judges signing on for part of the concurrences but not all. Because the Court failed to provide a definitive test, it seems that the machine-or-transformation test will continue to be the controlling subject matter test for process patents.

Once the court or examiner addresses the initial question of whether the claimed invention is patentable subject matter, the next question presented is: into which one of the different categories of patent does the application fall? Although very novel applications may fit within more than one category—for example, an oil-eating bacterium in the famous *Chakrabaty* case was found patentable as both a "composition of matter" and a "manufacture"— the practice is to examine an application in relation to only one category because there are special rules relating to each category. This particularly matters in the distinction between process patents and product patents—a distinction we need to spend some time examining.

A "process" is a method, and requires a series of steps to perform a task. Examples include a method for swinging on a swing or for implementing a one-click purchase over the internet.[14] Claims here are usually phrased something along the lines of:

A process for making compound *implausibilium*, comprising the steps of:

(1) mixing *unobtanium* and *adamantium* in the ratio 2:1;
(2) subjecting the mixture to zero gravity; and
(3) decanting the resulting compound into a high energy field of 1.21 gigawatts generated by a flux capacitor.

---

14. Amazon.com's one-click patent: Method and system for placing a purchase order via a communications network. U.S. Patent No. 5,960,411 (issued Sept 28, 1999).

Sometimes the process patent will result in a patentable product, for example, where a novel process for producing *implausibilium* produces a new chemical or pharmaceutical (i.e., the *implausibilium* itself). But not always: the first U.S. patent was granted for a process of making potash, a chemical compound that was well-known and not otherwise patentable.[15]

It's significant to note that it has been the category of process patents that has been the basis of recent concerns about patent quality, issues we mentioned in the introduction and will take up again in the final section below. Process patents for computer-implemented processes and for business methods have caused particular problems. In the first case, the grant of a patent for a computer-implemented algorithm may foreclose all uses of that algorithm, something that we've already seen is contrary to policy since an algorithm is equivalent to a mathematical formula or a law of nature. In the second case, business method patents for inventions such as Amazon's one-click shopping function or Priceline's reverse online auction are problematic because they don't seem to be novel, or they are obvious.[16]

The remaining three categories—machines, manufactures, and compositions of matter—are usually grouped together as *product* patents to distinguish them from *process* patents. *Machines* are human-created (not naturally occurring) devices that generally involve moving parts, and they include every mechanical device or combination of mechanical powers and devices to perform some function.[17] Well-known examples of machines that were the subject of machine patents include the telegraph, the airplane, and the laser. Machine patents cause few conceptual difficulties, although recently courts have been asked whether a general-purpose computer controlled by software amounts to a machine: the answer is

---

15. David W. Maxey, *Inventing History: The Holder of the First U.S. Patent*, 80 J. Pat. & Trademark Off. Soc'y 155 (1998).

16. Two features that, we'll see, are contrary to the grant of the patent.

17. Corning v. Burden, 56 U.S. 252, 267 (1853).

(more-or-less) *yes*. A *manufacture* is the production of articles of use from raw or prepared materials by giving to these materials new forms, qualities, properties, or combinations, whether by hand labor or by machinery.[18] This category is really a kind of catchall for product patents that don't fit elsewhere, but it is often conceptualized as any human-made invention that, unlike a machine, does not involve moving parts. Examples include toys, food (e.g., the crustless peanut butter and jelly sandwich patent), and computer memory.

Finally, *compositions of matter* include all compositions of two or more substances and composite articles, whether they are created by chemical union or mechanical mixture, or whether they are gases, fluids, powders, or solids. Examples include every pharmaceutical ever made, genetic material, metallic alloys, and even toothpaste. The actual physical structure of the composition is the relevant patentable invention, not the use made of it or its properties. Botox was first approved by the FDA in 1989 for use in the treatment of eye muscle disorders; the later discovery that it can also be used for wrinkle smoothing is not a patentable invention, although the original chemical structure could be. The other main issue that arises in relation to compositions of matter is whether one can patent purified forms of naturally occurring products, including drugs derived from nature or valuable types of biological or genetic material. Although there is a prohibition on granting patents over naturally occurring products, this does not extend to compositions of matter where human ingenuity is necessary to produce them. A product patent will be granted where the product is distilled, purified, altered, or improved, rendering the end product chemically or therapeutically distinct from the natural product.

18. Diamond v. Chakrabaty, 447 U.S. 303, 308 (1980).

## Novelty

For a patent to issue, the invention must be new or, as the patent laws call it, *novel*. This makes perfect sense if you think about it: in exchange for the grant of the patent monopoly, an inventor must be contributing something new to the sum of human knowledge. Section 102 of the Patent Law details the requirements of novelty, and these can be broken down into three main features: the invention must not be already known,[19] it must not have derived from another,[20] and it must not already be subject to a patent claim by another.[21] Further, the applicant must have applied expeditiously and in a way that does not bar the application.[22] We will look at each of these requirements in turn.

If someone has previously come up with the invention applied for in the patent, then the claimed invention is *anticipated*. The test for anticipation is as follows: an invention is not novel if the claimed invention is in a reference within the prior art that anticipates the invention on the relevant date. A *reference* is a publication, product, or other evidence of public knowledge. There are arcane rules about what amounts to an anticipating reference: secret use by another is not anticipating, but, for example, an obscure PhD dissertation that was buried in a library in a foreign country was sufficient to anticipate the invention.[23] The anticipating reference must be within the *prior art*—that is, the publicly accessible repositories of references (e.g., prior patents, published reports, libraries, conferences, and so on). For an invention to be anticipated, all of the elements of the claimed invention must be present in a single reference. This requirement is called "identity of invention," and it means that if one of the

---

19. The "anticipation" requirement found in §§ 102(a) and (e).

20. The "derivation" requirement in § 102(f).

21. The priority determination from § 102(g).

22. The various statutory bars in § 102(b)–(e).

23. *In re* Hall, 781 F.2d 897 (Fed. Cir. 1986).

claimed elements is missing from the reference then it is not anticipating. As an example, recall the earlier process patent for making
*implausibilium*. A scientific paper describing the first two steps of
the process (mixing *adamantium* and *unobtanium*; subjecting it to
zero gravity) but not the third (decanting it into a flux capacitor)
would not be anticipating.[24]

Anticipation relies on the date when the claimed invention was
made, and this date is, obviously, earlier than the date of filing.[25]
Indeed, the actual date of a complex invention may be hard to
determine because the question is when was the invention "reduced
to practice"? That is, when were all of the steps necessary first taken,
and when was all necessary testing performed? Various complex
rules of thumb are used to determine when reduction to practice
took place, and, at worst, the date of filing of the application is considered "constructive" reduction to practice. Finally, the fact that the
patent applicant is unaware of the anticipating reference is irrelevant since the question is whether the claimed invention is objec-
tively novel, not whether it is new to the patent applicant.

The second and third elements of novelty deal with derivation
and priority, issues that arise when there are two or more prospective inventors. The requirements for *derivation* are fairly simple:
basically, this element asks whether the person applying for the

---

24. Where there are multiple references that together describe the claimed invention, the problem is one of obviousness—that is, whether it was obvious to
combine the references. We'll look at this shortly.

25. But not so long ago as to bar the patent. Yes, I know, sometimes patent law's
strictures make you feel like you need to step outside just to clear your head.
But take a breath and you'll be able to get this: The date of filing a patent
application on your invention will be after you invent it, but there are good
reasons for society to insist that you ask for a patent expeditiously, because
otherwise you'll sit on the idea as a trade secret as long as you can, and only
when it looks like someone else might come up with the invention will you
seek to get a patent, which has its twenty-year monopoly. Society wants to
discourage that, so the patent law includes bars on protection so as to encourage reasonably expeditious filing of the application. We'll look at them a little
later, once we deal with this question on anticipation.

patent is the actual inventor. This can lead to odd situations, such as the famous case of the patent for the first U.S. computer, ENIAC: the applicant was denied the patent because he was not the true inventor, and the true inventor was unable to apply for the patent because he was too late. Thus, as a result of the derivation requirement, the invention fell into the public domain.[26]

*Priority* disputes are different. In a priority dispute, two or more people claim to be the inventor, and section 102(g) of the Patent Act is designed to work out who can claim priority. This matters in the U.S. system because we follow the first-to-invent principle (the person who is factually the first to invent has the right to the patent), whereas most countries follow the first-to-file principle (no matter who was the first inventor, the first person to file the patent application in respect of the invention is the appropriate patentee). First-to-file values clarity and administrative efficiency, while first-to-invent privileges some conception of fairness that the first person to have the inventive spark should get the benefit of the patent. The downside of the U.S. system is the determination of these priority disputes—called "interferences"—which can be very complicated and incredibly expensive. Section 102(g) says that the first person to reduce the invention to practice has priority unless (1) that inventor abandoned, suppressed, or concealed the invention (either affirmatively or by delay for an unreasonable period); or (2) the other inventor conceived the invention and proceeded with reasonable diligence in making and patenting it before the other inventor conceived the invention. Interferences are often nightmarish, take years to resolve, and eat up more money than you would believe.[27] For years, reformers have sought to do away with the U.S.'s adherence

---

26. An eventual result that was almost certainly a very good thing, when one considers the historical development of computers.

27. Almost any intellectual property lawyer has a friend in the business who spent the better part of his or her career litigating one interference proceeding.

to the first-to-invent principle and the peculiarly wasteful spectacle of interference proceedings—but with no success.[28]

Finally, on the question of novelty, there are various statutory bars to patenting. The main limitation is that an inventor must file the application within one year of the invention becoming public knowledge, whether this happens through public use, sale, or publication of the invention (section 102(b)). Further, the inventor must not abandon the invention (section 102(c)), must not obtain a foreign patent before filing the U.S. application if the foreign application was filed more than a year before the U.S. application (section 102(d)), and must exercise reasonable diligence in filing the patent application (section 102(g)). We don't need to go into more detail than this here.

## Non-Obviousness

Section 103(a) of the U.S. Patent Act forbids the grant of a patent that is obvious at the time of invention. This is determined based upon what is obvious to a person having ordinary skill in the art into which the invention falls, not to someone who knows nothing about these types of inventions.

Obviousness and novelty are two of the core issues in the grant of a patent that go to the heart of why patents are granted in the first place: society can justify the grant of a patent monopoly only if the invention actually produces something that is new and not obvious. However, it is important to note that obviousness is a very different concept from novelty: section 103(a) specifically notes that the requirement of non-obviousness applies "though the invention is not identically disclosed or described" in the prior art. This is another way of saying that an invention may be novel in that it is

---

28. As this book was going to press, there was another attempt to reform the Patent Act to move toward a first-to-file system. Because it faces stiff opposition, it is unclear whether the bill will pass.

not identically disclosed in a prior reference, but it might nonetheless fail for being obvious. The novelty requirements in section 102 deal with a single reference in the prior art, whereas obviousness in section 103 is a judgment about *all* the prior art. An example that might make this distinction a little clearer: consider a patent application for a six-legged chair. It's perfectly conceivable that no one has ever sought to patent such a chair before, and therefore the invention is novel. But adding two extra legs to furniture may well be obvious to a person having ordinary skill in the art (i.e., furniture making or design).

Obviousness determinations proceed according to the primary test given by the Supreme Court in *Graham v. John Deere*:[29]

(1)  Determine the scope and content of the prior art;
(2)  Ascertain the differences between the prior art and the claims in the application under consideration; and
(3)  Decide the level of skill in the pertinent art.

The scope and content of the prior art is assessed according to the categories established for section 102, and all prior art for that section is applicable for the purposes of this part of the test. The examiner will first ask what problem the inventor faced and see whether the reference falls within the field of the inventor's dilemma; if not, the examiner must ask if the reference is reasonably pertinent to that problem.[30]

Under the second part of the *Graham* test, the examiner or court must assess the difference between the prior art and the claims in the application. The difference might involve something missing from the prior art references, or it might involve combining multiple references. The latter situation is the more common, and

---

29.  383 U.S. 1, 17 (1966).

30.  *In re* Paulsen, 30 F.3d 1475 (Fed. Cir. 1994).

in *KSR v. Teleflex* the Supreme Court addressed this requirement.[31] Under previous Federal Circuit cases the prior references had to include some teaching, suggestion, or motivation for combining the references, otherwise the combination was not obvious. The Supreme Court in *KSR* rejected this test, and concluded that a person of ordinary skill is also a person of ordinary creativity, not a robot. Prior references therefore needn't provide a teaching, suggestion, or motivation; and combining references or adding things to them would be obvious if an ordinarily creative person would consider it so.

Finally, the *Graham* test requires an assessment of the level of ordinary skill in the pertinent art. This will differ depending on numerous factors: for example, the types of problems encountered in the art, the speed of innovation in that arena, the education level of people working in the art, etc. The question here is, of course, an objective one about the skills of the hypothetical average worker in the field, and not the individual brilliance or stupidity of the inventor who is applying for the patent.

The *Graham* case also noted that secondary considerations may be used to determine if an invention was obvious at the time of its creation; thus, evidence that the invention has met with commercial success will be relevant to the obviousness analysis, as will evidence that there was a long-felt-but-unmet need for an invention of this sort, evidence that others had failed to meet the need, evidence that the outcome of the experiment was unexpected given current knowledge, evidence that competitors licensed the invention, and so on. *KSR* added other criteria such as the effect of market demand and the likely inferences that a person of ordinary skill would make.

## Utility

Section 101 of the Patent Act states that an invention must be "useful" for it to be patentable, a requirement that can be traced back

---

31.   550 U.S. 398 (2007).

to the Progress Clause of the Constitution that allows Congress to make laws to promote the "useful Arts." The starting point for the modern interpretation of utility is Supreme Court Justice Joseph Story's statement that a useful invention is one "which may be applied to a beneficial use in society, in contradistinction to an invention injurious to the morals, health, or good order of society, or frivolous, or insignificant."[32] Although it is often quoted by courts, this test is not altogether a helpful analysis, in part because it is short on specifics and in part because the USPTO no longer assesses the "moral utility" of an invention. At one stage patents were denied for breaches of morality, so there are well-known cases denying patents for morally dubious inventions involving gambling, including inventions for betting machines, slot machines, and horse race games. Patents involving fraudulent practices were also denied: for example, an invention for the production of seamless stockings that looked like they had a seam was denied patent protection because consumers thought that seamed stockings were stronger and better than seamless, and therefore to allow a patent for this would be to defraud the public.

However, in 1999 the Federal Circuit put an end to the moral utility line of reasoning in *Juicy Whip*.[33] The case involved a patent over a drink dispensing machine for fast food restaurants that had a clear bowl at the top where a fresh-looking juice-like liquid would sit, but where the drink dispensed would come from a source of, presumably inferior, liquid. Consumers, of course, believed that they were receiving a delicious drink from the visible liquid in the bowl, but actually received an inferior drink. The court declined to follow previous moral utility rulings, concluding that the fact that customers may believe they are receiving fluid directly from the display tank did not deprive the invention of utility. The requirement of

---

32. *Note on the Patent Laws*, 3 Wheat. App. 13, 24.

33. Juicy Whip, Inc. v. Orange Bang, Inc., 185 F.3d 1364 (Fed. Cir. 1999).

"utility" in patent law, the court said, is not a directive to the USPTO or the courts to serve as arbiters of deceptive trade practices.

At its core, and leaving aside the question of morality, the utility requirement is that the invention actually perform the function that is claimed. But this is not the end of the question. Consider a new chemical compound, the beneficial use for which the inventor has no idea, but is able to claim as useful because the compound could be used as landfill in powdered form, or as balloon ballast in its liquid form. The inventor is engaged in a fishing expedition, patenting the invention with an insubstantial use in the hope that eventually someone will find a valuable use for the compound. The USPTO should reject the application as having insufficient utility: granting these sorts of patents will encourage a speculative land grab that will be inefficient and unjust.

Thus, the utility requirement is intended to limit patents to only those inventions genuinely of benefit to society, and here the USPTO's Utility Examination Guidelines provide a useful explanation: the utility asserted for an invention must be "specific, credible, and substantial." Utility must be *specific* to the invention, and not *general* to the broad class of the invention. Consider, for example, the case of *Brenner v. Manson*.[34] The inventor sought a patent over an untested steroid that was of the same class as some known cancer-inhibiting chemicals, but because the inventor had no idea of the use of the steroid, he claimed utility based on its similarity to the other cancer-fighting drugs. The Supreme Court rejected this claim as insufficiently specific. As the Court said, a patent is not a hunting license; it is not a reward for the search, but compensation for its successful conclusion. The requirement of *substantial utility* is a little different. This requirement demands that the invention has a real-world use and does not merely involve a throwaway utility, such as the one mentioned in the landfill example above. It's always possible to find *some* use for an invention—a transgenic

---

34.  383 U.S. 519 (1966).

mouse may be used as snake food, a mechanical invention may be used to create an artificial reef or a breakwater—but the actual utility claimed must be substantial and not de minimis. Finally, *credible utility* relates to far-fetched claims that may be difficult to verify or to disprove, but which should be denied as implausible; examples often given for this include inventions for time travel or perpetual motion machines.[35] The examiner here asks whether the assertion of utility is believable to a person of ordinary skill in the art. Since time machines and perpetual motion machines are contrary to the laws of physics, patent applications over them must be denied for failure of credible utility.

### Adequate Disclosure

If an inventor doesn't want to disclose the full workings of her invention, she can always keep the invention a trade secret, an area of law that has its own issues and which we examine in a later chapter. However, if she wants a patent she must disclose the invention fully, otherwise society gets a bad deal. The quid pro quo of patent protection is disclosure of how to practice the invention so that other inventors can use this in coming up with their own improvements and alternatives. Policing the "adequate disclosure" obligation is the job of the written description, enablement, and "best mode" requirements of section 112 of the Patent Act.

The application must contain a written description of the invention in "clear, concise, and exact terms."[36] The invention must be described in a way that allows one skilled in the relevant art to determine that the inventor was in possession of the invention at the time of filing, but it does not mean that the inventor has to

---

35. Of course, if the inventor provides no data proving that the perpetual motion machine actually works, then the analysis is even easier: the inventor has failed to show that the machine performs the function claimed (i.e., that it has any utility at all).

36. 35 U.S.C. § 112.

explain how she came up with the idea, or how the invention works. It's perfectly possible to have a patent over, say, a process for making a compound, but not know how it works. All that matters is that the invention is adequately described. The written description demonstrates that the inventor was actually in possession of the actual invention rather than some idealized version of it that might later be claimed.

The enablement requirement of section 112 is about enabling others to practice the invention; thus the section provides that the applicant must describe the invention in such "full, concise, and exact terms" as to allow someone skilled in the art to make and use the invention without "undue experimentation."[37] Enablement serves three ends: it stops nonfunctional inventions from being patented, it forces disclosure of the means of practicing the invention, and it narrows down the nature of the claims. As an example of the latter, consider Samuel Morse's patent over the telegraph. Morse claimed not only the techniques of telegraphy but the use of electricity to print symbols at a distance, no matter how these symbols were transmitted. The Supreme Court was happy upholding the telegraphy claims because Morse had actually reduced these to practice, but it denied the other more speculative claims on the basis of what these days we would call enablement.[38] Morse hadn't actually described what was necessary to practice this. How could he? He couldn't know how the as-yet-uninvented television or telephone might work, and so these claims were denied.

Finally on the issue of patent disclosure, the inventor must also set forth the best mode of practicing the invention. The purpose of this is to ensure that the inventor doesn't hold back her knowledge about the invention, at least as to the best way to practice it. So, where the inventor has discovered the best type of material for the invention—for example, the best type of rubber for a newly

---

37. The Incandescent Lamp Patent, 159 U.S. 465 (1895). U.S. Patent No. 317676.

38. O'Reilly v. Morse, 56 U.S. 62 (1854).

invented type of grommet—she must disclose that in the application.[39] The main issue here is a subjective analysis; if the inventor doesn't have a best mode, then there can be no violation by failing to state a best mode. Equally, if the inventor's best mode is not the best way of practicing the invention—let's say there's a better rubber available for that grommet that any competent engineer would know—there's no violation as long as this was the best mode that the inventor actually knew.[40]

## Design Patents and Plant Patents

There are two special types of patents that deviate from the prototypical requirements we've been discussing in relation to utility patents: design patents and plant patents.

Design patents protect the ornamental features of an article—the appearance of the article, not its function. Examples include designs for fountains, the distinctive shape of banana bicycle seats, and the shape of Croc footwear. In common with utility patents, design patents must be novel and non-obvious, but the test for design patents operates a little differently from what we've studied to date. For design patents, the role of one skilled in the art in the anticipation and obviousness requirements applies to determining whether to combine earlier references to arrive at a single piece of art for comparison with the potential design, or to modify a single prior art reference. Once the person skilled in the art has done this, the touchstone for anticipation and obviousness is the effect on the ordinary observer; that is, would the ordinary observer, comparing these references and the application, think that this design is

---

39. Chemcast Corp. v. ARCO Indus. Corp., 913 F.2d 923 (Fed. Cir. 1990).

40. An objective component will creep in when considering whether a best mode is generally known to those having ordinary skill in the art, but we needn't worry about that here.

anticipated or obvious? This makes sense: design patents are about ornamental features, and so an ordinary observer can compare a prior design with the one in the application, or decide whether a set of prior references means that a claimed design is or is not obvious.

Design patents have other differences from utility patents. They are only granted for fourteen years from the date of application, the statutory bar period is shorter, and any functional elements of the design must be a by-product of the ornamental features. This last requirement is to stop applicants from using design patents as an end run around the higher standards imposed on the grant of utility patents. To give some idea of the difference in examination standards, the specification in a design patent typically involves nothing more than drawings of the design, whereas utility patents are much more onerous and involve elaborate descriptions, reviews of prior art, discussions of best mode of practice, and so on. The separation between utility and design patents is not absolute, however. Design patents may have some functional features, and a design patent will only be rejected on functionality grounds where substantially every part of the ornamental design is dictated by utility.[41]

Plant patents also differ from both utility and design patents. Protection for plants has been a feature of the patent system since 1930; the justification for it was to recognize the unique role of the cultivator of plants in developing new strains and varieties. At the time it was generally accepted that plants couldn't be the subject of utility patents, both because the Patent Office considered plants to be unpatentable products of nature and because of the difficulties of meeting disclosure requirements for plant types. Nonetheless, there was the recognition even then that, unlike say the simple discoverer of minerals, the plant cultivator takes something that is naturally occurring and improves it, thus warranting the protection

---

41. *In re* Levinn, 136 U.S.P.Q. 606, 607 (1963).

of the plant in a way consistent with what we've discussed earlier.[42] Congress responded by creating the special category of plant patents, and 35 U.S.C. § 161 provides for the grant of a plant patent for any new and distinct plant type (except tubers or plants found in an uncultivated state) that is invented or discovered and which is asexually reproduced. Tubers (e.g., potatoes) and wild plants are excluded because of their significance to the food supply. Asexual reproduction includes horticultural practices such as grafting or budding, and this was included in the original 1930s' legislation because it was the only way at the time to ensure true-to-type reproduction of exactly the same article.

The requirements for the grant of a plant patent are different from utility patents: the applicant need only show that the asexually reproduced plant is "new and distinct." Novelty here is easier to establish than the standard for utility patents since the plant can simply be found in nature and need not be improved in order to be protected. The requirement of distinctiveness speaks to the claimed plant variety being distinct from other types of plants; features demonstrating this include the plant's color, flavor, shape, or form, as well as its resistance to heat, wind, and other environmental assaults.

The 1970 Plant Variety Protection Act was introduced to offer a similar form and scope of protection to sexually reproduced plants, and was a response to then-modern technology that allowed for true-to-type reproduction by methods other than asexual reproduction. Like the law on plant patents it protects new and distinct plants. However, it does have some differences in that the plant must also be uniform and stable, the protection can apply to tubers, and the period of protection is twenty years. One important technical difference is that the protection offered is not formally a patent

---

42. If we apply the utilitarian, Lockean, or Hegelian justifications, plant propagation warrants some kind of exclusive rights in the propagator. Look back at the discussion earlier in this chapter if you're unsure why.

because it falls in a different title of the code and the certificate is issued not by the USPTO but by the Department of Agriculture. It is nonetheless an important form of protection for the commercial agriculture industry.

Finally, inventors of plant- and agriculture-related technologies are able to obtain a regular utility patent provided that all the usual requirements are met. Numerous utility patents have been obtained for genetically modified crops, new types of seeds, and insecticide-resistant crops.

### Patent Prosecution and Examination

Patents are only granted subject to the creation of a detailed application, and only after a long process of examination. The process of navigating the legal and administrative requirements of the USPTO is called patent prosecution, and given its significance in the creation of the rights, it's important to have a basic idea of what it entails.[43]

As we discussed earlier in this chapter, the patent application provides the names of the inventors, the description or specification of the claimed invention, any prior art relied upon, any necessary drawings, and the specific claims defining the patent grant. The document is inevitably drafted by a patent agent or patent attorney.[44] There is a special type of application called a provisional application, which only needs to include the specification and any

---

43. We don't look at the equivalent process for the grant of copyrights or trademarks because the filing/prosecution processes there are so much less onerous, and make little difference in the protection of the rights under each of those regimes. Patents are different and worth studying because the prosecution process defines the rights the patentee has.

44. A patent agent is a person qualified to practice before the PTO, meaning the person must have the requisite scientific or engineering training and have passed the patent bar. A patent attorney is a patent agent who is also legally admitted.

drawings (no claim need be provided). This type of application is used to stake a claim, but it needs then to be perfected within twelve months by a non-provisional application that details the other required material.

Once patent applications are filed, time starts running for a number of important purposes. The application will be kept confidential for eighteen months after filing unless it fits into one of a small number of special situations, such as it being the subject of a secrecy order, a provisional application, or a design patent application, or it not being the prospective subject of a foreign application. And the patent term— twenty years for utility patents, fourteen years for design patents— runs from the date of filing, not the date of issuance of the patent. Extensions are sometimes granted where there are specific sorts of administrative delays in the prosecution of the patent, notably when the USPTO fails to respond within a certain time or when the application takes more than three years to issue from the time of filing.

The application is assigned to one of the examiners in the USPTO who will assess it against the patentability requirements discussed above, as well as some other more administrative and technical issues. It's unusual for the patent to be granted on the basis of the initial application, and the examiner will usually issue a number of "office actions" that may reject the application outright or demand changes in it for the patent to issue. The applicant will respond to these office actions in various ways by demonstrating that the examiner is incorrect, agreeing to the amendment, and so on. If the examiner rejects the patent, the applicant may apply for reexamination and submit further information. If the patent is rejected after reexamination, the applicant may file a "continuation" that keeps open the dialogue with the examiner. Eventually all processes with the examiner may be exhausted, at which point the rejected applicant may appeal to the Board of Patent Appeals and Interferences, and then to the Court of Appeals for the Federal Circuit, or the U.S. District Court for the District of Columbia, depending on the nature of the issue. (Determination as to the appropriate court is too arcane an issue for us to worry about here.) The length of the period it takes a successful applicant from filing to issuance varies, depending on the type of patent: the most recent data shows that from filing to the first office action takes, for example, 1.1 years for design patents, 1.4 years for plant patents, 2.2 years for aeronautics and molecular biology patents, and four years for interprocess communication patents.[45] Since the first office action is only an intermediate step in the process, all patents take years to prosecute, although numerous calls have been made to speed the process.

Patent applications are prosecuted ex parte for the majority of the examination process, and for the first eighteen months no one outside of the applicant and the PTO is made aware of the application. Because of the non-adversarial nature of the application there is a duty of "candor and good faith" on the part of the applicant to disclose all relevant information about the invention and the prior art. Any intentional misstatement or failure to disclose material information amounts to inequitable conduct, what used to be called "a fraud on the patent office." Inequitable conduct is grounds for denying a patent during the administrative phase, or invalidating it in subsequent litigation. When the patent application is published, a rival inventor may claim priority in invention, a process called an *interference* proceeding, governed by section 102(g) discussed previously.

Once the patent issues there is the possibility of a reexamination pursuant to section 302. The PTO can initiate the process, or anyone else can request reexamination of the patent on the basis that the examiner missed anticipating references in the prior art. The reexamination and cancellation of the Amazon "One-Click Checkout" patent is a notable example. Further, as long as there is no intentional deception, a patentee can apply to fix mistakes in the patent after it issues—for example, if the inventor is wrongly named or the claim is too broad—in a process called patent *reissue*.

---

45. Dennis Crouch, *How Long Do I Wait for a First Office Action*, PATENTLY-O, May 3, 2010, http://www.patentlyo.com/patent/2010/05/how-long-do-i-wait-for-a-first-office-action.html

## ⅋ Infringement

The grant of a patent gives the patentee the right to stop others from making, using, offering for sale, or selling the invention throughout the United States, to stop them from importing the invention into the United States, and to stop third parties from inducing the same activities. All of the five basic rights of exclusion—making, using, selling, offering for sale, and importing—are delimited by the claimed invention. Therefore any discussion of patent infringement must look first to how we interpret the claims in a patent, and this is what we take up in the first section below. After that, we look at the two ways in which patent claims may be infringed, either by literal infringement or by the doctrine of equivalents. Finally we look to the slight differences in how courts deal with infringement in the case of design and plant patents rather than the utility patents we will use as the prototype case here.

### Claim Interpretation

By now it is well-established that any patent infringement action has two parts: the interpretation of the patent claims, and then the comparison of the claims with the allegedly infringing device. The first stage is intended to determine the "metes and bounds" of the invention: the metaphor references an action for trespass to land, where we need first to determine the boundaries of the plot before we can say whether the defendant has overstepped them. In patent attorney language, the process of interpreting the claims is usually called *claim construction*, but we'll use the more generic term *interpretation* here for the sake of simplicity.

Since 1996 the interpreters of patent claims have been judges. In that year, the Supreme Court handed down *Markman v. Westview Instruments*,[46] which held that the Seventh Amendment of the

---

46.  517 U.S. 370 (1996).

Constitution did not guarantee a jury trial in matters involving patent claim interpretation. Claim interpretation is, therefore, a matter of law for judges, and as a matter of practice the majority of judges in patent cases schedule pretrial *Markman* hearings to determine the ambit of the claims prior to empanelling a jury and hearing testimony. The Court of Appeals for the Federal Circuit is the appeal court for patent matters, and on claim interpretation it need not defer to the lower court because this is a matter of law. Thus, the Federal Circuit has tremendous power to shape patent law through interpretation of the claims. Arguably this was in the intention of the Supreme Court when it decided *Markman*, since it noted that giving judges power over claim interpretation would encourage uniform interpretation, a notable complaint of the pre-*Markman* period when juries could decide claim interpretation, and when some critics suggested that claim interpretation was all over the map. Critics of the Federal Circuit suggest that litigating claims interpretation in the district court is pointless since the Federal Circuit can and will impose its own view of the law de novo.[47]

Numerous evidentiary sources are used to interpret the scope of the claims, and they are usually categorized as *intrinsic* or *extrinsic* materials. Intrinsic materials are so-called because they are contained, in some way, within the public record of the patent's issuance. So they include the patent specification itself, the drawings that accompany it, and the prosecution history (or "file wrapper") of the application. Extrinsic materials come from outside the administrative record and include dictionaries, scientific treatises, expert testimony, and the like. Intrinsic evidence is considered superior to extrinsic because it is created at the time of patent prosecution, it isn't influenced by the litigation (and is thus likely to be less partisan), it is likely to be more "objective" and neutral, and it does not implicate issues of procedural fairness because all parties became

---

47. Cybor Corp. v. FAS Techs., Inc., 138 F.3d 1448, 1476 (Fed Cir. 1998) (en banc) (Rader J. dissenting).

aware of it on the application's publication. Dictionaries, encyclopedias, and treatises that were available at the time of the filing occupy a midpoint between intrinsic and extrinsic material. Although they are formally part of the extrinsic evidence, they are often treated more like intrinsic evidence because of their perceived neutrality and the fact that they reflect the general knowledge of the person having ordinary skill in the art at the time of the patent filing.

Like statutory interpretation, patent claim interpretation involves the careful parsing out of complex language, and, just as for statutory interpretation, there are certain canons of patent interpretation. The most important canon states that claims are to be interpreted from the perspective of the person having ordinary skill in the art, and not that of the judge, the litigants, or laypeople. Further, the terms are given their ordinary and customary meaning (according to the person having ordinary skill in the art); however, a patentee may be his or her "own lexicographer," that is, may choose to define terms in an idiosyncratic way. The redefinition may be express or implicit, but must occur within the patent application. There are numerous other canons that are beyond the scope of our discussion, but all of them operate as defaults and are intended to assist competitors and courts in understanding the ambit of the claims in the event of ambiguity.

### Infringement of Utility Patents

The second stage of any patent infringement action is comparing the properly interpreted claim or claims against the allegedly infringing device. It is vital to recognize that infringement will only be found if each and every element or limitation of the claim is found in the accused device, either literally or under a rule called the doctrine of equivalents. This is called the *all-elements* or *all-limitations* principle, and it requires that the patent claim be compared on a limitation-by-limitation basis with the defendant's device. It is not permissible to look at the defendant's device and say that it infringes the "whole" of the patentee's claim, or its "gist," "essence," or general idea.

Every single element of the claim must be analyzed and if so much as one of these elements is not infringed by the defendant's device then the device does not infringe. An instructive example is *Larami Corp. v. Amron*,[48] which involved the Super Soaker range of water pistols. The relevant claim in the operative patent was for a water pistol with "an elongated housing . . . having a chamber therein for a liquid [tank]" and a pump for building up the necessary pressure. The allegedly infringing device included every one of the elements of the claim except that the water chamber was outside the gun rather than inside as the patent claimed. Consequently, no infringement was found.

Each one of the limitations can be infringed either literally or by the doctrine of equivalents. Literal infringement is just as you'd expect; that is, the defendant's device has literally the same element as the claimed limitation in the patent.[49] A patent over the chemical structure of a new drug is literally infringed by the production, sale, or importation of that drug, and so on. However, if this were the only way to infringe a patent, then clever competitors could design around the patent by making tiny changes to one of the claims, and no infringement would be found. Thus courts developed the doctrine of equivalents, which provides a patentee with a wider scope of protection to avoid these kinds of practices. The standard account of the doctrine of equivalents is that a patent claim may be infringed if the plaintiff's invention and the defendant's device perform the same work, in substantially the same way, and accomplish substantially the same result.[50] This "triple identity test" is not completely dispositive, however, and the Federal Circuit has indicated that it is simply one way of determining the fundamental question at the heart of the doctrine: are the differences between the plaintiff's and

---

48. 27 U.S.P.Q.2d 1280 (E.D. Pa. 1993).

49. A "limitation" means a discrete element of the claim, but the method of determining what is a limitation is beyond the scope of our discussion.

50. Graver Tank & Mfg. Co. v. Linde Air Prods. Co. 339 U.S.605 (1950).

defendant's devices merely "insubstantial"?[51] Because of the indeterminacy of a test of "insubstantiality," courts often adopt the triple
identity test, but whatever test the court adopts, the doctrine of
equivalents is interpreted differently depending on the inventive-
ness of the claim,[52] and a pioneering patent that establishes the
field tends to be granted a broader range of infringing equivalents
than a patent that is only a small improvement in the field.

The doctrine of equivalents is one of a host of changes to patent
law—other examples include the creation of the patent-friendly
Federal Circuit, the increase in duration, and the expansion of the
categories of patentable subject matter—that have vastly expanded
the scope and range of patent protection over the last fifty to one
hundred years. And although it's easy to agree in the abstract with
the proposition behind the doctrine of equivalents—that patentees
shouldn't be put at risk of colorable imitations bypassing patent
protection—the whole point of the patent examination is to define
the scope of the patent narrowly. In theory, everyone agrees that
competitors should be allowed to invent around a patent because
that is broadly pro-competitive and appropriate, but of course this
is a freedom that the doctrine of equivalents restricts. The issue is
especially pronounced when one considers the chilling effect on
competitors that occurs as a result of the uncertainty of the interpretation. The only way that a competitor can know that something
is an equivalent is to have it tested in court, and the Federal Circuit
has indicated courts should have broad discretion over what they
consider to be equivalent. Further, the relevant appellate court is
the patentee-preferring Federal Circuit, and so it's not hard to understand some of the concerns of the discontents of the patent system
(concerns we take up in the final part of this chapter) suggesting

---

51.  Hilton Davis Chem. Co. v. Warner-Jenkinson Co., 62 F.3d 1512 (Fed. Cir. 1995)
     (en banc).

52.  Cont'l Paper Bag Co. v. E. Paper Bag Co., 210 U.S. 405 (1908).

that the doctrine of equivalents has expanded the scope of patent protection beyond reasonable limits.

However, there are a number of important limits on the doctrine of equivalents. Probably the most important consideration is what's called *prosecution history estoppel*. During the administrative process of prosecuting a patent, the applicant is often asked to limit its application to accord with the requirements of patentability. Under the doctrine of prosecution history estoppel, the successful patentee cannot claim infringement based on an equivalent that it had surrendered in the prosecution of the patent. So, for example, the original application for our fictional "*Implausibilium* patent"—that includes limitations about the ration of mixing *unobtanium* and *adamantium*, and subjecting it to a high energy field of 1.21 gigawatts— might not have specified the strength of the high energy field. If the examiner required that the strength be included because of prior art that taught how to produce *implausibilium* at higher strengths, then the patentee would not be successful in applying the doctrine of equivalents against a defendant who was producing *implausibilium* at those higher energy levels. Prosecution history estoppel often goes by its older name, *file wrapper estoppel* in reference to the notations of the applicant's concessions that the examiner used to make on the wrapper of the patent application file.

It was once the case that a claim narrowed by amendment could only be literally infringed, and was not capable of infringement by an equivalent. However, in *Festo v. Shoketsu* the Supreme Court abandoned the "strict bar" approach to prosecution history estoppel and instead adopted a *flexible bar* approach.[53] This means that a court must examine exactly what the patentee surrendered in amending the claim, and then conclude whether the defendant's equivalent falls within that surrendered portion. The court concluded that there is a rebuttable presumption that a narrowing amendment surrenders the particular equivalent that is at issue. Thus, once the issue is raised,

---

53. Festo Corp. v. Shoketsu Kinzoku Kogyo Kabushiki Co., 535 U.S. 722 (2002).

the burden will be on the patentee to show that the equivalents are not excluded by estoppel in the amendment, and the patentee must also show that at the time of the amendment one skilled in the art could not reasonably be expected to have drafted a claim that would have literally encompassed the alleged equivalent.

Apart from literal infringement and the doctrine of equivalents, there are a small number of ways a defendant can incur secondary liability for patent infringement. The most obvious is to actively induce another's infringement. This basically requires evidence that a defendant intended to cause acts that it knew would infringe the patent. An example would be selling the necessary ingredients that go into producing a patented product together with detailed instructions on how to make it. The other main type of secondary liability is called the *sale of non-staples*, which is a specialized variation on the prohibition on active inducement. Some products, albeit a very small number, have no other function except to be used in the production of a patented invention. Where a defendant sells these products, it will be liable for inducement as long as there is, in fact, no other use for the products, and it acted knowing that the products were especially made or especially adapted for infringing use.[54] This prohibition does not apply to what are called "staple articles of commerce" suitable for noninfringing use (in other words, products that are used by others for other purposes).[55]

## Design and Plant Patents

Infringement of design and plant patents operates in a slightly different way than as to utility patents, and the core principles are

---

54. 35 U.S.C. § 271.

55. You may recall the concept of "staple article of commerce" that was so important to the test of contributory infringement in *Sony v. Universal*, discussed in the previous chapter. This is where that test came from.

drawn from the utility patent literature. The test for infringement of design patents has been remarkably stable over the years—it was established by the Supreme Court in 1871 in *Gorham Co. v. White*[56]—and infringement is found if, in the eye of the ordinary observer, the two designs are substantially the same and the resemblance is such as to deceive the observer into purchasing one, thinking it is the other. Recent cases have upheld this test; for example, a court concluded that minor differences between the patented shape of Crocs and a knockoff brand—differences such as the placement of ventilation holes or their shape—would not be enough for an ordinary observer to be able to tell them apart.[57]

Plant patents and plant variety protection have more difficult infringement standards than utility patents or design patents. Infringement of a plant patent occurs by the asexual propagation of the patented plant; an easy example of this is where someone takes a graft of the patented plant and produces a "cloned" plant from it. Thus, no infringement was found where a competitor produced a similar flowering plant to a patented variety of *heather persoluta*, and where there was no evidence of the direct taking of the patented plant.[58]

### Remedies

As for copyright law, the remedies for patent infringements are basically the same as for any other area of law. The one area where patent differs is in the arena of injunctions, both preliminary and permanent. Courts have long issued preliminary injunctions prior to trial for alleged patent infringements, an approach that has been exploited by speculating patent litigants who would obtain an

---

56. 81 U.S. (14 aWall.) (1871).

57. Int'l Seaway Trading Corp. v. Walgreens Corp., 589 F.3d 1233 (Fed. Cir. 2009).

58. Imazio Nursery, Inc. v. Dania Greenhouses, 69 F.3d 1560 (Fed Cir. 1995).

injunction and then delay the trial in the hope of forcing a favorable settlement. Although this is still possible, the recent Supreme Court decision in *eBay v. MercExchange* has changed the practice in relation to permanent injunctions, and to some extent preliminary ones.[59] For many years the default position was that courts should issue permanent injunctions against patent infringements absent exceptional circumstances. In *MercExchange* a unanimous Court concluded that the traditional four-part test should be applied to determine whether an injunction is necessary. Hence, the plaintiff must prove (1) that it has suffered an irreparable injury; (2) that the law does not provide other adequate ways to compensate it; (3) that considering the balance of hardships between the plaintiff and defendant, an injunction is warranted; and (4) that the public interest would not be harmed by a permanent injunction.

Although the holding applies only to permanent injunctions, and only those in relation to patent infringement, the decision has influenced the granting of preliminary injunctions and the grant of injunctions in other types of intellectual property cases. It seems that these days district and circuit courts of appeal are more careful about the grant of injunctions, both permanent and preliminary, in all types of cases. And under the watchful eye of the Supreme Court, lower courts are increasingly applying the four factors in most intellectual property cases.

## ✐ Defenses

In general, defenses available to a patent infringement defendant are neither as broad nor as numerous as those available for copyright infringement. This reflects the more rigorous examination process that patents must endure: in theory at least, the examiner limits the scope of the patentee's rights during the prosecution of

---

59.  547 U.S. 388 (2006).

the patent and, in exchange, defendants don't have as many defenses available. It's also the case that patents are intended to be a stronger monopoly than copyright—thus weaker defenses are appropriate for patent law. Moreover, patents generally do not implicate the kinds of First Amendment concerns that animate many of the copyright defenses.

With that said, section 282 of the Patent Act provides three main defenses in patent actions: invalidity, absence of infringement, and unenforceability.

## Invalidity

It is always open to the defendant in a patent infringement action to claim that the plaintiff's patent was invalidly granted because it lacks one or more of the fundamental requirements we discussed above: novelty, non-obviousness, utility, and so on. The defendant claiming invalidity is not limited to the material used by the examiner, and may, for example, find additional prior art references that the examiner never found, which demonstrate that the invention was actually anticipated.

## Absence of Infringement

The second category of defense arises from arguments that there is an absence of liability for infringement. Here, *absence of liability* means that (1) the defendant had a license to perform one or more of the exclusive rights held by the patentee, (2) the defendant had prior user rights, (3) the defendant was engaged in experimental use, or (4) the plaintiff has slept on its rights or is otherwise barred by equity. The license issue is not complicated and generally tracks the model familiar from contract law: one can have express or implied licenses, the latter are implied based on equitable principles such as acquiescence, estoppel, and so on. The only unusual feature

of patent law is that an authorized user of a patented device is entitled to repair the device but not to reconstruct it. Reconstructing
the device effectively means that the owner is "buying" a new version of the device, which is not permitted because the patentee has
the exclusive right to sell devices containing the patented invention. *Prior user rights* exist where a defendant used the invention
prior to the patentee's application, but never bothered to apply for
a patent. This occurs in situations where the defendant maintained
the invention as a trade secret. The requirements were recently
codified in section 273: the defendant must have acted in good faith,
reduced the invention to practice more than a year before the plaintiff filed its application, and used the invention commercially before
the infringement action was filed.

Perhaps the most problematic of these "absence of liability"
defenses is the one for experimental use. In theory, this defense allows
a competitor to make use of a patented invention for the purposes of
study, in labs or research institutions or the like. The defense comes
about because the stated purpose of the patent system is to encourage innovation in science and the useful arts, and it would be contrary to this aim if competitors and tinkerers were forbidden from
investigating the nature of the patented invention and using it for producing new inventions. Difficulties emerge where the defendant has
mixed commercial and research motives, and courts construe the
experimental use exception extremely narrowly, confining it to experiments "solely for amusement, to satisfy idle curiosity, or for strictly
philosophical inquiry." Thus, in the *Madey* case,[60] Duke University
continued to use devices that were covered by patents owned by
Madey, a former professor at the university. When Madey sued for
infringement, the court rejected Duke's experimental use defense,
saying that research of the kind performed in the university labs fur-
thered the commercial aims of the school by attracting and educating
fee-paying students, providing the basis for further research grants,

---

60. Madey v. Duke Univ., 307 F.3d 1351 (Fed Cir. 2002).

and contributing to the prestige of the place. Numerous researchers have criticized this decision as too broad, suggesting that it eviscerated the experimental use exception and took away the public's right to tinker with patented inventions—a right that leads to the production of more socially beneficial inventions. Critics charge that the Federal Circuit's approach makes it impossible for research institutions to do research without the permission of the patent owner, leading to patent thickets, patent anticommons, and holdouts that are profoundly damaging to innovation policy. We will look at criticisms such as these in more detail in the final part of this chapter.

The last defenses for "absence of infringement" are all based on equitable principles, and include laches (delay), equitable estoppel, and the "reverse doctrine of equivalents." The delay defense includes a specific statutory time bar in section 286 that requires the plaintiff to bring an action within six years of the infringement, as well as the more general equitable principle of laches that does not specify a time by which the plaintiff must file but simply forbids recovery where there has been an unreasonable and inexcusable delay that prejudices the defendant. Equitable estoppel in this situation forbids recovery where the plaintiff has misled the defendant to believe that it won't enforce the patent and the defendant has relied on this representation to its detriment.

Finally, you should recall our discussion of the doctrine of equivalents in the infringement part above. The defense of "reverse doctrine of equivalents" is the flip side of that form of infringement, but it only applies as a defense to a claim of literal infringement. It occurs where the defendant's device is a literal infringement of the plaintiff's patent, but where the defendant's device is so completely changed in principle from the claimed invention that it would be inequitable to find infringement.[61] The principle was established in the late nineteenth century case of *Boyden Power-Brake Co. v. Westinghouse*, where Westinghouse had a patent over a form of airbrake for steam engines.

---

61. Boyden Power-Brake Co. v. Westinghouse, 170 U.S. 537, 562 (1898).

The Westinghouse brake was inefficient, and Boyden came up with a vastly improved airbrake which, unfortunately, happened to literally infringe the terms of the Westinghouse patent claims even though Westinghouse never took the inventive step that Boyden had. The Supreme Court concluded that Boyden's contribution took its device outside the equitable bounds of the patent. Although numerous commentators have praised the reverse doctrine of equivalents as a useful balance against patent expansion, the truth is that courts almost never apply their equitable powers to excuse liability.

### Unenforceability

The final type of defense in section 282 provides that a defendant is not liable if the patent is "unenforceable." There are two basic defenses that occur within this framework: inequitable conduct and patent misuse. Both of these focus on the behavior of the plaintiff, which must be problematic in certain ways, and to a degree that warrants a finding that its patent cannot be enforced against the defendant. The first defense involves inequitable conduct by the patentee in the prosecution of the patent, which goes to the question of whether the plaintiff complied with the duty of candor in its filings with the USPTO. The penalty is very severe in order to ensure compliance; however, because of the severity the standard of proof is very high, and there must be clear and convincing evidence of wrongdoing. Further, the evidence must demonstrate that the nondisclosure or wrongful submission was material, and that there was an intention to deceive.

The other "unenforceability" defense is patent misuse on the part of the plaintiff. This is an issue, grounded in a combination of equity and antitrust, which occurs where a patent holder misuses the monopoly granted by the patent in various anticompetitive ways. These include tying arrangements that condition the grant of a license to use the patent on licensing another product, or that require the purchase of unpatented goods for use with a patented device (provided that the patentee has market power).

It also covers arrangements that effectively extend the term of the patent beyond the statutory period. The defense can only be used as a shield not a sword—that is, it does not generate a separate cause of action, but exists only as a defense to an infringement claim—with the defendant being required to show that the patentee has impermissibly broadened the "physical or temporal scope" of the patent grant to anticompetitive effect.

There are other ways in which antitrust concerns intersect with the patent system, all of which are beyond the scope of our discussion. However, at the time of this writing, the practice of reverse exclusionary payment agreements has come into the news. The issue only arises within the pharmaceutical industry, and it occurs as a result of a complicated interaction between patent law and the Hatch-Waxman Act, which regulates patented drug prices and availability. This interaction means that the owner of a drug patent can pay off the first qualified generic producer of the drug, thereby effectively blocking other generic producers from entering the market in a timely fashion. Although this is not directly a patent misuse issue, it is one that implicates the same combination of patent monopolies and antitrust concerns. Reverse exclusionary payments were held in the Second Circuit to be permissible but on narrow grounds,[62] and it seems likely this issue will eventually make its way up to the Supreme Court, likely changing the way that both patent misuse and Hatch-Waxman are interpreted.

## ℳ Discontents

If you think about the kinds of problems that we discussed at the beginning of this chapter, it should come as no surprise that there is a robust set of critics seeking the reform—and occasionally the

---

62. *In re* Ciprofloxacin Hydrochloride Antitrust Litig., Docket Nos. 05–2851-cv(L), 05–2852-cv(CON), Apr. 29, 2010 (2d Cir. 2010); Arkansas Carpenters Health & Welfare Fund v. Bayer AG, 604 F.3d 98 (2d Cir. 2010).

overthrow—of the patent system. These fall into a number of distinct categories.

First are the scholars, patent practitioners, and groups who are concerned about patent quality, an issue that we saw demonstrated at the beginning of the chapter with the "Method of Swinging on a Swing" patent. Proponents of this reform agenda range across the spectrum and are not merely fringe groups, or necessarily against intellectual property in general. For example, the Federal Trade Commission, the National Research Council of the National Academies, and even the previous director of the USPTO have all indicated concern about the quality of patents that have issued. Granting unmeritorious patents—that is, any patent that fails to meet the core requirements of novelty, non-obviousness, utility, and adequate disclosure—creates numerous social costs. Notably it generates an increase in litigation and uncertainty, a decrease in perception that the patent system is working properly, and a fundamental distortion of the incentives at the core of the system. There are numerous reasons for there being a patent quality problem, the most obvious of which include issues with the resourcing of the USPTO—inadequate time for examination, or inappropriate databases for the search of prior art—and perverse incentives for examiners to grant patents quickly rather than reject them. There are also problems outside the USPTO, including incentives for firms to apply for large numbers of low-quality patents, incentives not to disclose the invention completely, incentives that encourage difficult claim examination, and so on.

Virtually every patent law scholar has spent time wrestling with this issue, and numerous reform proposals have been aired to greater or lesser fanfare. At one end are proposals championed by Lemley and Kieff, inter alia, who argue that we don't need to make many changes to the patent system because the system involves a trade-off between cost and quality.[63] We *could* improve the quality of

---

63. *See, e.g.,* Mark A. Lemley, *Essay, Rational Ignorance at the Patent Office,* 95 Nw. U.L. Rev. 1495, 1531 (2001); F. Scott Kieff, *The Case for Registering Patents and*

issued patents, but only at great expense, and since most patents are valueless, we should allow competitors to deal with issues about patent quality via litigation, since litigating this small number of cases is socially more efficient than pouring large amounts of money into reforming the patent system for all patents. Less sanguine commentators have proposed ways for applicants to gold plate their patents by paying for increased scrutiny at the examination stage in return for various sorts of benefits in enforceability.[64] Other proposals focus on marginal improvements in what we already have in place: increases in the number of examiners, improvements to the search tools through technological means, crowdsourcing the search of prior art, or the expansion of post-grant review and the reexamination process. Though each proposal has its supporters (and each its critics), the final conclusion seems to be that fixing the patent quality problem may simply be too hard, given what we already have and where we already are.[65] The USPTO is likely to see increased funding in the coming years and, though wholesale change is unlikely, its spending money on reducing obvious errors in the administrative process may result in modest gains.

Another arena of discontent over patents is much more politically charged—it focuses on the way that patents can undermine basic human rights and human needs. One focus of this has been in relation to medicines. A number of civil society groups such as Universities Allied for Essential Medicines have pointed out the human rights problems inherent in reduced access to patented medicines, and have criticized the role that universities, research institutions, and the pharmaceutical industry play in privatizing health technologies. Perhaps the most obvious example is HIV-drug

---

the *Law and Economics of Present Patent-Obtaining Rules*, 45 B.C.L. REV. 55, 56–58 (2003).

64. Mark Lemley, Doug Lichtman & Bhaven Sampat, *What to Do about Bad Patents?* REGULATION 10 (Winter 2005–06).

65. R. Polk Wagner, *Understanding Patent Quality Mechanisms*, 157 U. PA. L. REV. 2135 (2009).

access in Africa.[66] Pharmaceutical groups fought the introduction of generic versions of their patented antiretroviral drugs produced in India and China on the basis that the generics infringed on their patent rights. Physicians and governments in Africa countered that without these "knockoff" drugs, there would be no effective treatment of HIV in Africa, given the high cost of the patent-approved or "genuine" drugs. The clash of ideology leads to political standoffs in the drug arena generally, between public interests (represented by civil society groups), and private interests (represented by the pharmaceutical industry). Both sides have strong arguments—the human right to healthcare technologies versus the need for incentives for private investment to create those technologies—and it's virtually impossible to come to a conclusion about who is right in the abstract. The view of what's right and what's fair in this area is mostly a question of one's political ideology.

A similar set of issues and warring ideologies arise in relation to certain genetic materials and in some agricultural chemicals. For many years the USPTO has allowed the patenting of genetic material, including human genetic material. While this initially caused some concerns about whether human genetic material was appropriate subject matter, the issue was eventually resolved in favor of the patent applicants. However, recently the ACLU and the Public Patent Foundation filed suit against the USPTO and the holders of seven patents over the BRCA1 and BRCA2 genes that are used in screening breast cancer.[67] In a remarkable turnaround, the district court for the Southern District of New York found the patents

---

66. This example is used since many people are aware of it, but it is largely historical. Although it was true in the early part of the 2000s, these days a combination of bulk purchasing, commercial negotiation, marketplace competition, and international pressure and funding have meant that drug companies can often provide their patented versions of antiretroviral drugs at realistic prices. *See, e.g.*, http://www.avert.org/generic.htm The lesson of the HIV-drug example is nonetheless applicable to a host of other medicines and diseases.

67. Ass'n for Molecular Pathology v. U.S. Patent & Trademark Office, 94 U.S.P.Q.2d 1683 (S.D.N.Y. Mar. 29, 2010).

invalid on the basis that the isolated DNA of the patents was not markedly different from the native DNA found in human cells. This case may well be overturned on appeal, and the conclusion of the court was framed as a subject matter concern; consistent with what we saw above, the court concluded that the claimed discovery was not meaningfully different from the naturally occurring material and therefore not appropriate for patenting. However, it was clearly significant that the patents in issue created a monopoly in breast cancer screening tests, as the judge noted:

> The widespread use of gene sequence information as the foundation for biomedical research means that resolution of these issues will have far-reaching implications, not only for gene-based health care and the health of millions of women facing the specter of breast cancer, but also for the future course of biomedical research.

Agriculture is another battlefield where patent theory and practice is pitted against conceptions of human rights. Agrichemical companies have embraced the patent system for the protection of their advances in genetically modified seeds, including notable examples such as Monsanto's "Roundup Ready" herbicide-resistant line. Regular seed stock allows farmers to reserve a percentage of the seeds of a harvest and use this in planting for the following year, but patented crop seeds typically make this impossible, either through technological methods that render the stock incapable of reproducing or through agreements with farmers at the time of the purchase of the seed. These licenses—or "bag-tags" as they are called—forbid reuse, and ignoring the terms of the bag-tag license can land the farmer in federal court defending, of all things, a patent infringement suit.[68]

---

68. The issue is confined to those types of plants/seeds that are covered by utility patents. Plant patents under §§ 161–164 only cover asexual reproduction

The fault lines over bag-tag infringements pit the agribusiness and patent lobby against the farmers' lobby, and is the scene of ongoing and bitter division. One view of the dispute is that under the patent exhaustion/"first sale" doctrine, the owner of a product protected by a patent is free to do anything he likes with the product, including reverse-engineering it, pulling it to bits, or destroying it, as long as he is the lawful owner. In this view, the patent holder can't sue for patent infringement for something that the rightful owner of the product—the farmer who legally bought the seed— does with it;[69] although under the terms of the bag-tag the patent holder can always sue for a contract breach. One of the differences between a contract dispute and a patent dispute is, of course, the appropriate forum to hear the case, with the latter action being a federal matter. This is particularly significant because a number of states with strong consumer protection and/or farming interests have proposed or promulgated laws limiting the scope and enforceability of bag-tag licenses. Thus another fault line involves the question of federal preemption of the issue, with interests and outcomes both closely balanced and uncertain in operation.

Aside from concerns that sound in patent quality or human rights, there are numerous criticisms made about the patent system, certainly too many to review here. Probably the most significant is the concept of the tragedy of the patent anticommons, pioneered by Heller and Eisenberg, and the idea of patent thickets that arises from this theory. Many are familiar with the tragedy of the commons, a metaphor created by Garrett Hardin to explain why communal

---

(budding, grafting, etc), and the rights granted under the Plant Variety Protection Act are limited by the "brown-bag" exemption in 7 U.S.C. § 2543 that allows farmers to resow saved crop seed that is produced on their farms.

69. This argument was unsuccessful in Monsanto Co. v. Scruggs, 459 F.3d 1328 (Fed. Cir. 2006) on the basis that the reused seed was never sold because it was a second-generation product; however, the recent Supreme Court case of Quanta Computer, Inc. v. LG Electronics, 553 U.S. 617 (2008) may have changed the outcome in subsequent cases.

resources such as fisheries or forests can be depleted: in a commons every member has a right to use all the resource, creating a perverse incentive to overuse. Heller noted that the mirror image of this tragedy occurs in private property regimes where multiple parties have the right to veto the use by others, creating a situation where no one has an effective right of use. He and Eisenberg have shown that the tragedy of the anticommons can afflict some industries, notably biomedicine, because of multiple overlapping patents that effectively preclude innovation.[70] Not all industries reach the point of an anticommons, but a number of them are clearly the subject of a lesser variant called a patent thicket. Rational companies will patent multiple variations of a single invention to create a portfolio of patents that will protect against competitors designing around a single invention. A small number of incumbent players with large numbers of patents may then cross-license their inventions, creating a largely impregnable barrier (a thicket) that protects against any other entrant into the marketplace. This is not something that was anticipated in the creation of the patent system, and, according to some, needs to be remedied.

As patents continue to increase in number and value, we can expect these sorts of concerns to multiply. It is, however, anyone's guess whether they will in the future lead to changes in the patent system.

---

70. Michael A. Heller & Rebecca S. Eisenberg, *Can Patents Deter Innovation? The Anticommons in Biomedical Research*, 280 SCIENCE 698–701 (1998).

# FOUR

# Trademark

WALK DOWN ANY AISLE in the supermarket, turn on the television, or emerge from the subway into the neon-wonder of Times Square, and you will be *assailed* by trademarks. They are absolutely everywhere, and everyone can name any number of famous and not-so-famous marks—COCA-COLA, IBM, CHEVROLET, CAMPAGNOLO, STATE FARM, FORD, LOUIS VUITTON, TIDE, CREST, APPLE, DELL, IPOD, NIVEA—the list is endless.[1] Each of these marks provides consumers with a recognizable link to goods or services, and provides the owner of the mark with a competitive advantage. Trademark law is essential to modern day capitalism, and the billion-dollar businesses of marketing, advertising, and retailing are all built on the law of trademarks[2] that in the federal system is governed by the Lanham Act.[3]

---

1. In keeping with the usual convention, capitalized words indicate words operating as trademarks. Thus, for example, Hermès bags have the mark HERMÈS applied to them.

2. People in these industries usually call marks *brands*. I'm not going to draw a distinction between marks and brands, although some people suggest that the term *mark* or *trademark* should be reserved for specific signifiers that have legal protection (e.g., the federally registered trademark for "Coca-Cola"), whereas brand refers to the entire set of associations and goodwill surrounding a mark or set of marks (the advertising "the real thing," etc.). This isn't something that should trouble us much, and I will use the two terms interchangeably. While we're dealing with definitions, the Lanham Act has separate provisions for marks that relate to goods ("trademarks") and those that relate to services ("service marks"). We also don't need to be too fussed with this distinction—the differences between the law on each is negligible—and references to "marks" generally relate to either type.

3. 15 U.S.C. § 1051 *et seq.*

The proliferation of marks and brands should give us a hint that trademark law has a different purpose from the two intellectual property regimes we've looked at so far. Recall that the commonly accepted rationale for copyright and patent is the public goods/ incentive thesis. The first copy of the Great American Novel costs thousands to produce because during its production the author has to forego other work opportunities, pay rent and utilities, buy food, and so on; the first pill of the Cure for the Common Cold will cost millions because of the need for large teams of chemists, the expensive-to-maintain laboratories, the double-blind testing, FDA approval, etc. However, the second copy of each of these costs only pennies. If we don't provide the author/inventor with a monopoly or some exclusive rights, once the original is produced, substitutes will immediately flood the market and the author's or inventor's investment will be lost. Assuming that they're rational, the prospective author of the Great American Novel or drug company investigating the Cure will recognize the free-rider problem before they begin working, and will choose instead to invest their money and time toward something less socially worthwhile—the author will become a law professor or a cosmetic surgeon, the pharmaceutical company will close the lab and invest its money in a hedge fund. Thus, society will lose the benefit of their remarkable book/drug, and we will all be worse off.

But brands don't operate like this. There is no shortage of brands, and the Lanham Act doesn't try to encourage the production of yet more brands. Instead, trademark law has two purposes. First and foremost, it is supposed to protect consumers from being confused or deceived about the source of goods or services. Let's say that yesterday you purchased a drink you enjoyed. It came in a red can labeled "Coca-Cola" that featured a swirling ribbon device. You want to purchase the same drink today. In a world without a trademark system, you couldn't rely on your recollection of the COCA-COLA word mark, or the ribbon device, or the distinctive red color of the can.[4] Without a trademark

---

4. What is usually called the "trade dress" or "getup" of the product.

system that protects marks, any producer could use these features and you could be easily confused as to what you were buying. You would only realize that you'd be duped into buying my Dan's-Inferior-Soda-Bottled-in-the-Same-Getup-as-Coca-Cola when you took the first swig of my inferior soda. But in a world with trademarks you don't need to do anything other than recognize the marks and/or trade dress of the Coca-Cola Company to ensure that you get the same delicious piece of liquid heaven today as you bought yesterday. The Coke you have today will come from the same producer as the one you bought yesterday, and so it will be more or less the same.

Or, as the Supreme Court said:

> Thus, the core concern of trademark is to ensure that consumers aren't confused as to the source of products, and the second purpose of the trademark system comes about as a consequence of this. The course attribution justification means that businesses are encouraged to invest in the quality of their products by providing a right against unfair use of the mark by competitors. Because a trademark provides a stable signifier of the source of the product—the Coke that you buy today is going to come from the same source as the Coke you bought yesterday—the owner of the mark is provided with an incentive to build up goodwill.[5]

The court noted, following on immediately from the prior quotation:

> At the same time, the law helps assure a producer that it (and not an imitating competitor) will reap the financial, reputation-related rewards associated with a desirable product.[6]

---

5. Qualitex Co. v. Jacobson Prods. Co. Inc., 514 U.S. 159, 163–64 (1995) (quoting 1 J. THOMAS MCCARTHY, MCCARTHY ON TRADEMARKS AND UNFAIR COMPETITION 2.01[2], pp. 2–3 (3d ed. 1994), emphasis in the original).

6. *Qualitex*, 514 U.S. at 164.

We'll see in later sections that these purposes are sometimes at odds with each other, generating some deeply worrying features that emerge from the mismatch. But at this stage if you understand these basic justifications, then a range of trademark principles will be easy to understand. Many core trademark principles emerge from the basic premise. For example, unlike copyrights and patents, trademarks can last forever. This makes perfect sense because they come from different justifications. As we saw in the previous two chapters, copyright and patent require a balance between the need to provide a private property right to motivate production and the need to promote creativity, with the private property right needing to be circumscribed lest we lock up the inputs to further creativity so tightly that no one is able to create anything new. So we place a temporal limit on these two types of property rights. With trademark, however, there is no benefit to placing an arbitrary limit on how long a mark will denote the source of the product. Trademarks are generally not used as inputs into newer trademarks. And imagine what would happen if the trademark COKE fell into the public domain after a certain period: the day after there would be hundreds, if not thousands, of knockoff Cokes out in the marketplace, and soda consumers (and the Coca-Cola Company) would be significantly worse off than the day before. Endless numbers of consumers would purchase sodas that they actually didn't want, and Cokes that should have been sold would rest on the shelves along with thousands of their knockoff cousins. The only ones who would be made better off are the knockoff artists, and this is not a constituency that we particularly want to encourage. Thus, the Lanham Act provides for an initial registration period of ten years, with the right to renew registrations indefinitely as long as the mark is being used in commerce.

The second basic principle that falls out from the core purposes of trademark is the nature of the property right it grants. As we've seen, copyright and patent provide strong monopoly rights against the world at large. But the point of trademark is to protect the consumer from confusion (and, as a corollary, to protect the trademark owner from unfair competition), and so the right that trademark grants is not a property right "in gross" (i.e., in itself). In this respect it's not like most other types of property that, in Blackstone's memorable turn of phrase, involve "sole despotic dominion" over the property, and which can be freely sold or given away.[7] Trademarks exist only as far as they are used in relation to a product, and only to the extent that consumers would be confused by another's use of the mark. Delta Airlines does not have a monopoly over the word *Delta* even though it has a registered trademark for it. It is perfectly fine for the same DELTA mark to be registered to other companies for the application of the mark to faucets, baby products, science kits, and canned meat because no consumers will be confused by these other uses of the mark.[8] Further, even though all manner of entrepreneurs would like to carve out monopolistic property rights for potentially valuable words—think of buzzwords and neologisms that emerge overnight such as *staycation, locavore, truthiness, recessionista,* and *sexting*—they can't get rights over the mark unless they can demonstrate that they have used it in relation to a product, or can provide evidence that they have a good faith intention to use the mark in this way.

Finally, even though many trademarks are extraordinarily valuable in themselves—think of the value of marks such as APPLE, McDonald's Golden Arches, or Disney's Mickey Ears—the mark owners cannot sell or license the mark outright. If they sell the mark, they have to sell the goodwill of the business that the mark attaches to, and if they license the mark, they must impose some kind of quality control over the product that is sold with the licensed mark. Again, this principle is derived from the consumer confusion basis of trademark law: if Coke could license the COKE mark to anyone (even me, with my admitted history of appalling soda manufacture) without ensuring some degree of quality control, then consumers may be confused as to the source of

---

7. WILLIAM BLACKSTONE, COMMENTARIES ON THE LAWS OF ENGLAND 2 *et seq.* (Wayne Morrison ed., Cavendish Publishing 2001) (1893).

8. At the time of this writing, federally registered marks that involve the word mark DELTA include U.S. Reg. No. 0970418 in respect of air travel, U.S. Reg. No. 76233807 in respect of faucets and plumbing, U.S. Reg. No. 78949706 in respect of math and science kits, U.S. Reg. No. 78869096 in respect of baby products, and U.S. Reg. No. 78659093 in respect of canned and fresh meat, and canned vegetables.

the product and will purchase inferior soda by mistake. We'll see later in this chapter that courts often ignore this limitation—or at least dance around it, pointing somewhere else in the hope that no one notices—because of the significance of merchandising and the power of modern marketing that demand the ability to license the brand independently of the product and the goodwill. But as difficult as it might be to reconcile trademark law with marketing practices, it is true nonetheless that the doctrinal core of trademark remains true to its consumer confusion roots. Trademarks simply are not property separate from the product to which they are attached. Or, as the intellectual property theorists would say: trademarks are not property in gross.

From this discussion we can make a number of important observations. First, trademark law cleaves to a different set of foundational purposes than its other intellectual property cousins, and second, that these purposes generate some fundamental trademark doctrinal principles. But of course it's not as simple as that. Both the purposes and principles are artifacts of a long common-law history and a series of contested theoretical arguments about why certain doctrines were necessary for trademark. So in the section that follows we will look a little at the changes in our understanding of trademark and how this has influenced the current law. We still see echoes of old debates in recent cases, and we will see that it's impossible to understand why judges and legislators make the laws or decide the cases the way they do without our first understanding the way that the battle lines have shifted in trademark law. After we understand the historical and theoretical arguments, we can move on in subsequent sections to examine our typical topics of the creation and infringement of the rights, the nature of the defenses, and the emerging problems.

## History & Theory

It is probably true that the earliest artisans applied marks to their products. We have examples of marks applied to bricks from

Ancient Egypt and Rome, and to Grecian and Etruscan pottery from as far back as 800 to 400 BC. Doubtlessly other examples existed before these, but the evidence has been erased by the march of time. The reason for the applications of marks during the prehistorical period are likely little different from the basic reason artisans and craftspeople mark their products today: there appears to be a basic human need to declare to the world that "I made this." Of course even in the earliest period manufacturers of goods must have possessed the commercial interest of attracting other business from consumers who saw the product with the fancy brand and looked to the same manufacturer for their needs. And some marks were clearly intended to denote a claim to physical property—not so much "I made this" but "This is mine"—especially for property such as animals, which could stray and be lost. Ranchers have long used red-hot irons to brand their cattle, a practice from which we, of course, get the words "branding," "brands," and all their cognate terms.

Whatever the motivations of the artisans or manufacturers who apply their brands to products and property, marks become valuable signifiers of quality, and a reputation for high quality products becomes commercially important very quickly. An unscrupulous competitor can appropriate a mark that the public has come to associate with high quality by applying it to his low-quality product, not only reaping where he hath not sown, but also destroying the excellent reputation of the original craftsperson or manufacturer who worked so hard to generate the mark's goodwill. Thus, for the longest period, trademark law was mostly concerned with trade diversion and deceit, or what is sometimes called "palming off": the situation where an unscrupulous competitor uses another's mark that denotes high quality to pass off its shoddy goods as being the original owner's. Initially Anglo-American common law tended to focus on the damage to the reputation of the original owner, the so-called "senior user" of the mark. There were concerns about consumer confusion—palming off leads to consumers purchasing inferior products—but much of the early language about trademark focused on the unfair competition concern. As recently as 1946, a trademark lawyer asked about the basis of the protection conferred by a mark would point to the moral and property rights inherent in it before mentioning any perceived dangers to consumers. As a Senate Report of that time noted, "where the owner of a trade-mark has spent energy, time, and money in presenting to the public the product, he is protected in his investment from its appropriation by pirates and cheats."[9] A reflection of this is found in the observation that, to this day, trademark law is almost always characterized as a branch of unfair competition law, and almost never as a part of consumer protection law. State law also maintains this approach, with the main codification of common law found in the third chapter of the current Restatement regarding unfair competition.[10]

Numerous doctrines in trademark law rely entirely on this understanding. As we'll explore below, one of the ways in which I can infringe a famous trademark is to use the mark in a way that dilutes its power of distinguishment. So, for example, if I use the famous TIFFANY mark by applying it to my restaurant, then Tiffany & Company—the iconic Fifth Avenue jewelers and owner of the famous mark—has a dilution action against me for blurring of its mark. And if I use the TIFFANY mark for my strip club, then Tiffany & Co will have a dilution claim for tarnishment. We'll examine some of the doctrinal issues with these forms of infringement in the sections below, but at the moment the important thing to consider is that no consumer confusion occurs in either of these situations. The prospective consumer, standing outside either the restaurant or the strip club, doesn't mistake the source of his upcoming dining or adult entertainment experience as Tiffany & Co, the famous jewelers. Thus, dilution must stem from the unfair competition theory of trademark law, and the dilution action recognizes the quasi-property

---

9. S. Rep. No. 79–1333, at 3 (1946), reprinted in 1946 U.S.C.C.A.N. 1274.

10. Restatement (Third) of Unfair Competition, § 9 et seq. (1995).

rights in its reputation that Tiffany & Co has acquired through its careful maintenance of quality, marketing, and the like. The interesting feature of dilution infringement is that it was added to the Lanham Act only very recently, and at a time when the standard theoretical account said that trademark law existed to protect the consumer. It's hardly surprising that scholars widely decried the changes that occurred in the 1996 amendment that introduced this new form of infringement and then the 2006 revisions that broadened it.

Even though the dilution example demonstrates that the protection of business's property interests remains central to an understanding of trademark law, the theoretical understanding of the Lanham Act has nonetheless shifted over the years. These days the standard theoretical account posits that the consumer is sovereign within the trademark system, and where business reputation is protected it is usually done so as a by-product of protecting the consumer. It's impossible to pinpoint exactly when and why this change happened, although it has something to do with the rise of legal realism in the 1930s, which questioned essentialist and natural rights theories of property, then later had general policy concerns about the grant of wide-ranging monopolies that might be anticompetitive. Whenever and wherever the change happened, we can say with confidence that the most significant theoretical advance occurred within the trademark literature in the 1980s when, as with many legal disciplines in the United States, law and economics began its ascendancy. Within trademark law, the particular reflection of law and economics is called the "consumer search cost theory," and its dominance is impossible to overstate. It was pioneered by William Landes and Judge Richard Posner in a series of articles and a book,[11] and since then, virtually every trademark

---

11. William M. Landes & Richard A. Posner, *Trademark Law: An Economic Perspective*, 30 J. L. & ECON. 265 (1987); William M. Landes & Richard A. Posner, *The Economics of Trademark Law*, 78 TRADEMARK REP. 267 (1988).

scholar has adopted this theory that has profoundly influenced the legislative agenda along with outcomes of innumerable cases all the way to the Supreme Court.

Any understanding of the principles of trademark must grapple with the consumer search cost theory; to understand it, recall our earlier Coke example. You bought a Coke yesterday, and you want to purchase the same drink today. Being an ordinary consumer, you didn't note the chemical composition of the drink or the name of the company that produced the drink. So you can't use either of those two search strategies to find your preferred drink today. But being a human, you quickly and easily recognize the COCA-COLA mark on the cans in the supermarket aisle, and so you are able, unerringly, to reach for the drink that exactly meets your preference. Landes and Posner characterize this transaction as one about the reduction of your search costs. In trying to find the same drink as yesterday, you have to engage in a search for the same product—a search that is hard to do if you have to investigate all the constituent components of the drink, or the details of its manufacturer:

> Rather than reading the fine print on the package to determine whether the description matches his understanding of brand $X$ . . . the consumer will find it much less costly to search by identifying the relevant trademark and purchasing the corresponding brand . . . A trademark conveys information that allows the consumer to say to himself, "I need not investigate the attributes of the brand I am about to purchase because the trademark is a shorthand way of telling me that the attributes are the same as that of the brand I enjoyed earlier."[12]

Under this approach, the cost of a product to consumers is the nominal price of the good or service added to the cost of gaining

---

12. WILLIAM M. LANDES & RICHARD A. POSNER, THE ECONOMIC STRUCTURE OF INTELLECTUAL PROPERTY LAW 167 (2003) ( footnote omitted).

information about the source or quality of the good or service. In order to reduce the final cost of the product, trademark law reduces the information cost of determining quality and/or source, thereby increasing efficient bargaining and thus competition. The theory also explains in economic terms why producers of trademarked products can charge a premium over generic-branded products: consumers will pay the information cost of the trademark as long as it is lower than the search cost of investigating the quality or source of the generic product. This model has the virtue of certainty and reciprocity. Not only is there ascertainable value to the consumer (the information cost of the search) but also "[t]he value of a trademark to the firm that uses it to designate its brand is the saving in consumers' search costs made possible by the information that the trademark conveys or embodies about the quality of the firm's brand."[13]

This theory, the "consumer search cost theory," is now the dominant approach in both scholarly literature and the courts,[14] and it provides a justification for a range of trademark doctrines that we will examine later. There are a number of problems with the theory, but we will focus on the ways that the theories of trademark have influenced the development of the black-letter law, and anyone trying to understand the current approach to the Lanham Act needs to understand the consumer search cost theory and grapple with it in some form. As we look at the principles and doctrines, we'll also see how this theory, and the earlier unfair competition theory, have driven the territorial expansion of trademark.

---

13. LANDES & POSNER, *supra* note 12, at 168.

14. *See, e.g.,* Scandia Down Corp. v. Euroquilt, Inc., 772 F.2d 1423, 1429 (7th Cir. 1985). "Trademarks help consumers to select goods. By identifying the source of the goods, they convey valuable information to consumers at lower costs. Easily identified trademarks reduce the costs consumers incur in searching for what they desire, and the lower the costs of search the more competitive the market."

## ⚉ Creation and Rights

When the framers wrote the Progress Clause of the Constitution, they specifically gave Congress power to make laws in relation to copyright and patent, but failed to mention trademarks at all. Common law trademarks and associated state trademark laws had long existed, so it wasn't clear whether the Founding Fathers had intended to remove trademarks from the control of the states and hand it over to the federal government. But this didn't trouble Congress much: the "oversight" in the Constitution was ignored, and federal trademark acts were passed in 1870 and 1876 based on the assumption that the Progress Clause provided the basis for federal trademark laws.

In 1879 the federal takeover of these rights was challenged in the *Trade-Mark Cases*.[15] The Supreme Court ruled the federal laws were unconstitutional because Congress had been given no express power to regulate in relation to all marks. The reliance on the Progress Clause was rejected and as a result subsequent statutes—including the 1946 Lanham Act, the basis of modern federal trademark law—relies on the Commerce Clause, and, in theory, applies only to marks used between states, or internationally, or between the states and Native Americans, following the limits of that clause. These days this constitutional limitation provides few constraints on federal trademark power: in an increasingly connected world, national advertising campaigns are commonplace, interstate and international trade is an everyday reality, and the internet and electronic commerce have been adopted by every wholesaler and retailer known to man. As a practical matter the constitutional basis of federal trademark law is now unquestionable.

Recognizing trademark law's constitutional history and basis is, however, vitally important to understanding one feature of the system: federal trademark law is not intended to preempt common

---

15. The Trade-Mark Cases, 100 U.S. 82 (1879).

law rights, and it does not codify them. Instead, the Lanham Act is intended to be a mechanism for federal recognition of some common law rights. That is, the initial creation of rights in a federally recognized mark depends on the trademark owner using the mark and establishing an association between the source of the product and the mark, in keeping with the way that common law marks have always been created. However, the Lanham Act does go further than merely codifying common law, and it does materially extend common law rights and infringements. Notably, it generates national protection for marks that may only have local reputation. In this respect we can say that the federal trademark law creates a form of property rights in gross, at least in regions where the trademark owner has no reputation. The federal law also extends the state and common law systems in other important ways: it makes rights in a registered mark incontestable after five years. It provides access to the federal courts without the need to establish the usual requirements of federal jurisdiction. It establishes a national register that provides notice of existing marks, and changes evidential presumptions in favor of registered marks. It further creates certain types of collective and certification marks that were not found in common law. And it extends the types of infringements available in relation to trademarks. In summary, the Lanham Act relies on the system of common law marks, but extends it in significant ways.

We'll focus on the federal system in the remainder of this chapter, but we'll occasionally draw attention to situations where the federal system diverges from the approaches in common law and under state systems.

## Registering Trademarks

A trademark is defined as a "word, name, symbol, or device, or any combination thereof" that is used in commerce to identify and distinguish goods and to indicate the source of the goods. Trademarks are usually words and/or graphical symbols (or "devices" as they're often called). So NIKE is the word mark, and the swoosh is the device mark; just as COKE is the word mark, and the ribbon is the device mark.

In common law there is no need for registration of a mark for it to operate as a trademark, because the source identification of the mark in the mind of the consumer is sufficient. This is true to an extent in the Lanham Act—especially in the area called trade dress that we'll look at later—but by and large, to gain federal protection you need to register the mark with the United States Patent and Trademark Office (USPTO). The Lanham Act provides for the registration of marks, but this should not be confused with the type of registration that applies in the patent system. A patent registration is the *grant* of the right, whereas a trademark registration is intended merely to signal the *recognition* of an existing right. Thus, registration is not the be-all and end-all of the trademark system, but it is important in numerous ways because the scope of the rights available differs depending on whether the mark is registered and in what category the mark is registered.

Under the Lanham Act there are four main types of registrable marks: trademarks, service marks, collective marks, and certification marks. Trademarks and service marks are conceptually identical, and differ only in that the relevant products for trademarks are goods—KODAK, in relation to cameras, for example—whereas, unsurprisingly, with service marks they're services, as in CITIBANK, for banking services. Collective marks are not intended to denote the source of the product, but rather indicate that the producer is a member of a collective or an association. So, for example, the mark, REALTOR is owned by the National Association of Realtors, and members of that body are entitled to use the mark in relation to the services they offer, primarily as a signifier of membership in that group, and secondarily, as an imprimatur of quality or high service in real estate services. Certification marks are also not intended to be source identifying, but rather to denote that the product has certain qualities or attributes, such as that it's made from a certain type of material or conforms with certain standards. Thus, the

WOOLMARK certification mark can only be applied to fabrics that have a certain percentage of wool in them; the UL certification mark, owned by Underwriters Laboratories, may only be applied to products that have passed the safety standards of that organization and been granted the right to affix the certification mark.

A special type of certification mark is geographical indicators. These marks, commonly called GIs, are significant in international intellectual property arenas but mostly ignored in the United States. Geographical indicators regulate the use of terms such as "champagne," "cheddar," or "parmesan" and denote products coming from certain geographical regions—in these cases, the wine from the Champagne region of France, the cheese originally stemming from the region around the English town of Cheddar, and the cheese from the Parma region of Italy. For many years these terms were used as generic descriptors of the type of product, and so consumers would, for example, ask for "champagne" at their local wine seller, not caring whether it came from vineyards in California, South Africa, or Australia. Fairly recently (within the last twenty years or so) we've seen efforts by European governments to force the adoption of geographical indicators worldwide because this grants trade protection for their products coming from their economically significant regions. The United States has grudgingly acceded to this, and so the Lanham Act now treats geographical indicators as a form of certification mark. However, the scope of the provision is limited—it is mostly relevant to allow trade groups to register a geographical indicator as a certification mark—and in many situations does not stop competitors from describing their product by its commonly used name. This is why you still see cheddar cheese from Wisconsin in the supermarket.

Finally, when thinking about words used within business, there are trade and company names to consider. These are the names of companies or businesses that are regulated and registered under various state laws. They are not eligible to be registered under the Lanham Act unless they serve as a signifier of the source of the product: for example, the word *Nike* is part of the trade name of the company that makes the running gear, but only when the NIKE mark is applied to the running gear is it eligible for trademark registration. Trade names don't give the owner any proprietary rights against others using the same name, and it's common to have similar or identical names for businesses in different states.

Of the types mentioned, far and away the most important are trademarks, and so the principles discussed in the remainder of this chapter will focus on them. Service marks are treated by the Lanham Act in almost exactly the same way as trademarks, so the discussion here will be applicable to that form of mark also. Collective and certification marks are such a small category of marks that we may ignore the special rules for them.

Now that we know the categories of marks, we can turn to what type of thing can function as a mark. As we saw, usually we're talking about words or logos, but it's possible to register marks that are formed by other types of symbols or indicators, as long as these indicators are capable of distinguishing the goods to which the marks are applied. The easiest example is sound: there are trademark registrations for the familiar NBC chimes, the Intel bonging sound, and the MGM lion roar.[16] The smell of flowers as applied to sewing thread has been registered as a trademark.[17] The shape of the Coke bottle is a trademark.[18] And in an important case, the Supreme Court found that the green-gold color of dry-cleaning pads was capable of operating as a trademark as long as it adequately distinguished the applicant's goods in the marketplace from its competitors.[19] Thus we can say that features that distinguish a

---

16. U.S. Reg. No. 72349496 (NBC chimes), U.S. Reg. No. 78721830 (Intel five-note sound), U.S. Reg. No. 1395550 (MGM lion roar).

17. U.S. Reg. No. 1639128 (plumeria scent as a trademark for OSEWEZ sewing thread and embroidery yarn, subsequently abandoned).

18. U.S. Reg. No. 73088384 (distinctive hourglass shape for Coke bottle).

19. Qualitex Co. v. Jacobson Prods. Co. Inc., 514 U.S. 159, 163–64 (1995).

product from other similar products may be used and registered as a trademark.[20]

It is important also to note the scope of registration. Marks are registered in respect of certain products, in various classes that have been agreed to internationally. There are forty-five classes, with thirty-four used for trademarks and eleven used for service marks. Each class is a broad category of similar types of products that are considered to be closely related. So, for example, Class 13 covers "Firearms; ammunition and projectiles; explosives; fireworks" while Class 44 is for "Medical services; veterinary services; hygienic and beauty care for human beings or animals; agriculture, horticulture and forestry services." In the United States, the class categories are mostly an administrative convenience since our system is heavily dependent on the actual use to which a mark is put. Thus registration in one class doesn't necessarily give the mark rights over all of the products in that class, but only over those products to which the mark is actually applied. It would be possible, therefore, for two different people to have registrations in the United States for HUNTER in respect of firearms and explosives even though they are in the same class. It depends on whether the two registrants had reputations that spilled over from one area to the other: the registrations would only be refused if there were a likelihood of confusion between the two registrations. In practice, though, it's very hard to register similar marks in the same class in the United States, and virtually every other country formally forbids doing so.

Registered marks are granted specific rights, but to enforce them the owner must provide notice of the registration, a requirement usually satisfied by applying the symbol® to the mark. The symbol™ may be applied to unregistered marks, but it isn't necessary to do so to enforce rights in an unregistered mark.

---

20. However, you should note that this principle is limited by the functionality doctrine, discussed below.

Marketers often do this however as a way of marking out their territory—or at least the territory they'd like to claim, whether or not this is supported by actual use.

Registered trademarks can last forever. The Lanham Act provides for an initial registration period of ten years, followed by an unlimited number of renewals of ten years. The mark must be in continuous use as otherwise it's subject to cancelation. Therefore, businesses are not permitted to register a mark and then "warehouse" it for later use or sale. However, as long as, for example, Sony Corporation continues to sell consumer electronics under the name SONY, the mark can continue to be registered forever. This accords, of course, with our discussion of the theoretical justification for trademarks: since trademarks are said to exist in order to reduce consumer confusion, no purpose would be served by placing limits on the period that Sony can have trademark rights as long as the company continues to use the mark. In this, trademarks are very different from most other types of intellectual property.

Finally, note that registration is primarily a national system, and a U.S.-registered mark does not confer automatic protection in other countries. There are various international treaties that provide for expedited and simplified registration in the national systems of other countries. The basic treaties are the Paris Convention, the North American Free Trade Agreement, the General Inter-American Convention, the Madrid Agreement, and the recent Madrid Protocol. The mechanics of these treaties are well beyond the scope of this short introductory primer; but they provide a range of means of gaining recognition and registration of a trademark in signatory countries based on an initial trademark registration in the United States.

## Distinctiveness

As we discussed above, any indicator that is capable of being perceived by human senses is also capable of being recognized as a trademark. However, no matter what form the indicator takes, the mark must be distinctive of the product. That is, the mark must distinguish the branded product from the competition, and it must be separate from the product itself. This explains in part why tactile marks, for example, are so rare: usually the feel of a product is part of the product itself. The USPTO has registered a sensory mark for a velvet sheath applied to a bottle of alcohol as being distinctive of the product, but this is very unusual.[21] Other types of indicators are more easily adapted to distinguishing products—words and devices especially—and so they are more amenable to registration.

A mark may be inherently distinctive or may acquire distinctiveness. An invented word such as *EXXON* is inherently distinctive because it automatically distinguishes the mark's registrant from all other competitors: no one else has ever used this mark before. Other words, such as *apple* or *American*, may acquire the ability to distinguish the product from competitors through long-term use, advertising and marketing, and the like. A mark having acquired distinctiveness is usually referred to as having "secondary meaning." Consider the APPLE word mark applied to computers and electronics. There is the primary meaning of *apple* in the minds of consumers—that is, the fruit we call an apple—and there is its secondary meaning as the well-known mark APPLE, as applied to Macintosh computers, iPhones, and iPads.

In grappling with this concept, courts and commentators have developed a categorization of four different levels of distinctiveness. Ranging from the least distinctive to the most, a potential mark can be (1) generic, (2) descriptive, (3) suggestive, or (4) arbitrary or fanciful, and we'll look at all of these levels below.

### Generic Marks

Generic terms define the basic nature, the class, or the genus of which the product is a member. These terms can never be registered as

---

21. U.S. Reg. No. 3155702 (turgid velvet covering for wine bottles, for American Wholesale Wine & Spirits).

trademarks because to do so would freeze out competitors from being able to describe the nature of their products. Thus, terms such as *soap* or *computer* or *dental clinic* are considered generic when applied to soap, computers, and dental services, respectively. But no term is generic of itself, and whether a term is considered generic depends on the relationship between the potential mark and the product. The word *ivory* is generic when used in relation to products made from elephant tusks, but is perfectly acceptable as a trademark when applied to soap.

Sometimes marks are generic from the get-go, and other times marks become generic through usage. Familiar expressions such as *escalator, murphy bed, aspirin*, and *cellophane* began life as registered trademarks that were canceled when they became generic descriptors of the class of goods. These are instances of what is occasionally called *genericide*, and this used to happen fairly often: the mark became popular in the marketplace, consumers just called the product by the mark name, and the mark owner didn't do anything to stop it. Modern branding practice however has developed sophisticated means to try to end this problem by making the brand and the product distinct. Johnson and Johnson no longer refer to its product simply as "Band-Aids" but as "Band-Aid Brand Adhesive Bandages." A number of years ago when photocopying first emerged, the Xerox Corporation was concerned that the word *Xerox* would become generic, and so it brought out an advertisement patiently explaining that you couldn't "Xerox a Xerox on a Xerox" but you could "copy a copy on a Xerox copier." For all these efforts, brand owners can only do so much policing of the consumers' use of their marks, and in the end the relevant question to determine if a mark has become generic is to ask whether the general public uses the mark as a generic descriptor of the class or nature of the product. If so, the mark is generic and subject to cancelation, no matter the efforts of the brand owner.

### Descriptive Marks

Descriptive terms are those that identify a characteristic or quality of the product to which they're applied. So, the terms *red* in respect of apples or *tasty* for cheese are considered descriptive. Merely descriptive marks are not distinctive of the source of the product and therefore are not registrable as trademarks. However, where the descriptive term has been applied to a product and has acquired secondary meaning in the minds of the public—and as a result is now an indicator of the source of the product—then the mark may be protected as a registered trademark. CHAP STICK, for example, was initially descriptive of the product itself, but it is now a recognizable mark performing the usual source-identifying function of trademarks.

The Lanham Act provides for a prima facie presumption of acquired distinctiveness of a mark after five years of continuous use, but secondary meaning is more commonly proven through market survey evidence of consumer perception and recognition of the mark, combined with details of the volume of sales in the trademarked product, expenditure on advertising and marketing, and so on.

While thinking about descriptiveness of marks, it's worth considering some special cases, including personal and geographical names. Personal names are treated as descriptive marks and therefore require secondary meaning for registration. And though there was once an absolute right for people to use their names in business, recent approaches have treated these situations in a way that is consistent with the consumer protection theory of trademark. Thus, John McDonald is not completely free to open a diner called "McDonald's," because of the concern that consumers might be confused with the chain of fast food joints operating under the MCDONALD'S mark. Use by John McDonald of his family name will generally only be allowed where there is no risk of confusion, and will often require elaborate disclaimers. Although this seems to be harsh as to Mr. McDonald, remember that the basis of the Lanham Act is to protect the consumer from confusion in purchasing decisions, and so these requirements are consistent with the general principles relating to likelihood of confusion. Similar principles apply with geographical designations that generate similar concerns: imagine a well-known brand of wine from "Napa Wineries" or dairy products from "Great Lakes Dairies." Giving complete control of the geographical name to the first registrant will provide a monopoly that will forbid second comers from accurately describing their wines or dairy products, but to allow the junior users to appropriate these terms will confuse the consumer. To accommodate these sorts of balancing acts, the USPTO will generally allow registration only with disclaimers, or with prefixes, suffixes or other modifiers that will ensure that the potential consumer won't be confused.

Finally, in the category of descriptiveness, in certain contexts the Lanham Act takes its consumer protection role very seriously: it forbids registration of marks that are deceptively misdescriptive (e.g., ALWAYSFRESH for seafood that has been frozen), and misdescriptive as to geography (e.g., NAPA ESTATES for wine that doesn't come from California) as long as the misdescription is material and leads to deception.[22]

### Suggestive Marks

The third category in the spectrum of distinctiveness is for those marks that are considered *suggestive*, that is those that suggest some characteristic of the product but are not descriptive because they require the consumer to exercise some imagination to draw a conclusion about the mark. Examples of these types of marks include SEASON-ALL for spices, and COPPERTONE for sunscreen. Suggestive marks are, of course, somewhat descriptive—they describe, in some attenuated way, some characteristics of the product—and one of the main difficulties in assessing distinctiveness is deciding whether a mark is descriptive or suggestive. A lot rides on the conclusion: suggestive marks do not need secondary meaning in order to be

---

22. Various other types of marks are ineligible for registration because they are immoral, scandalous, or disparaging; they involve national, state, or municipal insignia, or the Olympic logo; or they are likely to cause confusion.

registered, whereas, as we've seen, descriptive marks must have secondary meaning to be registrable. In confronting a mark that might fall into either the suggestive or descriptive category, courts use a number of tests. These include (1) the "dictionary test" where the court looks at definition for the ordinary significance of the word; (2) the imagination test, which asks whether a term requires imagination for a conclusion to be reached about the nature of the goods; (3) the monopoly test, which queries whether competitors need the claimed term in order to be able to describe their goods; and (4) the empirical test, which examines the degree that competitors use the term in marketing a similar product. None of these tests are definitive, and the conclusions reached are often unpredictable.

### Arbitrary and Fanciful Marks

The final category of distinctiveness is for those marks that are arbitrary or fanciful. These marks convey no information about the character of the products to which they are attached, and these marks are inherently distinctive. Thus, they may be registered without a showing of secondary meaning. An invented word such as EXXON or KODAK is fanciful. An existing word used in an unusual context, such as CAMEL for cigarettes or APPLE for computers, is considered arbitrary. Fanciful marks are, in one sense, "stronger" than arbitrary marks, since fanciful marks can be applied to any product. Arbitrary marks used in their dictionary definitions can be in danger of falling into the descriptive or generic category: APPLE is considered arbitrary for computers, but descriptive for the juice and generic for the fruit.

### Trade Dress

*Trade dress* usually refers to the features of a product's packaging, or what is sometimes called its "get-up." It can also refer to the configuration and image of the product itself, which the Supreme

Court has defined as including "features such as size, shape, color or color combinations, texture, graphics, or even particular sales techniques." As an example, for a Mexican restaurant the distinctive features of interior dining and patio areas, an outdoor dining area accessed by garage doors, decorations with artifacts, bright colors, paintings, murals, neon stripes, and so forth, were considered the business's trade dress. For UPS, it's the distinctive brown of its trucks and logos.

It's possible to register trade dress in the federal system in the same way as we've seen above—that is, essentially as a mark—but a more significant feature of the Lanham Act is found in section 43(a). This section prohibits a range of deceptive and misleading practices such as false designation of origin, false description of fact and—most saliently for our purposes—the use of an unregistered word, term, name, symbol, or device in a manner likely to cause confusion. Thus, section 43(a) extends the protection afforded registered marks by the Lanham Act to unregistered trade dress as long as it fulfills the Constitutional "use in commerce" requirement. In this way the Lanham Act protects unregistered trade indicia.

It's hard to overstate the significance of this. All indicia of a product and its packaging may become something which competitors are forbidden from using, even without a trademark registration. Section 43(a) provides for the same kinds of protections for unregistered trade dress as found in the common law system. There are, however, some limitations on the rights granted to unregistered trade dress. First, they don't enjoy the specific benefits of registered marks that are described above: they don't become incontestable after five years, they don't have rights outside locations where the claimant trades, they don't get the evidentiary presumptions in their favor, and so on.

More than this, there are some special considerations that apply to trade dress. As with registered marks, the trade dress has to be distinctive of the source of the product, but certain types of trade dress can't be inherently distinctive. As indicated above, trade dress comprises both the packaging of the product as well as the actual product itself. Trade dress in the product packaging may, as a question of fact, be inherently distinctive, but the Supreme Court has ruled that, as a matter of law, trade dress that comprises the actual product itself must have secondary meaning for it to be protectable. The example often used is the one used by the Court in *Wal-Mart v. Samara* of an unusual cocktail shaker.[23] Imagine a cocktail shaker in the very distinctive shape of a penguin; the penguin shape of the shaker is part of the design of the product, not part of the packaging it came in. It may be distinctive, but its distinctiveness is not used to identify the source of the cocktail shaker, but rather to make the shaker more appealing to the consumer and therefore more likely to be purchased. The configuration trade dress is not inherently distinctive as to source because the penguin shape doesn't inherently tell the consumer that this product comes from a specific manufacturer. It is perfectly possible that the penguin-shaped cocktail shaker might acquire distinctiveness through secondary meaning—for example, through extensive advertising, the relevant consuming public may associate penguin cocktail shakers with only one manufacturer— but the design of the shaker in and of itself isn't inherently distinctive. Configuration trade dress must therefore be accompanied by evidence of secondary meaning for it to be protected.

The other main issue for trade dress claims in respect of product design is where the element is a functional component of the product. This issue is one that applies to all trademarks, and is the subject of the next section.


## Functionality

Trademark law deals with brands and marks, and is intended to protect consumers from confusion and protect businesses from being ripped off by unfair competitors. It's very different from patent and copyright law, and generally we don't need to undertake the delicate

---

23. Wal-Mart Stores, Inc. v. Samara Brothers, Inc., 529 U.S. 205, 213–214 (2000).

balancing act between scope and length of protection that is necessary in those regimes. However, occasionally there arises in trademark law the same kind of balancing act between private and public rights that animate our discussions of patent and copyright law. This occurs most evidently in trademark's functionality doctrine, which says that trademark protection is not available for the useful or functional features of an article. Consider the design of a traffic sign that is mounted on a set of springs, and which is intended to bend rather than break when pushed over by the wind or when it's hit by a car. It's perfectly possible that consumers will come to associate this design with one producer, especially if the design is the subject of a patent granting the producer twenty years of exclusivity. Should we let other businesses use this design when the patent expires, even though a competitor's use might generate consumer confusion?

The functionality doctrine says that a mark owner can't use trademark law to forestall competition by gaining a monopoly over a useful product feature. Useful features are, as we've seen, properly the subject matter of patent law, and the danger of allowing trademarks into this arena is that of granting via the trademark system a de facto infinite patent over a functional element. As we discussed in an earlier chapter, there are good reasons patent protection has the shortest period of protection of any intellectual property regime, and to allow an infinite term of protection via the backdoor of trademark law would be a Really Bad Idea. The concept then is to refuse trademark protection where the protection is over a functional element, even though this might cause consumer confusion.

While it's easy to agree to this general principle, things get hairy quickly, and the functionality doctrine is contested in a range of areas. But, before we delve into these difficulties, there is some low-hanging fruit that we can pluck. First, it's commonly accepted that it simply doesn't matter that a useful product feature has become distinctive of a particular producer. Even if every single consumer on the planet associates a product feature with your company, you cannot obtain trademark protection if the feature is functional. Functionality doctrine trumps distinctiveness.

Second, the most obvious problems with functionality arise in relation to a section 43(a) infringement claim for configuration trade dress. Since the trade dress in this type of claim is the actual design of the product, not the packaging or branding around it, the risk of protecting functional components is especially acute. Most cases arise in this context, and judges are particularly mindful of protecting functional elements when dealing with design elements in a section 43(a) trade dress claim.

The problems begin when we examine the tests for what amounts to a functional component of a product. It's clear that a product feature is functional, and therefore forbidden trademark protection, if it's essential to the use or purpose of the article or if it affects the cost or quality of the article. This is what we can call the *primary functionality test*. Drawn from three Supreme Court decisions, it is relatively easy to apply to situations such as the spring-loaded sign example mentioned above. It's obvious that the springs are essential to a sign designed to bend with the wind—indeed in the case from which the example is drawn, the springs had previously been protected as a patent[24]—and so they are precluded from trademark protection. But what of the color or shape of an object that provides some aesthetic benefit to the producer? What of an aesthetically pleasing but distinctive gold-trimmed heart-shaped box of chocolates, or the distinctive black color of Mercury boat engines?

For situations such as this, the Supreme Court has crafted a secondary test that asks whether the feature places competitors at a significant non-reputation-related disadvantage were it to be protected as a trademark. This is the test for "aesthetic functionality," and it is a notoriously difficult one to apply. Do consumers buy Coke in the hourglass bottle because it feels good in the hand—a competitive advantage generated by the aesthetic functionality of the shape of the bottle, which means no protection—or because it's a Coke—a reputation-related advantage that is clearly protected

---

24. TrafFix Devices, Inc. v. Mktg. Displays, Inc., 532 U.S. 23 (2001).

by trademark law? Courts sometimes try to find a way to decide based on the primary test to avoid the uncertainty of the secondary test for aesthetic functionality. For example, in the case involving the black Mercury outboard engines, the court concluded by applying the primary test, noting that the color was essential to the use of the article because black dissipates heat better and can be used on boats of any color.[25] It wasn't necessary therefore to ask whether consumers just liked black better in their boat engines.

The difficulty of both tests for functionality can be seen in the divergent ways that the circuits treat the question. Some circuits apply the two-part test exactly as noted above, some include additional factors to determine functionality—asking, for example, whether the feature was the subject matter of an expired pattern or advertising touting utilitarian benefits—and some even make a distinction between de jure and de facto functionality. All that one can say simply is that where functionality is in issue, there's going to be a fight—and the outcome is often a crapshoot.

## Use

Use is one of the two fundamental requirements to gain trademark rights. (As we saw above, the other fundamental requirement is distinctiveness). Use is required whether the trademark is registered under the federal or state systems, or is unregistered as in the common law, but the different systems have slight variations in what amounts to use.

The common law looks to "use in trade," which basically means the actual use of the mark in connection with offering the product to the public. The scope of use determines the scope of the common law trademark right. Thus, if I market a line of chili-flavored chocolates under the name "Hotstuff Chocolates" in New York City and

---

25. Brunswick Corp. v. British Seagull Ltd., 35 F.3d 1527(Fed. Cir.1994).

nowhere else, my rights in the common law mark will only extend geographically as far as consumer recognition of the name is a reliable indicator of source. Unless you ship chocolates across the United States and have a reputation in other geographical markets, there is nothing stopping you from producing a line of chocolates named "Hotstuff" in San Francisco or Oklahoma or New Orleans. Further, I will only have rights in respect of the actual products to which I apply the mark. Thus my use of the mark in respect of chocolates will mean that someone else's use of the mark in relation to bicycles is not actionable, because no consumer would be confused by that use. Finally, in common law I can't get any prospective rights in marks I intend to use, but for which I haven't yet established actual use in trade. So there's no way for me to claim rights in the term "Hotstuff" prior to establishing a reputation in the term— something I might want to do if I'm setting up, printing labels, buying advertising, and generally investing money in a mark that won't have a reputation for some months (at best).

The "use in trade" requirement is also found in the federal system, but is complicated slightly by the constitutional basis we've previously discussed. That is, the requirement of "use" is translated into "use in commerce" in order to satisfy the Commerce Clause. As previously mentioned, this isn't a huge hurdle for most applicants these days, and the only significant requirement is that the goods or services be used or transported in commerce. Section 45 of the Lanham Act provides an inclusive definition of "use in commerce," noting that the term "means the bona fide use of a mark in the ordinary course of trade, and not made merely to reserve a right in a mark."[26] The first part of the definition is expanded by a number of instructive examples of use, including placing the mark on the goods or their containers, on tags or labels, or on advertising associated with the product. The legislative history of the section explains that "use in commerce" was intended to be interpreted flexibly, and the history provides examples of sales in

---

26.  Lanham Act, § 45; 15 U.S.C. § 1127.

test markets, infrequent sales of large or expensive products, and various other types of commercial relationships.

The latter part of the definition makes clear that the old approach of *token use* is no longer available. Token use was the mechanism that existed prior to the revisions of 1988, where the applicant applied a mark to a small number of sample products and then marketed them in very limited fashion, often internally to its staff. This was done for the express intention of reserving the mark. This approach is no longer kosher, in part because it conflicts with the core understanding of the U.S. trademark system—that it's predicated on *actual* use that generates single-source identification in the minds of consumers—and also because the Lanham Act provides an alternative mechanism, the intent-to-use registration system. These days, actual use isn't necessary as long as the applicant has a bona fide intention to use the mark within a short period after the filing of the application. It's possible for me to file an intent-to-use as much as thirty-six months prior to the marketing or sale of my chocolates—although shorter periods are more common—so that I can effectively reserve the name as I'm developing the business. Intent-to-use applications are particularly important to large businesses, such as those involving consumer products or pharmaceuticals whose products rely heavily on advertising and who need to develop elaborate marketing plans prior to the release of a new brand of toothpaste or anti-cholesterol drug.

This is a major benefit of the federal system over the common law, but it's not the only one in relation to use. A federal registration is sufficient to generate constructive use in markets where the registered owner has never sold or advertised its products. Therefore, unlike the common law example above, if I take out a federal registration for HOTSTUFF chocolates, then you will be unable to sell your chocolates under that mark anywhere in the United States. This is true even if I never sell my chocolates further west than Jersey City. The constructive use provisions of the Lanham Act also provide significant benefits for priority dates for intent-to-use applications: essentially the date of the filing of the intent-to-use application is considered to be the date that the registrant actually began using the mark. This is extremely important and useful, and a large proportion of applications these days are intent-to-use applications because of the constructive use provisions.

## 🕮 Infringement and Other Actions

Your day began, as it usually does, with a quick session surfing the internet. You found yourself looking at handbags on the Louis Vuitton web site. Fantastic, and fantastically expensive, these bags all feature some combination of the "LV" monogram and a distinctive "quatrefoil" flower symbol. So pretty, you thought to yourself. You idly Googled "Louis Vuitton" and you noticed that the sponsored links on the right side of your screen offered any number of web sites offering counterfeit Louis Vuitton handbags, at domain names such as <louisvuittoncollections.com>, as well as some fashion sales outlets that don't sell knockoffs but seek to entice the prospective purchaser with sample sales of high-end fashions. Your search also disclosed that at least one particularly obsessed fashionista has a *quatrefoil* flower tattooed on her thigh. You shook your head: some people need help. Trawling further into the search results, you discovered that it's possible to buy dog toys from a brand called "Chewy Vuitton," which features a "CV" monogram as well as a similar quatrefoil design. You laughed at the incongruity of a fluffy dogbed that references the famous logo, closed your laptop, and got on with your day.

Only later did you ask yourself whether you had seen any trademark infringements.

Previously we looked at the requirements that trademark owners must satisfy to obtain their rights. In this part we'll look at the actions that can be brought against and by others in relation to those rights. These are basically three types of actions: opposition, cancellation, and infringement. These are conceptually related, but distinct in practice. Opposition and cancellation proceedings are actions brought by another user of the same or similar mark in relation to a federally registrable mark. Opposition actions occur prior to the grant of the trademark, where the other party is—no surprise here—opposing the registration of the mark. A cancellation action occurs where a mark has been registered, often for some time, but the non-registered party seeks to have the mark canceled. And of course, an infringement action occurs where a trademark owner, whether federally registered or not, claims that a junior user is infringing its rights.

We'll spend most of the time here discussing infringement actions since these provide the clearest examples of general trademark principles. Further, the issues examined in an infringement proceeding are very similar to those addressed in opposition and cancellation proceedings; it's just that the identity of the parties may differ. So, for example, arguments about whether a mark is distinctive or generic, or whether a competing brand is likely to confuse consumers can find their way into any of the actions; in an opposition proceeding, a claim of confusion might be the basis for refusing registration of the mark, whereas in an infringement action it's a core basis for the finding of infringement.

Therefore in the sections below we'll briefly mention opposition and cancellation proceedings before moving on to infringement actions. Whether we're talking about federally registered trademarks, unregistered trade dress subject to section 43(a), or any of the state- or common law- based actions, the categories of infringement are basically threefold. The canonical infringement is the so-called "likelihood-of-confusion" infringement, where two marks are so similar that a potential consumer may be confused about the source of the products. A more recent addition is the action for dilution-based infringement, and the final form is a range of special cases of infringement that apply regarding domain names and some related situations. We'll look at each of these below.

## Opposition and Cancellation

The Lanham Act is not intended to preempt common and state law principles, and everything we've talked about to this point applies to federal, state, and common law marks. It's nonetheless the case that some parts of the federal system are unique, and it's worth understanding trademark practice here, if only because federally registered marks are so valuable. A significant part of trademark practice under the Lanham Act involves dealing with the requirements in section 2, which excludes federal registration for certain types of marks. We've already mentioned some of these exclusions when discussing distinctiveness: deceptive marks, family names, and geographically misdescriptive marks are denied registration under section 2. Other marks that are denied registration include immoral, scandalous, or disparaging marks; marks comprising a coat of arms or the insignia of the United States; and marks comprising the name, signature, or portrait of a deceased U.S. president during the life of his widow. There is one very significant prohibition, the section 2(d) bar, which forbids registration for marks that are sufficiently similar to existing marks or names that their use would cause confusion, mistake, or deception. Essentially this requirement invokes the same analysis we'll examine when looking below at the likelihood-of-confusion infringement.

We needn't go into detail why each of these types of marks is denied registrations, but it's necessary to understand the basics of the trademark examination process. In a regular application, after the application is filed an examining attorney in the USPTO will check for all the elements we discussed above—distinctiveness, use, etc—and will also assess the application against the section 2 bars. If, in the examiner's opinion, the application satisfies all the criteria and is not barred by section 2, then the mark is published for opposition. Here is where section 2(d) becomes significant because other brand/mark/name owners may find that the Office is about to register a mark that unduly impinges on rights they've already established in their brands.[27] At this point they can bring an opposition proceeding seeking to have the mark denied registration.

---

27. They may also have an objection based on the other § 2 bars, but this is less common.

If no opposition is brought, or if the opposition is unsuccessful, the mark will duly be registered. After registration it's still possible for an aggrieved party to challenge the federal registration; this type of proceeding is called a cancellation action, since the remedy sought is cancellation of the federal registration. This may be brought on the basis of the section 2 bars or upon some of the other issues we've looked at or will look at—functionality, abandonment, genericide—but the downside is that it's harder to obtain a cancellation than it is to win an opposition proceeding. This is true because there are a number of presumptions in favor of the registered mark that make it more onerous for the party seeking the cancellation.

### Use

We saw that a trademark owner must establish use in order to assert its claim over the mark. Use on the defendant's part is also significant since, for there to be an actionable infringement, the defendant must have used the plaintiff's mark in commerce, in connection with sales or advertising, and without authorization. This is an initial hurdle that the plaintiff must surmount before there is any discussion of the form the infringement takes, because, without this type of use, a defendant can't be liable.

Recall the examples with which we opened the chapter, starting with the girl with the tattoo. It's very unlikely that our tattooed fashionista will be liable for a trademark infringement should Louis Vuitton Malletier S.A.—the corporate owner of the VUITTON marks—discover that she has been tattooed with the LV quatrefoil. Using the mark in this way—as a kind of homage or expression of appreciation—is almost certainly not going to be a use against which the trademark system protects. Unless she seeks to engage in some kind of sale or marketing through the use of the tattoo, her fangirl appreciation of the famous marque isn't going to ground a trademark action, and any action should be dismissed on the basis of non-use.

The situation with the Google Adwords example is slightly more complicated. Google auctions off advertising displays based on search terms within its site so that when a user searches any term, the search results are retrieved along with the "sponsored links" that are displayed based on who paid the most for that display of their advertisement in conjunction with the term. This isn't a trademark issue when the search term in question is, for example, "mesothelioma" or "medical malpractice," but it becomes an problem when (as in the above example) the term is covered by a trademark. Google isn't applying the LOUIS VUITTON mark to any product Google offers, but it is definitely making money from the fake handbag vendors and others who pay to display their ads when a user searches for "louis vuitton." Some courts initially characterized these sorts of uses as internal to the search company and suggested that this type of use was analogous to an individual's private thoughts about the product. Just as courts don't tell me that I can't think about Louis Vuitton, the reasoning went that this kind of commercial use was equally not a use that the trademark system was designed to stop. However, with the proliferation of actions against Google, most courts have concluded that this does amount to a trademark use, and have gone on to examine whether any of the infringement types apply.

## Likelihood of Confusion

The canonical form of trademark infringement is the consumer confusion action: is the defendant's use of the plaintiff's mark likely to confuse the consuming public? More correctly, the "likelihood-of-confusion" test asks whether an appreciable number of ordinarily prudent consumers are likely to be misled or confused into believing that the defendant's product came from the plaintiff, or that the plaintiff sponsored, endorsed, or was affiliated with the defendant's product. Courts interpret the open-ended requirement of "an appreciable number" in numerous ways in keeping with the usual sort of conclusory reasoning that drives courts of first instance. Relatively small numbers of confused people are usually sufficient: as few as 10 percent of people polled in a market survey is a commonly accepted baseline for a court to conclude that there is a likelihood of confusion.

All circuits adopt a factor-based analysis for the likelihood-of-confusion test, all of which are similar in broad terms but differ in their specifics. Each circuit looks at issues of the defendant's intent and whether there was actual confusion, then at a series of factors focusing on the nature of the market in the products. Unfortunately every circuit has its own specific list of factors. Thus, the *Polaroid* factors of the Second Circuit interrogate the strength of the original user's mark, similarity of the two marks, proximity of the two products, likelihood that the original user would enter into the alleged infringer's market ("bridging the gap" between the two markets), evidence of actual confusion, alleged infringer's intent, relative quality of the products bearing the marks in question, and sophistication of consumers of the products. The *Sleekcraft* factors of the Ninth Circuit pose similar questions but change them slightly by focusing on market expansion rather than "bridging" and asking the degree of care that a consumer would exercise in choosing the product. Other circuits include analysis regarding the nature of the advertising media used, the nature of the retail environment, and the similarity in function between the competing products. As with most multifactor tests, courts regularly suggest that no one factor is determinative. However, recent scholarly work indicates that most cases can be called on the basis of a small subset of the factors, most notably the similarity between the competing marks, strength of the senior user's mark, and defendant's bad intent.[28]

The prototypical confusion claim relates to consumer confusion as to the source of the plaintiff's and defendant's products, but courts have been confronted with a number of variants on this prototype.

---

28. Barton Beebe, *An Empirical Study of the Multifactor Tests for Trademark Infringement*, 94 CALIF. L. REV. 1581 (2006).

These actions include those relating to reverse confusion, post-sale confusion, and initial interest confusion. Reverse confusion occurs when the senior user—that is, the first user or the registered owner—is overwhelmed by a junior user's use of the same mark. Usually this occurs when the junior user advertises so heavily that it becomes associated with the mark, leading to consumers thinking that the senior user's products come from the junior user. These cases fit easily within the dual aims of the trademark system regarding consumer protection as this type of use potentially generates consumer confusion *and* amounts to unfair appropriation of the senior user's mark and goodwill. In the very few situations where this has happened, courts have had little difficulty concluding that an infringement has occurred.

Post-sale confusion occurs when, for example, knockoffs of well-known products are seen on the street by potential consumers, leading to the senior user's product becoming less desirable because of the knockoff user's use. Recall our earlier example of the Louis Vuitton knockoffs advertised for sale on the Google-sponsored link. Courts have been quick to conclude that there is an actionable harm here because of the potential damage to the plaintiff's reputation or reduction in its business. These cases are ridiculous if we recall that the main purpose of the trademark system is to protect consumers from confusion in relation to their consumption decisions. Since the person carrying the counterfeit bag is presumably aware that it's not from the luxury brand—after all, that person bought it from some skeevy guy on Canal Street or Santee Alley for $50—it's a stretch to suggest that any consumer confusion has occurred. Courts get around this by suggesting that potential and subsequent consumers may be confused, but this is a thin basis for decision. The reality seems to be that judges don't wish to condone this type of activity, and few of them have difficulties bending the principle of confusion to fit this sort of situation.[29]

---

29. There are specific prohibitions in the Lanham Act and in most state laws prohibiting the sale of these type of counterfeit products, and so it's odd that courts find it necessary to stretch the definition of consumer confusion this way.

Initial interest confusion is another extension of the likelihood-of-confusion action, which doesn't comport particularly well with the standard theory of trademarks. This occurs where a junior user adopts the senior user's mark, creating confusion that seeks to capture the consumer's initial attention, even though at the time of purchase the consumer is aware that she is not buying from the senior user. For example, imagine a billboard on the highway advertising a McDonald's at Exit 8, which the consumer discovers, upon turning off, is actually a Burger King. Or a bar called the "Velvet Elvis" that, upon entry, is clearly not sanctioned by the Elvis Presley estate. Or a domain name for a well-known brand of clothing that resolves to a competitor's site. In each of these examples the consumers are arguably lured to the location through confusion and deception but at the time they actually buy their burger, or drink, or clothing, they know exactly who they're buying from and so are not suffering any confusion. Should we use the likelihood-of-confusion action to stop marketers from attracting consumers' attention in this way? Many courts endorsed and adopted the initial interest confusion theory when the cybersquatting problem first emerged during the mid 1990s. There was no specific protection for domain names, and the theory of "initial interest confusion" could be pressed into service to resolve some of the more difficult cases. Not all circuits have approved this approach, and it's clear that it enshrines the property theory of trademark rather than the consumer protection theory. With the advent of domain name-specific remedies, initial interest confusion is no longer as necessary as it once was as the basis for infringement, and as a result, its prevalence and significance has waned.

## Dilution

In 1996 Congress passed the Federal Trademark Dilution Act (FTDA), an amendment to the Lanham Act, which added a new form of infringement for the "dilution" of famous marks. Similar state trademark and unfair competition laws had been in place for many years that protect well-known or famous marks from various types of dilution of the distinctive quality of the mark even without there being any likelihood of consumer confusion. As a result of some limitations in the FTDA, Congress passed the Trademark Dilution Revision Act (TDRA) in 2006. We'll look at both the FTDA and TDRA in this section.

The FTDA created an actionable harm in situations where a famous mark was used in a context that is not confusing in any way, but which in some way reduces the ability of the mark to distinguish. There are two forms of dilution infringement in the federal system. Dilution by blurring occurs where the power of the famous mark to distinguish is lessened by a junior use, such as using the mark DUPONT in respect of shoes, BUICK in relation to aspirin, or, in the example given earlier, of using TIFFANY in relation to a restaurant. Few consumers are ever going to think that the jewelers or the car manufacturer or the chemical company have branched out into these new markets. Nonetheless, the argument goes, the power of these famous marks to distinguish in the marketplace is lessened by the use of others—their power has been "blurred"—and the law protects against this accordingly. The other form of dilution, dilution by tarnishment, operates a little differently: it is a kind of defamation upon the famous mark, reducing the status of the mark as a consequence of negative associations. Imagine that I opened up a low-rent bar called THE CADILLAC, or used the mark TIFFANY in connection with a strip club. Each of these uses is again not likely to be confusing to the consumer, but it links the famous marks with the shoddy quality or unsavory associations of the businesses I'm operating.

Initially there was some judicial reluctance to apply the dilution law. The FTDA required actual dilution for the action to lie, and the Supreme Court placed a high evidential burden on the plaintiff seeking to establish dilution. The Court said that it was insufficient for the plaintiff to show that there was some association between the senior and junior uses of the mark; rather the plaintiff had to establish that there was actual injury to the economic value of the mark as a result of the junior use. This was difficult to establish unless there was a direct use of exactly the same mark, and junior uses of similar marks were often allowed. On the flip side, courts were reasonably lenient when it came to assertions of fame. A number of courts held that marks with niche fame—fame in a certain geographic region, or within a small marketplace or community of interest—could be famous for the purposes of the FTDA. The conclusion of niche fame was particularly common for domain name cases prior to introduction of the remedies specifically tailored to address cybersquatting. This probably occurred for the same reason as the rise of the action for initial interest confusion in relation to domain names: there was a harm that courts wanted to address and felt otherwise hamstrung to do so. The 2006 TDRA amendments to the dilution action altered the positions in relation to both these issues. Fame is now confined to the situation where the mark is "widely recognized by the general consuming public of the United States," thereby abolishing niche fame and making the dilution action harder to assert. But the action was altered to apply in situations where there was *likelihood* of dilution, not just *actual* dilution. As a result, we've seen a corresponding increase in the success rate for owners of famous marks.

The dilution action is a lightning rod for scholarly criticism, largely because it enshrines the trademark-as-property conception that, as we discussed above, has been largely abandoned as the core normative foundation for the trademark law. Numerous critics and commentators have criticized the introduction of the dilution action as unnecessary or bad. Granting property rights in gross to this special category of trademarks, they say, undermines the balance in IP regimes, reduces expressive capabilities in society, or serves as another example of a land grab by the favored few in intellectual property. And of course all of these cases involve large corporate owners of famous marks asserting that they've been irreparably damaged by the (often amusing) use of their mark by some small-scale operator. The seminal Supreme Court case on the subject involved Victoria's Secret suing a sex shop operator over their name "Victor's Little Secret." The fact that the alleged infringement came to light when a military officer saw the sex shop and was so offended that he contacted the company only makes the huge lingerie group appear even more humorless and overreaching. Ditto the example of the "Chewy Vuitton" dog bed mentioned earlier, where the enormous—and, it has to be said, completely humorless—Louis Vuitton organization sued the tiny (and amusingly named) Haute Diggity Dog, LLC.[30]

A few scholars and judges have sought to rehabilitate the dilution action by moving away from the protection of the business interest of the plaintiff, suggesting that it may be a consumer protection action in disguise. The idea here, developed by Judge Richard Posner, is that dilution generates a "thought burden" on the consumer. In an influential hypothetical in the *Ty* case, Judge Posner sought to validate the newly introduced blurring and tarnishment infringements by reference to search cost theory. In the example with which we're now familiar, he imagined that the owners of the famous mark TIFFANY are in conflict with a restaurant called "Tiffany." Although consumers may not be confused, they are *forced* to think about both the jewelry and the restaurant, thereby reducing the strength and efficacy of the TIFFANY mark. Or as Posner puts it:

> Consumers will have to think harder—incur as it were a higher imagination cost—to recognize the name as the name of the store.[31]

On the related issue of tarnishment, the judge suggested that once exposed to the use of TIFFANY in relation to a strip club, consumers will never be able to wash their minds clear of the association. This, he said, will always affect the consumer's mental

---

30. Louis Vuitton Malletier S.A v. Haute Diggity Dog, LLC, 464 F. Supp. 2d 495 (E.D. Vir. 2006), 507 F.3d 252 (4th Cir. 2007).

31. Ty Inc. v. Perryman, 306 F.3d 509, 511 (7th Cir. 2002).

processes and so will always drive up their search costs. In experimental validation of this claim, a couple of professors of marketing have demonstrated that, in recognizing brands, people in general took longer to recognize famous marks if they had been primed with a diluting mark. So it seems that there is an objective basis in suggesting that consumer search costs can be increased by dilution. The problem is that it doesn't really make a lot of sense if what we care about is the consumer making an appropriate purchasing decision. Trademark law was never intended to stop consumers from *thinking*, it was intended to aid consumers in making accurate purchase decisions. Focusing on consumer search at the cost of consumer decision making is plainly strange.

Whatever one's view on this, the dilution action is here to stay. And it stands as a good example of the strength of the trademark lobby and the way that trademark, like other intellectual property regimes, is subject to expansionism over time.


### Other Infringements

Although the likelihood-of-confusion and dilution actions are the most significant, numerous other minor infringements have been added to the trademark canon over the years. Many of these are specific to special circumstances, such as the prohibition on producing counterfeit luxury accessories, or the protections granted by the Olympic and Paralympic Marks Act, prohibiting any person from adopting or using the Olympic rings, or any of the other Olympic and Paralympic marks that are reserved for the use and licensing by the U.S. Olympic Committee. Important though these infringements may be for the special groups concerned, they needn't detain us here. There are, however, a couple of infringements that are worth mentioning in a small amount of detail.

Of general application are the secondary liability principles that courts have grafted onto the statutory regime. There are no statutory provisions for contributory or vicarious liability in the

Lanham Act, but doctrines dealing with both have long been a feature in common law and state regimes, and increasingly are applied to cases involving both registered marks and unregistered trade dress. This is hardly surprising: trademark and unfair competition is usually seen as a component of tort law, and courts have long imposed liability on tortfeasors who encourage, condone, or assist others in the commission of torts.

Contributory liability for trademark infringement, similar to its copyright cousin, occurs when someone actively induces another to infringe, or supplies a product to a person that she knows or should have known is using the product in an infringing activity. As with secondary liability in all contexts, a lot turns on the degree of knowledge of the defendant and the degree of control of the defendant and the primary infringer. Defendants are routinely found liable where they are willfully blind to the primary infringements. However, where the defendants are simply assisting the infringement rather than somehow being responsible for it, courts are loath to hold the defendant responsible: the owner of a flea market, whose vendors are primary infringers, is much more likely to be found liable than the hired hands who set up the stalls. Finally, it's unclear the extent to which contributory liability can be applied to the dilution action since almost all cases have involved likelihood of confusion as the primary infringement.

Vicarious liability in trademark law is construed more narrowly than in copyright, and generally follows common law principles of agency. That is, a defendant will usually only be vicariously liable for another's trademark infringement where the primary infringer can be viewed as acting directly at the behest of the defendant. The fundamental test is whether the defendant and the infringer have an actual or apparent partnership, have the authority to bind one another in transactions with third parties, or exercise joint ownership or control over the infringing product. Given the degree of connection necessary between the defendant and primary infringer, vicarious liability is almost never found in trademark cases, certainly less often that it is found in copyright cases.

The other special case that is worth considering is the prohibition on cybersquatting that was enacted in the 1999 amendments of the Anticybersquatting Consumer Protection Act (ACPA). Various types of objectionable behavior emerged after the internet was opened up to commercial use in 1992: this included registering a mark as a domain name to stop a competitor from having its trademark reflected in the domain name space, registering someone else's famous mark to attract a lot of internet traffic, or simply registering the domain name of a famous mark and then ransoming it to the mark owner. Trademark law was ill-adapted to respond to this innovation. Apart from the difficulties of jurisdiction and enforcement against squatters who could register domain names from anywhere in the world, there were problems with the use requirements as well as evidential issues about whether consumers were actually confused by the use of another's domain name. After the unfortunate application of various existing doctrines—as we've seen, the unhappy rise of initial interest confusion and the evisceration of the fame requirement in the first trademark dilution statute can be laid at the door of the cybersquatting problem—eventually Congress stepped in with the ACPA, which created a new infringement in section 43(d). The new section gives a cause of action against anyone who, with a bad faith intent to profit from the mark, registers, traffics in, or uses a domain name that is identical or confusingly similar to a mark, or is dilutive of a famous mark. The defendant can prevail if he demonstrates an absence of bad faith, which is established by a multifactor test that examines, inter alia, whether he has intellectual property rights in the domain name or has used the domain name in connection with a bona fide offering of goods or services, or otherwise that there is evidence of fair use of the name.

Although section 43(d) has been successful at mitigating cybersquatting by U.S.-based defendants, there is still the problem of jurisdiction. Since many cybersquatters reside overseas and are outside the reach of in personam jurisdiction, the ACPA created a strange quasi-in rem jurisdictional basis by providing that the action can be brought on the basis of the location of the domain name. Many domain names trace their lineage back to a central registry in Herndon, Virginia, and this potentially makes all ACPA infringements actionable in the federal district court for the Eastern District of Virginia. As a practical matter however this hasn't happened, in part because of disagreements by courts over the scope of the section, but more importantly because of a low-cost, international alternative that emerged around the same time as the ACPA.

In 1999, the main authority for domain names, the Internet Corporation for Assigned Names and Numbers, created a mechanism for the fast and cheap resolution of domain name cases, which is called the Uniform Domain Name Dispute Resolution Policy (UDRP). Whenever someone registers a domain name, that person now agrees to be bound by the terms of the UDRP, which provides for a private arbitration in relation to disputes filed by trademark owners anywhere in the world who are aggrieved by the domain name registration. The core remedy is transfer of the domain name to the trademark owner, and the requirements for finding an infringement are similar to the ACPA: the domain name is identical or confusingly similar to a mark in which the complainant has rights, the domain name holder has no legitimate interest in the domain name, and the domain name was registered and is being used in bad faith. Compared to court proceedings under the ACPA, the UDRP process is extremely speedy (a couple of months) and very cheap (a couple of thousand dollars). As a result many more cybersquatting cases are resolved through the UDRP than the ACPA. Absent special considerations, unhappy trademark owners will typically opt for UDRP proceedings every time.

## ✹ Defenses and Loss of Rights

Here's an exercise for you to try at home. Try making a comment on modern day consumerism without using a trademark. If you want to refer to popular culture in a way that your viewers, readers, or listeners will understand, you're pretty much guaranteed to be using some well-known brands, and you will probably be infringing some important trademarks. And even if you're not using the trademark as shorthand—"That restaurant is the Cadillac of BBQ joints"—you may be a business that wants to refer to a competitor to draw attention to the quality of your product in comparison ("six out of seven people who take the Pepsi challenge prefer Pepsi to Coke," for example).

Trademarks are part of our language, of our society, and of our modern cultures. Inevitably courts confront uses that are objectionable to the trademark holder, but which are beneficial to some function within society. Whether we're concerned with a Chicago newspaper celebrating the Bulls' sixth NBA championship win with the headline "The Joy of Six," or an artist portraying Mattel's Barbie doll as an ingredient in a cocktail or an enchilada in a series of prints called "Food Chain Barbie," trademark law and free speech intersect in ways that pose all manner of concerns.

A series of defenses are included within the trademark system to try to mediate this problem. In the next section we'll tease out the different categories of what can be labeled "fair use" defenses within trademark. There are also a number of ways that a potential defendant can demonstrate that the plaintiff no longer has any rights in the claimed mark. Although these may be characterized either as affirmative defenses or as limitations on the owner's rights in the mark (depending on the context in which they are applied), we'll look at them in this part because they are often pleaded by the defendant by way of a defense, or may be used by a junior user in a cancellation or opposition proceeding.

## Fair Use Defenses

The trademark "fair use" defenses comprise a combination of interpretations based on First Amendment values, as well as some specific statutory and common law defenses. These elements tend to overlap and so the reasoning in relation to each is not very satisfying.

The most obvious limit on trademark infringement is when it intersects with First Amendment concerns. This often occurs in the context of commercial parodies where a competitor uses a mark to make fun of the product with which it's in competition. So, using the Mastercard "Priceless" trope or elements of Dr. Seuss's "Cat in the Hat" for commercial purposes will generate concern for the mark owners. The plaintiff's motivation is to police its mark for reputation and property reasons, but the defense will be structured around the concern that the consumer will be confused by the use. In cases such as this, the First Amendment is not, as one might expect, a complete trump to the action; rather, it is one of the considerations in the likelihood-of-confusion test. Here, the parody-satire distinction that the *Acuff-Rose* court drew in relation to copyright[32] seems to apply to trademark also: satires do not comment on the appropriated work and so, it is said, are more likely to generate confusion and not be excused from liability by free speech values. Thus, a T-shirt labeled as "Mutant of Omaha" did not comment on the MUTUAL OF OMAHA mark, nor its corporate owners, and so was not excused from liability. This approach has been criticized extensively, and there appears to be a move toward recognizing that trademarks are used these days as part of our vocabulary. As one court has noted, how else do you express the thought that something is the "Rolls-Royce" of its type, or that a quick fix is a band-aid solution?[33]

There are also a number of specific defenses that are either mentioned in the Lanham Act or developed by common law. These include "descriptive" fair use, nominative fair use, and fair use in relation to dilution. Descriptive fair use involves situations where an alleged infringement is done for descriptive purposes, is not a trademark use, and is undertaken in good faith. An example is the

---

32. See discussion in Chapter 2.

33. Mattel, Inc. v. MCA Records, 296 F.3d 894, 900 (9th Cir. 2002).

use of the word "fish fry" in a case where there was a registered mark FISH-FRI. The court held that it was impossible for the defendant to describe its product—seasoned bread crumbs for frying fish—except in terms that would infringe the plaintiff's mark. As a result the descriptive fair use defense applied, and the defendant was free to use the term. Another example was a Christmas-themed air freshener in the shape of a pine tree, where a competitor held a registration for that shape in relation to air fresheners. The court found that the pine tree shape of the defendant's freshener was descriptive of the olfactory and seasonal character of the air freshener, and thus the descriptive fair use defense applied.

Nominative fair use is a creature of common law; it relates to the situation where the defendant is using the mark to refer to the plaintiff's product. The defense was, controversially, created by the Ninth Circuit in the *New Kids On The Block* case.[34] There, two publications had created polls asking readers to call in and vote for their favorite member of the boy band. The band sued—neither publication had licensed the use of the band's mark NEW KIDS ON THE BLOCK—but the Ninth Circuit concluded that there must be a defense for the use of the mark as a name, otherwise it would be impossible to refer to the trademarked product for the purposes of "comparison, criticism, or point of reference."[35] Three elements need to be satisfied for the nominative use defense: the product must not be readily identifiable without the use of the mark, the defendant may only use so much of the mark as it is reasonably necessary to identify the product, and the defendant must not use the mark in a way that suggests an endorsement or sponsorship by the plaintiff. Not all circuits allow the defense however—the First and Sixth for example have explicitly declined to adopt it—and the application of the defense in the adopting circuits is confused and unsatisfactory.

---

34. "Controversially" because, if the defense is a common law one, then how could a federal court applying federal law invent it?

35. New Kids on the Block v. News Am. Publ'g, Inc., 971 F.2d 302, 306 (9th Cir. 1992).

Some apply it as an affirmative defense after liability is found; some conflate it with the descriptive use defense; some apply it as a consideration in the analysis of whether the defendant has used the plaintiff's mark. Most courts apply it as a component of the likelihood-of-confusion test.

Finally, the introduction and refinement of the dilution action by the FTDA and the TDRA included an explicit defense of fair use in relation to dilution. Congress recognized that these new and broad rights carried a significant risk of chilling speech, in part because of the special category of tarnishment that could be brought against uses that involve negative commentary, but more generally because the dilution infringement has nothing to do with consumer confusion. Thus, the federal dilution action includes defenses for fair use in comparative advertising, noncommercial use of the mark, and all forms of news reporting and commentary. Critical blog posts, critical advertising, and even art works—the Food Chain Barbie example given above—have been held to be non-dilutive under this defense.

When we review all of these defenses, it's very difficult to draw a clear line between them. Not only are they conceptually related, but courts routinely mix and match elements and approaches among the defenses. One commentator has noted that courts usually come to the right decision in fair use cases, but their reasoning is chaotic and impossible to predict. He suggested that this amounted to a regime of "substantive successes and procedural failures."[36] It's hard to disagree with him.

## Affirmative Defenses and Loss of Rights

Aside from the "fair use" defenses discussed above, a number of other affirmative defenses are available to a defendant in a trademark

---

36. William McGeveran, *Rethinking Trademark Fair Use*, 94 Iowa L. Rev. 49, 53 (2008).

infringement action. These involve demonstrating that the plaintiff no longer has rights in the mark, or should never have been granted rights in the mark in the first place. We'll treat these as defenses to an infringement here, but they are also the basis for a cancellation proceeding or, sometimes, an opposition.

As we've seen, the U.S. trademark system is very concerned about use. Thus, discontinuing use is deeply problematic; it means that the consuming public may no longer associate the mark with the unique source of the product. The common law requires both factual abandonment by non-use and an intention to abandon the mark. This earlier requirement can be demonstrated by a period of years of non-use, and the latter requirement is usually demonstrated by a lack of evidence or efforts to begin re-use. The burden to demonstrate abandonment is on the defendant (or the applicant in a cancellation proceeding), and the standard of proof is high. Abandonment under the Lanham Act is derived from the common law principle and tracks the dual requirement of factual abandonment and intention to abandon. The main difference is that the federal system has a presumption of abandonment after three consecutive years of non-use, at which point the presumption shifts the burden to the plaintiff, making the work of the defendant that much easier. In the federal system, abandonment is also defined to include genericide, a topic we talked about above. Thus, a mark becoming generic is the basis both for an affirmative defense to infringement and for a cancellation proceeding.

Two additional defenses are worth considering: assignments in gross and naked licensing. These are conceptually similar, and also are formally considered to be trademark abandonments. An assignment in gross is where a mark is transferred separately from the goodwill that it represents; that is, the mark is sold separately from the business and essential assets that are used to make the products to which the mark is applied. A naked license is very similar, but involves a license of a right to use the mark rather than a sale of the mark outright: it's where a mark owner licenses the mark to another without engaging in reasonable policing and control of the activity of the licensee. Both of these actions are problematic because they break the purpose of the trademark: to provide an informational signal to the consumer. If we allowed the mark owner to license without controlling quality, or to assign the rights in the mark without the plant and know-how used to make the product, then the mark is no longer an indicator of the quality of the product. Courts take a dim view of this sort of behavior, equating it to a fraud on the consuming public, and both of these activities are the basis for an affirmative defense or a cancellation action.

Various other defenses exist, including estoppel by laches where there is inability to press the claim because of delay, and for claims of fraud on the USPTO. There are also a number of minor defenses relating to the first sale doctrine and the importation of gray-market products. These are of limited application and beyond the scope of our discussion.

## ℳ Discontents

Brands matter. A lot. But they don't matter in the way that trademark theory suggests that they do.

We started with the theory that posited that trademark was about ensuring consumers not be confused, and we expanded on this by examining the law and economics version of this, which is the consumer search cost theory. Our focus is perfectly consistent with what courts and legislatures say, but has very little do with what they do. And it is almost perfectly inconsistent with modern branding practice.

Brands and licensing form a multibillion-dollar industry, and this industry is founded on trademark law. But if you ask a brand manager at the multinational drinks company Diageo about GUINNESS—or her equivalent at Philip Morris about MARLBORO, her equivalent at Nike about the Swoosh, etc—she will not find the consumer search cost theory a particularly useful description of how she and her superiors think of the brand. The brand is theirs, and it is used in a way that has little to do with the interests of the consumer: it's cross-licensed, it turns up in rap music videos, it's valued at millions, independently of where or how the liquid inside the bottle is made. In short, it's insanely valuable property and it has a life of its own.

This leads to many of the sorts of problems we've stumbled across in the preceding sections. Trademark law and branding practice are not exactly at odds with each other, but they certainly make strange bedfellows. And the mismatch increases over time. The trademark system, like the copyright and patent systems, has expanded dramatically over the last fifty years. We can see this obviously in the legislative expansion of actionable confusion—from merely regulating source confusion to patrolling confusion as to affiliation and sponsorship—and the creation of the federal dilution action. But judicial solicitude for brands has become even more pronounced, even though courts often say that they're protecting the consumer when they're actually protecting the brand. Thus a court enjoined a gay rights patrol from continuing to use the name "Pink Panther Patrol" on the basis that consumer were likely to be confused that the group had licensed the mark from MGM, the owners of the federal mark.[37] Really? Which consumers can you think of who would actually be confused by this use? What about the case where a judge said that consumers might be confused by a low-rent dental clinic called "McDental" because, no kidding around here, McDonald's occasionally puts toothbrushes in its Happy Meals. Hundreds, if not thousands, of similarly ridiculous cases litter the Federal Supplement.

But if trademark law has a weird one-way ratchet in terms of greater and greater protection, it differs from similar expansions in other intellectual property regimes, although it leads to a similar outcome. As a result of legislative and judicial largess, both owners

---

37. MGM-Pathe Commc'ns v. Pink Panther Patrol, 774 F. Supp. 869, 875 (S.D.N.Y. 1991).

and the public at large come to expect large and increasing degrees of control over the marks. When trademark first emerged, the court's concern was with unscrupulous competitors stealing away business from upright merchants. Now courts and congresses worry about almost any unauthorized use of a brand.

Numerous scholars have addressed this, and voiced their concerns about the dangers of corporate control over speech, the diminution of the public sphere, and so on. Some theorists have suggested that we reform trademark law to accord with the confusion theory of trademark, then enforce the system in accordance with this theory and not with modern branding practice. Others have suggested that we go the other way and push for reforms that make trademark law conform with the brand owners' expectations about their ownership of marks as property. Still others suggest that we retain the current system but make certain parts of it more coherent—drop the prohibition on assignments in gross, for example, or codify the defenses in a more structured and rational way. Space constraints make it impossible to review all these proposals, and in any event, it would just be confusing. The only things that everyone agrees on is that trademark has dramatically expanded in scope over the years, and that there is a profound mismatch in trademark law between what we're doing and what we say we're doing.

One final observation about trademark reform is worth noting. In the similar section in the chapters on copyright and patent, we examined the public groundswell against expansion. In those areas of law, the critics aren't just pointy-headed scholars, but various civil society groups, representatives of developing nations, and certain trade groups, among many others. Oddly enough, we don't really see this in relation to trademark. No one outside of trademark scholars seems to worry much about the way that trademarks and brands have taken over our world. It's hard to know why that is, but nonetheless it remains true.

# FIVE

# Trade Secrets

IT IS ONE OF those fabulous urban myths that only three people know the secret formula of Coca-Cola—and they never travel on the same airplane. Myth or not,[1] the story is useful to understand some basic features of the law of trade secrets. Trade secret law is state law—statutory law in forty-seven states and territories[2] and common law in the remainder—that stops some sorts of valuable information from being used by others. The information must be both economically valuable, and the possessor of the information must have taken steps to keep it from being widely known or easy to acquire. These requirements are evident from the expression itself. It is "trade secrets" that are protected after all, with the "trade" element speaking to the commercial value of the information and the second element indicating that the information must be "secret."

Once the plaintiff has established these features, the court will ask whether the defendant has misappropriated the plaintiff's secret. It is on this question that trade secret cases are usually won or lost, and the most significant predictor of the outcome here is the judge's view of the actions of the defendant. Of course, one can often tell

---

1. It's almost certainly a myth. The "secret" ingredient of Coke is nutmeg sourced from the Banda Islands, a fact well known to all of Coke's competitors and anyone else with access to chemical assaying equipment or a subscription to the *New Yorker*. John Seabrook, *Soldiers and Spice: Why the Dutch Traded Manhattan for a Speck of Rock in the South Pacific in 1667*, NEW YORKER, Aug. 13, 2001, at 60, 65.

2. All variants of the Uniform Trade Secrets Act.

how all manner of intellectual property cases are going to turn out by listening carefully to what judges are saying about the morality of the parties in a dispute, but morality plays a startlingly large part in judicial decisions over trade secrets. Consider the reasoning of the court in one of the best-known (if not best-reasoned) trade secret cases, *Du Pont v. Christopher*. A commercial photographer and his brother flew their plane over the site of Du Pont's new methane plant as it was being built, and took aerial photos of what they saw. Du Pont claimed a trade secret over the process that was to be used in the plant for the production of methane, and argued that taking photos of the layout of the plant from the air was a misappropriation of the secret. The opinion of the Fifth Circuit began with the words:

> This is a case of industrial espionage in which an airplane is the cloak and a camera the dagger.[3]

No prizes for guessing who prevailed.

At other times the role of commercial morality is more veiled, but the core of most trade secret cases won by plaintiff is the Biblical admonishment "Thou shalt not steal." This prescription is one that has limited and problematic application to the special case of goods constituting information, since one doesn't steal ideas in the way that one steals a car. My improperly acquired knowledge of Coca-Cola's secret formula doesn't deprive Coke of it. Coke might be bent out of shape by my knowing it, but we can both use it at the same time. Unlike a car, our uses of the information are not rival. Or as Thomas Jefferson more poetically put it:

> He who receives an idea from me, receives instruction himself without lessening mine; as he who lights his taper at mine, receives light without darkening me.[4]

---

3. E.I. Du Pont de Nemours & Co. v. Christopher, 431 F. 2d 1012, 1013 (5th Cir. 1970).

4. Thomas Jefferson, "Letter to Isaac McPherson, Monticello, August 13, 1813," in *XIII The Writings of Thomas Jefferson*, edited by A. Lipscomb (1904), 326–338.

Further, the Biblical admonishment is inapplicable to the legally permissible action of reverse engineering a product containing a trade secret, as well as a number of other actions that might be morally dubious but are legally sanctioned. Nonetheless, simplistic moral assessments of the actions of the parties are at the core of many trade secret cases, and it's not hard to see why. The standard examples of trade secret misappropriation include departing employees who take client lists or secret plans, commercial firms who hire private detectives to engage in commercial espionage or rummage through competitors' dumpsters (and worse), and disaffected former partners who each claim that the other ripped him off on the dissolution of their friendship and their business. No different from any area of tort law, any decision maker is going to be heavily influenced by her judgment about the morality or otherwise of the parties' behavior.

At the outset then, we need to recognize the reality that judges in trade secrets cases are heavily influenced by their moral judgment of the behavior displayed by each party. This is not necessarily a criticism—although one might be troubled by the degree to which legal outcomes are determined by judges untrained in moral reasoning—and it is not just a recognition that law as practiced is different from law as written on the books. Assessment of "commercial morality" is explicitly encoded in both the justifications for trade secret law and the specific requirements of the law; and so it plays a huge role in the determination of the existence of trade secrets and in the liability for misappropriating those secrets. To understand this we look next at the normative justifications for trade secret law before we start examining the requirements of the law.

## ✺ Theory and History

The primary justifications for protecting trade secrets from misappropriation come from some variant of either utilitarian or moral reasoning.

The utilitarian position should be familiar from our previous discussion of other intellectual property rights: society grants some kind of limited monopoly over the trade secret, in the form of a legally enforceable right, in order to provide economic incentives for the production of the trade secret. As judges often remind us, business depends on a range of significant innovations that are protected only by trade secrets. These secrets confer significant competitive advantages to the secret holder and significant economic benefits to society as a whole. Standard utilitarian accounts forecast underproduction of innovation without protection. These accounts also forecast espionage activities on the part of competitors, which is socially unproductive since it doesn't contribute to additional innovation (except presumably in spying equipment). Utilitarian reasons are therefore often used to justify trade secret protection.

But utilitarianism is not a simple fit for this area of law. The trade secret monopoly is potentially very broad, since it may involve protection of all of a commercial significant idea, and it does so potentially forever. Moreover, unlike a patent, a trade secret has no registration formalities, there is no need to satisfy an examiner that the idea is novel, non-obvious and useful, and there is definitely no requirement that the idea be disclosed to the world at large. (Indeed it is a continuing requirement of trade secret protection that the secret not become publicly known). This seems to be at odds with the usual way we balance public and private interests within the utilitarian approach to intellectual property law. Which is to say, we typically set off the scope of the grant against the term of the grant and the formalities: get a long term and you get limited protection (copyright); go through serious registration requirements and you get strong protection (patent). But unlike copyright or patent, trade secret law balances the interests of society and owner by making the monopoly extremely fragile in two ways. First, any disclosure of the secret destroys it, and makes it available for all the world to use. If the defendant discloses the secret, then she may be liable for damages for the plaintiff's loss, but unlike other forms of intellectual property, trade secret law won't forbid the world from using the intellectual property once it's been disclosed. Second, unlike patents, numerous parties can independently create the same secret and all of them are free to exploit their version of it.

Utilitarianism thus provides a decent justification for the existence of trade secret law and for some of its structural features. Alternatively, one can justify conferring protection on trade secrets via moral reasoning, through what is often called "misappropriation" or "tort" theory. This approach is famously captured in Justice Holmes's opinion in the early *Masland* case:

> The word "property" as applied to trademarks and trade secrets is an unanalyzed expression of certain secondary consequences of the primary fact that the law makes some rudimentary requirements of good faith. Whether the plaintiffs have any valuable secret or not, the defendant knows the facts, whatever they are, through a special confidence that he accepted. The property may be denied, but the confidence cannot be. Therefore the starting point for the present matter is not property or due process of law, but that the defendant stood in confidential relations with the plaintiffs.[5]

As we'll see in the discussion below, this tends to be the animating theory for many legal decisions. This is somewhat unfortunate since reliance on thinly reasoned intuitions about fairness is a poor basis for judicial decision making. Yet morality here remains a core justification and operating methodology in trade secret law.

The two normative foundations tend to result in two competing conceptions of trade secret law. The utilitarian-incentive justification often results in courts and scholars concluding that trade secrets are a special form of property. So, for example, in *Ruckelhaus v. Monsanto* the Supreme Court was asked whether a federal law

---

5.  E.I. Du Pont de Nemours Powder Co. v. Masland, 244 U.S. 100, 102 (1917).

mandating disclosure of certain information amounted to a taking for the purposes of the Fifth Amendment.[6] The Court concluded that trade secrets have many of the characteristics of property because they can be alienated and traded in various ways.

This tension has been present within trade secret law for as long as it has existed. Trade secret law derives from Roman law, which prohibited slaves from breaching the confidences of their owners. Later European versions through the medieval period and into the Enlightenment adopted similar approaches to deal with information created and discovered by serfs (at first) and then employees (later). The intertwined conceptions of trade secrets as involving both property and tort—and the concomitant strands of ownership and trust—have always been part of trade secret law, and they always will.

## ℳ Creation and Rights

Trade secret law is state law, and so the requirements may differ depending on the approach of individual state legislatures and courts. Generally though the states use one of three main canonical sources: the Uniform Trade Secrets Act (the UTSA), the Restatement of Torts §§757 and 758, or the Restatement (Third) of Unfair Competition. They are broadly similar, and the UTSA was based in large part on the Restatement of Torts; thus the Restatement is still influential in interpreting UTSA-based state laws. The second revision of the Restatement of Torts dropped trade secrets, but in 1995 the principles were picked up in the Restatement (Third) of Unfair Competition. Because the provisions are all very similar in this part, we will talk about generalities that apply pretty much across the board. Where there are important differences we'll draw attention to them, and we'll point out how the specific implementation of

---

6. Ruckelhaus v. Monsanto Co., 467 U.S. 986 (1984).

either the Restatement or the UTSA differs on a state-by-state basis.

There are three basic requirements in any trade secret infringement action. First, the subject matter must substantively qualify for trade secret protection. Second, the plaintiff must have taken reasonable precautions to keep the secret "secret." Finally, the defendant must have acquired the information wrongfully or, as it is usually called in trade secret law, the defendant must have misappropriated the secret. We'll look at the first two features below, then examine the defendant's actions in the Infringement section.

### Trade Secret

For information to be a trade secret, and thus for it to qualify for protection, it generally has to (1) be information of a certain type, (2) be secret, and (3) be commercially valuable. The UTSA defines the type of information to include "a formula, pattern, compilation, program, device, method, technique, or process,"[7] and although the definition is not intended to be exclusive, it is pretty much a definition of all of the sorts of ideas or information that could exist in the world. Examples of things that have been found to be trade secrets include various types of recipes for food and drink, design drawings, methods of ensuring that muffins have lots of butter-soaking cavities, customer lists, and the layout of chemical plants. The reality is that any kind of information can qualify as a trade secret as long as it satisfies the requirements of secrecy and value. The only real limitation on subject matter is that general professional skills of employees cannot be trade secrets. This principle arises because it would be inappropriate and dangerous to allow an employer to forbid a departing employee from working just because she gained some knowledge within the employer's business that the employer

---

7. UNIF. TRADE SECRET ACT § 1(4) (amended 1985), 14 U.L.A. 437 (1985).

might consider a trade secret but which is commonly used through-out the employer's field of business. Generally, we privilege the human right to work against the business' right to protect its secrets. However, at times these conflicting rights give rise to hard cases, and where an employee has been exposed to highly secret information, there is a small number of cases where the employee is forbidden from disclosing this information to a competitor, removing to some extent his ability to work for a period of time in the specific industry, perhaps the one for which his training has prepared him.

## Secrecy

The information must be secret; that is, it is not generally publicly known. In states that follow the Restatement, actual knowledge by others is sufficient to invalidate the secrecy requirement. In states that apply the UTSA, the information must not be readily ascertainable by the people employed in the relevant business or within the relevant industry. The secret need not be absolute—more than one person or business may know about it—but there are practical, if not numeric limits, on how many people may know of the information before it is no longer considered secret. It is important to understand that trade secret protection is not like patent: several people or entities can independently have trade secret rights over the same information, because they are not claiming sole rights over the secret, just rights against any person who misappropriates the information. But the information must be "substantially" secret, known only by a small and select group, otherwise it can't be protected. Information found in published sources, such as trade journals, technical references, or blog entries is no longer protectable as a trade secret. Also, if one can inspect a product and discover the claimed "secret," then it's not going to be "secret" enough.

Finally, on the question of whether the claimed information is appropriate subject matter for a trade secret action, the information must have "economic" value and that value must arise from the fact that it is secret. Jurisdictions differ slightly here: those based on the UTSA demand that the information have "independent economic value, actual or potential,"[8] whereas Restatement-based laws demand that the information give the owner the opportunity to obtain an advantage over competitors.[9] With its focus on value rather than competitive advantage, the UTSA's definition is broader than the Restatement's, and allows trade secret protection for information that is not covered by the Restatement. For example, the UTSA protects (1) information that is not related to a business as long as the information has value; (2) "negative know-how," that is knowledge that a line of experimentation is going to prove fruitless (again if this knowledge is valuable); and (3) one-off information, such as the terms of a corporate deal. None of these would be covered by the Restatement's definition even though they may be profoundly important and valuable.

When considering whether something is a trade secret, courts often apply the six-factor test laid out in the Restatement of Torts,[10] even if the jurisdiction is one that follows the UTSA. The Restatement test asks:

(1) How widely is the idea or information known outside the claimant's business?

(2) Who within the claimant's business knows the idea or information?

(3) What measures has the claimant taken to ensure that the information remains secret?

(4) How difficult would it be for others to properly acquire or duplicate the information or idea?

---

8. Unif. Trade Secret Act § 1(4)(i) (amended 1985), 14 U.L.A. 437 (1985).

9. Restatement (First) of Torts § 757 cmt. b (1939).

10. *Id.*

(5)  How valuable is the idea or information to the claimant and its competitors? and

(6)  How much effort or money has the claimant expended in developing or acquiring the idea or information?

Although these factors often prove useful, it should be clear that they conflate issues of secrecy, value, and whether the plaintiff has taken appropriate precautions, which occasionally leads to confused and sloppy reasoning. Teasing out the separate issues about whether the plaintiff can claim that the subject matter is suitable for trade secret protection tends to generate clearer analysis.

### Reasonable Precautions

After concluding that the information or idea is appropriate subject matter, courts turn to the question of whether the plaintiff has maintained reasonable precautions to protect secrecy—a process sometimes called *fencing*. A plaintiff need not demonstrate absolute secrecy, and courts will determine what are reasonable precautions given all the circumstances and in the context of the operation of the plaintiff's business. It is perfectly acceptable to communicate the information to employers, and even to third parties where there is a need to do so. For example, if work is contracted out or if suppliers need the information to be able to provide parts, then it is appropriate to share that information with them. This won't stop the plaintiff from asserting that it has fenced appropriately provided there are some secrecy provisions in place. However, there must be some evidence that the plaintiff engages in reasonable precautions, say by limiting the number of employees who have access to the information, insisting on nondisclosure agreements, or controlling access to the part of the factory that uses the secret.

There is an inevitable tension in the analysis of whether the plaintiff has taken sufficient precautions: the law of trade secrets is intended to provide sufficient protection that the owner doesn't have to spend a lot of money for fencing. But the law requires that owners actually spend money undertaking precautions, as otherwise the law won't apply. Courts recognize this, and generally won't require that the plaintiff engaged in unduly expensive precautions in order to protect itself from industrial espionage or employees walking off with secrets. An instructive case is the *Du Pont* one we mentioned above. The defendant photographers flew over the soon-to-be-constructed chemical plant being built by Du Pont, taking pictures of its layout. The Court found that Du Pont had taken reasonable precautions because to require it to place a roof over the building site in order to gain trade secret protection would impose ridiculous and unnecessary expense. Of course, not every case involves such an unusual trick, nor such expensive fencing costs, and courts will always engage in a very fact-specific and highly contextual analysis.

## 𝄞 Infringement

Once it's been decided that the subject matter is a trade secret and that the plaintiff has taken adequate precautions, the question is whether the defendant has *misappropriated* the secret. Misappropriation is the sole basis for the infringement of a trade secret; it means the improper acquisition, disclosure, or use of the secret. In general we can say that misappropriation comes down to one of two situations: either the defendant had a preexisting obligation to the plaintiff to keep the information confidential, or the defendant was involved in some kind of skullduggery.

The former situation is easier to explain, and arises in the case of numerous contractual relationships such as employment agreements or mergers and acquisitions, or where people are providing information in a deal covered by nondisclosure agreements. It shouldn't come as a surprise that where someone has promised to keep something confidential, or where there is a relationship of trust such as to warrant an implied obligation of confidentiality, disclosure or use of that information outside the boundaries of the agreement or relationship will be considered misappropriation.

Outside of situations involving a breach of confidence, it is much harder to define what sort of conduct amounts to misappropriation. The UTSA, various state laws, and numerous courts have tried to explain the difference between "appropriate" and "inappropriate" types of acquisition, disclosure, and use. These usually emphasize "improper means" or refer to a breach of "generally accepted standards of commercial morality." This is a remarkably broad and indeterminate definition, ranking right up there with Justice Stewart's infamous "I know it when I see it" of pornography. Although courts make it clear that they are trying to respect the interests of healthy competition, and refer to the breach of business practices and community norms as the standard for liability, it is also clear that judges do impose on the actions of the defendant their private views of what amounts to acceptable behavior and morality. For example, according to judges confronting the issue back in 1970, flying over and photographing the landscape was perfectly legal, except when the purpose was to find out the way that the Du Pont methane plant was laid out. What? Really? Why? How about another example that cuts the other way: It is perfectly permissible to buy a bottle of Coke and "reverse engineer" the drink by putting it through a chromatograph to discover the component chemicals. But it's a misappropriation to reverse engineer a piece of software distributed in object code by running it through a disassembler. If there is a principled distinction between these two actions, it's hard to understand what it is.

Although the concept of misappropriation is remarkably slippery, there are some guides to interpretation that are of assistance. There are generally thought to be three different acts constituting misappropriation: acquisition, use, and disclosure. There are no bright-line distinctions among the three, and there will often be significant overlap. Misappropriation by acquisition usually occurs when commercial competitors seek to gain access to a plaintiff's secrets, and here the only issue will be whether the means they use are proper or improper. As we've seen, this is a very open-ended question, and the means may be improper in and of themselves—that is, they are tortious or a breach of contract or of confidence—or they may be improper only in the circumstances of the particular case, as in the situation of flying over unrestricted airspace in *Du Pont*. Misappropriation by use or disclosure usually arises where someone gains possession of the trade secret by working for the owner, or through their relationship with the owner. But not always: a person who acquires information by improper means may also use or disclose it improperly, and sometimes a person who acquires the information accidentally can be liable for her disclosure or use, provided that she knew or should have known that the information was a trade secret.

It's worth noting that trade secret law differs from the other types of intellectual property we've seen before in that there is no clearly separate type of contributory or secondary liability. In trade secrets, all liability is primary liability, and the concept of "contributory" infringement here is really just another way of finding that the defendant has misappropriated by improper means. So, for example, if I am an employee of a company and assist another employee to disclose trade secrets improperly, or if I hire someone to steal another person's trade secrets, then I am liable for the infringement on the basis that I've misappropriated the information.[11] Equally, if I run a web site that, let's say, encourages others to disclose commercial information about a certain industry, then I will probably be liable for misappropriation as long as I know or had reason to know that the information being disclosed was a trade secret. Courts have been very robust in situations of what is often called "third party misappropriation" and have routinely enjoined companies from using information brought to them from the departing employees of their competitors.

---

11. Some courts will occasionally frame this analysis in terms of "contributory" infringement, but it's generally easier just to think of this as another form of misappropriation.

This approach reflects the general proposition that trade secret law exists to police the appropriate bounds of commercial morality as intuited by the courts. But following on from this, the special case of trade secrets held by employees is particularly vexing, and courts must balance concerns over commercial misappropriation against employees' abilities to work in their chosen trade or profession without the interference of past employers invoking trade secret claims over everything an employee might know. A distinction is usually made between the employer's trade secret and the employee's "know-how," that is, the employee's general understanding of work practices and skills. Like much of trade secret law, this is a fine distinction to make, and it's hard to be more specific than to say that courts dislike restricting the ability of an employee to make a living, and interpret the definition of *know-how* accordingly. But even here there are exceptions. In a few cases courts invoke the principle of "inevitable disclosure" to enjoin a departing employee from working for a competitor at all, if it is virtually impossible for a departing employee to work for the new employer without disclosing or using the previous employer's trade secrets. Not all courts are comfortable with this principle, and the number of cases enjoining an employee from working because of "inevitable disclosure" may be counted on one hand.[12]

Finally, there are situations of co-ownership of trade secrets that arise between employers and employees as a result of poorly drafted agreements with no thought given to ownership, or situations where employees create new secrets on their own time or in fields not related to their employment. Various split-ownership forms have emerged as a result, but we really don't need to worry about them here.

12. *See e.g.*, Pepsico, Inc. v. Redmond, 54 F.3d 1262 (7th Cir. 1995) (applying Ill. law); Bimbo Bakeries USA Inc. v. Botticella, No. 10–1510, 2010 U.S. App. LEXIS 15314 (3d Cir. July 27, 2010) (applying Pa. law).

## Remedies

As with all intellectual property regimes, the main legal remedies are damages and disgorgement of profits, and the main equitable remedy is an injunction. In the event of an improper acquisition where there has been no public disclosure, the court will generally enjoin the defendant from using and/or disclosing the trade secret.

Unlike other regimes of intellectual property, trade secrets can potentially last forever, and so in the event of public disclosure where the secret is lost, there is an interesting question about how to calculate the appropriate quantum of damages, or whether an injunction against the defendant is relevant. Should the court assess damages based on the plaintiff's lost profits forever? Or should it enjoin the defendant from using the secret forever, even though the secret might have naturally come out later, or might been successfully reverse engineered by the defendant or other competitors? Courts differ markedly on this issue, with some concluding that the defendant who disclosed the secret should be forbidden from using it forever,[13] and others that the appropriate remedy is to allow the defendant to use the secret but make the defendant pay damages or account for profits from this use.[14] The midway response is to apply a "headstart" theory, assessing damages or enjoining the defendant for the period from the misappropriation until the secret became, or would have become, public.[15] The idea is to stop defendants from profiting during the period of their headstart, but not to punish them for all time. Which of these approaches a court will choose is highly fact- and court-dependent.

---

13. *See, e.g.*, Shellmar Prods. Co. v. Allen-Qualley Co., 36 F.2d 623 (7th Cir. 1929).

14. *See e.g.*, Conmar Prods. Corp. v. Universal Slide Fastener Co., 172 F.2d 150 (2d Cir. 1949).

15. *See e.g.*, Winston Research Corp. v. Minnesota Mining & Mfg. Co., 350 F.2d 134 (9th Cir. 1965).

## ✄ Defenses

In general we can say that there are no affirmative defenses for trade secret law, but there are some special types of "negative" defenses. The Comment to UTSA section 1 notes a number of examples where the defendant has acquired the secret by legitimate means, which amount to specific types of situations where the plaintiff cannot show misappropriation. The most important examples are discovery by independent invention, discovery by reverse engineering, discovery by observation in public use, and discovery from the published literature.

*Discovery by independent invention* merely references the fundamental distinction between trade secrets and patents. The grant of a patent is a complete monopoly over that invention and forbids even independent inventors from practicing the patent. Not so with trade secrets: any number of people can independently come up with the same idea as that over which I have trade secret rights, as long as they don't misappropriate the secret. The only problematic issue with independent discovery is an evidentiary one: the court has to believe that the discovery actually was independent, and this can be tricky where the defendant is a competitor who hired away the plaintiff's star employee, or where the defendant has previously been known to engage in industrial espionage. In these situations the defendant's testimony is often not credible. To have a chance of persuading the court, the defendant will usually have to show evidence of previous experiments and efforts that lead up to the creation of the same secret as the plaintiff's.

Reverse engineering is another variation on the theme of discovery by legitimate means. Reverse engineering involves the discovery by inspecting a copy of the product that embodies the secret, and this is considered legitimate in most cases as long as the defendant purchases the product in the open market. A commonly cited example of reverse engineering is *Chicago Lock v. Fanberg*, a case involving a locksmith who sold a manual containing the special codes to unlock the plaintiff's highly secure tubular locks.[16] The codes had been compiled by Victor Fanberg from the work of a group of locksmiths who had picked numerous tubular locks that had been legitimately purchased from Chicago Lock. The Ninth Circuit rejected the lock company's claim that this was a misappropriation by improper means, noting that there was no way of imputing a duty of nondisclosure on the owners of the locks that were picked, or on the locksmiths who picked them and contributed to the manual of codes. Reverse engineering of the codes by picking the locks was an example of acquisition by a legitimate means.

The final two examples of acquisition by legitimate means given in the Comment to UTSA section 1 are observation of the item in public, and discovery from published literature. These make intuitive sense—a secret isn't a secret if anyone can find the information in a library or out in the open—and they can be considered simple variants of the reverse engineering defense. The only consideration that emerges in situations involving reverse engineering, or in other sorts of discovery from public sources, is whether in fact the defendant acquired the secret through these legitimate means. For example, in *Kadant v. Seeley*,[17] a plaintiff sued over a trade secret that the defendant produced shortly after the plaintiff's employee resigned and went to work for the defendant. The defendant argued that it had acquired the design of the device through reverse engineering, not through misappropriation via the employee, and the plaintiff failed to provide sufficient evidence to rebut this. However, the court noted that the defendant would be liable if it were shown that it could not have reverse engineered the device in the time available.

*K-2 Ski v. Head Ski*[18] involved a similar analysis, except this case related to the "public observation" defense. The plaintiff sued for misappropriation for the innovative design of skis involving

---

16.  Chicago Lock Co. v. Fanberg, 676 F.2d 400 (9th Cir. 1982).

17.  Kadant, Inc. v. Seeley Mach., Inc., 244 F. Supp. 2d 19 (N.D.N.Y. 2003).

18.  K-2 Ski Co. v. Head Ski Co., Inc., 506 F.2d 471 (9th Cir. 1974).

fiberglass lamination, and the defendant claimed that the knowledge was gained through public observation. Apparently, a supplier to the plaintiff had taken examples of the skis to a trade conference, and while there had shown a ski that was sliced lengthwise, demonstrating the lamination. However, the court concluded that this was not sufficient public display: the defendant and other competitors had not been at that conference, and so the defendant couldn't rely on this demonstration to defeat the misappropriation claim.

Reverse engineering and observation from the public are more serious issues for some types of secrets than for others: the makeup of Lynchburg Lemonade—a mixture of Jack Daniels whiskey, triple sec, sweet and sour mix, and 7-Up—is evident to an experienced bartender upon one taste,[19] whereas the layout of the Du Pont plant that produces methane more cheaply than its competitors is not evident at all from the methane that is produced by it. There is an obvious question that arises from this observation: why is reverse engineering permitted as part of the cut and thrust of competition, whereas other sorts of investigations, such as flying over a methane plant, are not? The dichotomy clearly favors those lucky trade secret owners who do not have to release products containing their secret. It's not self-evident why we should favor one type of secret over the other.

Why we allow reverse engineering but forbid other types of commercial investigation is an example of how mutable trade secret law is, and how poorly theorized it continues to be. Judges consistently make decisions based on their gut, and it's hard to read the opinions in trade secret cases as anything other than *ex post* justifications of the judges' intuitions about the relative rights and wrongs of the plaintiff's and defendant's behaviors.

---

19. See Mason v. Jack Daniel Distillery, 518 So. 2d 130 (Ala. Civ. App. 1987). The issue in this case wasn't reverse engineering, but rather whether the trial court appropriately denied a motion for a directed verdict; however, there was evidence that at least one bartender could tell the ingredients of Lynchburg Lemonade just by tasting it.

## Discontents

Trade secret law is, perhaps, the least visible area of intellectual property law. Cases typically involve commercial disputes between two businesses, and, because of the sensitive and secret nature of the idea in dispute, courts often hear evidence in closed session. Recall what we discussed in the first chapter about how all of intellectual property during the Modern Period was of little interest to the public because it was out of sight, and appeared only to be about allocation of interests by two private parties. Trade secret law conforms with this understanding. As a result, there is little for public interest groups to get their teeth into, and there are few if any calls for reform.

But as we've seen, the cases are thinly disguised moral judgments. There is room for people to wonder about the appropriate reform of this area of law—it's just that it hasn't happened yet.

# SIX

# Related Rights

AL MICHAELS IS A well-known sportscaster, and is as valuable as an old cartoon rabbit. We know this because Disney wanted to create a video game that featured a narrative of its defunct cartoon characters being rescued by Mickey Mouse from the back catalog. One of these characters was "Oswald the Lucky Rabbit," a character that Disney had shelved years ago because of a dispute with a subsidiary of NBC-Universal over who owned the rights. Disney "owns" Al Michaels, but NBC wanted him. So a deal was done: Michaels would move over to NBC and host the coverage of football games, and Oswald would come back to Disney so that he would be able, in due course, to be rescued by Mickey Mouse.[1]

This swap was made possible by the intersection of numerous types of legal rights. We've previously discussed the sorts of rights applicable to Mickey and Oswald: these are cartoon characters, and so copyright and trademark will probably apply to them. But a whole series of other rights also exist in this situation, including publicity rights in Mr. Michaels's persona as well as various types of contractual rights. The Michaels-Oswald story shows that multiple intellectual property regimes interact in interesting and unexpected ways: who knew that copyrights in a cartoon could be exchanged for publicity rights in a human being?

---

1. Richard Sandomir, *Michaels, Traded, Says, Th-Th-That's All, ESPN*, N.Y. TIMES, Feb 10, 2006.

This chapter takes up questions about the interactions among various intellectual property regimes, and it has two functions. First, it discusses the areas of intellectual property law that we haven't yet covered. These are a strange collection, some drawn from state law and some from unusual federal statutes. Reviewing these laws as a group allows us to undertake the important second function of this chapter: to sketch out how intellectual property laws interact with each other. Often, people think that if one area of intellectual property applies to something, then other areas of intellectual property must be excluded. This is not true. Sometimes legislatures and courts express a preference for the application of one type of law—for example, the federal Copyright Act is the only copyright law within the United States, and all state laws that seek to do the same thing as federal copyright law are invalid—but other times multiple laws can coexist and flourish. The latter part of this chapter discusses these interactions and overlaps between intellectual property regimes.

Most overviews of intellectual property have a chapter that does what we're seeking to do in the first part of this one: they recount the weird grab bag of disparate forms that have found their way into the laws of some states and occasionally into federal law. When confronted with the list of different types of protection—including such oddities as the misappropriation of news, the protection of vessel hull designs, or proposed sui generis rights over fashion designs—most authors and students scratch their heads and conclude that laws sometimes come into existence for weird reasons. They also might conclude that these laws share nothing with better-known ones such as copyright, patent, and trademark. However, number of threads run through these odd forms of protection—threads that connect them to the intellectual property regimes we've studied previously. Understanding these threads will make it easier to understand why they exist, and how to apply them.

The first thread is the observation that each of these types of protection arose as a response to a sense of unfairness, typically where someone had created something valuable and another person came along and used it without permission. This intuition—that the defendant is engaged in some inequitable misappropriation or, to put it another way, "reaping where he has not sown"—is at the core of many of the other intellectual property systems we've studied. However, systems such as copyright, patent, and trademark have, over time, been altered by other justifications and by some rigorous policy analysis. The laws we look at here are often poorly thought through, and the justification for their existence is, all too often, something along the lines of "Well, there is value here, and so the person creating that value should be able to get it." In the parts that follow we will examine a number of disparate systems of intellectual property that all stem from the desire to stop the unfairness to the plaintiff, but unlike the federal regimes examined in other chapters, these have never been subjected to much in the way of analysis. The examples of odd categories that we'll examine in the sections that tend to rely on this justification are the misappropriation claim, the protection of idea submissions, and the rights of publicity and celebrity.

The other relevant thread in this chapter is the way that important trade interests are reflected in the intellectual property system. We've seen this in other chapters where we've noted the relentless expansion of regimes such as copyright, patent, and trademark, largely as a result of lobbying by the multibillion-dollar industries that rely on those regimes for their livelihoods. The strange sui generis laws that make up the second part of this chapter—notably the protections for geographical indicators, vessel hull design, semiconductor chip layouts, and fashion designs—all arise because of the interests of various trade groups who have discovered that their products don't fit into one of the standard categories of intellectual property protection, and so have campaigned for unique laws to protect their trade interests. We'll look at how these different laws have come about, the political economies that gave rise to them, and the justifications given for them.

Finally, we'll pick up these threads and examine how these and intellectual property regimes overlap, and why.

## 𝄞 Misappropriation and Related Wrongs

We've already seen how misappropriation is the core infringement of trade secret law. But the idea of misappropriation, or "improper taking," finds expression in at least three other common law intellectual property laws that operate at the periphery of copyright and patent. These are common law misappropriation, trespass to chattels, and state protection for idea submissions.

Common law misappropriation comes from the 1918 decision *International News Service v. Associated Press.*[2] Then, as now, the Associated Press (AP) was a news wire service that gathered stories and circulated them to its newspaper members, who then printed the stories or used them as the basis for their rewritten versions. Newspapers on the East Coast would post AP wire stories on publicly available bulletin boards where employees of the International News Service (INS) could read and then eventually rewrite the stories and circulate them to their members across the United States. Before the invention of the telegraph, this practice didn't affect AP's business, but with the advent of transcontinental communication, AP found its Midwest and West Coast membership dropping because newspapers in those locations could subscribe to the cheaper INS service and get the same information. AP's stories weren't protected by copyright since they were purely factual information and, as we've seen, copyright generally does not extend to facts.

Searching around for a way to stop their competitors, AP fastened on an old common law protection for "hot news," and the Supreme Court upheld AP's claim. In doing so the Court crafted a three-part rule for the tort of misappropriation: (1) the plaintiff has created an intangible asset through the expenditure of effort and with the expectation of profit, (2) the defendant took the asset with comparatively little creative effort and with the expectation of

---

2. 248 U.S. 215 (1918).

profit, and (3) the defendant's taking economically harmed the plaintiff.

Over the years state courts have waxed and waned in their support of the misappropriation tort. These days the trend is against the tort. The *Restatement (Third) on Unfair Competition*, together with various scholars, have posited that the action should never have been recognized in the first place, on the basis that it's vague to the point of indeterminacy, poorly justified by anything other than an inchoate judicial intuition of unfairness, is inadequately theorized, and is generally anticompetitive. Nevertheless, it has been adopted by a number of courts, typically in circumstances where a plaintiff spends a lot to commercialize time-sensitive but noncopyrightable data. The leading opinion these days is *NBA v. Motorola*, a case involving a single-purpose sports-score pager that displayed NBA scores which Motorola had copied and rebroadcast from television and radio results of games in progress. The Second Circuit held that the principle from *International News* survives today, but limited it to misappropriation of "hot news," and not any wider form of misappropriation. The court's amended test for hot news misappropriation requires (1) a plaintiff gathering or generating information at a cost, (2) the information being time sensitive, and (3) the defendant free riding on the plaintiff's efforts, where (4) the defendant is in competition with the plaintiff, and (5) the defendant's free riding reduces the plaintiff's incentive to create the information to the point where the plaintiff's product is threatened. Various other state courts have their own versions of the misappropriation tort; for example, California's take on it is notably broader, protecting the handicapping formula of a golfing association from use even by noncompetitors.[3]

The misappropriation tort reflects the judicial intuition that it's wrong to take someone's intellectual work product, and this

---

3. U.S. Golf Ass'n v. Arroyo Software, 40 U.S.P.Q.2d 1840 (Cal. Super.Ct. 1996), aff'd 69 Cal. App. 4th 607 (1999).

intuition also animates the second common law principle under discussion here, the modern revival of the old tort of trespass to chattels. This principle forbids a person from interfering with another's use of the person's personal property to the point of dispossessing the person of it. The tort was created to take account of situations where the more common tort of conversion was not available, and for many years it was a dead letter on the law books of many states, routinely ignored and of little significance. The tort was revived with the rise of the internet as spamming emerged as a lucrative business practice. Spamming, of course, involves sending unwanted bulk e-mail to e-mail servers in vast quantities, and it causes all manner of problems for Internet Service Providers. They retaliated by suing spammers using the old trespass to chattels actions. Subsequently, other types of internet practices emerged that were susceptible to the action, notably "screen scraping" and "web crawling." These types of cases usually pitted established web players against competitors who appropriated some of the larger company's publicly accessible data. So, an incumbent such as eBay might spend large amounts of money building its site and brand, only to find that competitors could send large numbers of requests to the site via automated "bots" that collected all its information in order to set up competing sites. The incumbents were, obviously, unhappy about this and sued on the basis that the competitors were trespassing on their personal property, that is, their web servers.

The early spamming and scraping cases that applied trespass to chattels tended to come out in favor of the plaintiffs, and for a period it seemed that these types of activities would always result in a loss for the defendant. Courts routinely saw defendants' actions as unfair competition in much the same way as the misappropriation tort, and tended to decide based on how they felt about those actions. The elements of the tort are generally the same in each jurisdiction, and require an intentional dispossession of the plaintiff's server, or an impairment of its ability to operate to the point of being equivalent to dispossession, leading to some kind of harm (although courts have split over the nature and scale of harm necessary). One of the very few cases where the plaintiff lost was *Intel v. Hamidi*,[4] where a disgruntled ex-employee sent e-mails to Intel workers complaining of the company's labor practices and Intel sued for trespass to chattels. The California Supreme Court found against Intel, essentially on freedom of speech grounds. Absent these special considerations, courts have been robust in their condemnation of spammers and scrapers.

The final common law tort that relies explicitly on a conception of unfair taking is the doctrine that is usually called "idea submission." People will often submit valuable ideas to businesses in circumstances where the ideas can't be or haven't been protected by copyright, patent, trade secret, or express contract. Examples include the submission of a treatment for screenplays to a television network, the idea of how to streamline a business process to a manufacturing company, or an idea for a new product line to a consumer-products company. Without some kind of special relationship—such as when ideas are submitted within an employment relationship or as part of an advertised competition—the question facing the court is whether the business owes something to the person contributing the gratuitously offered great idea if the company then goes ahead and uses it. Copyright is clearly not able to help the submitter, since it expressly forbids protection of ideas, and patent is also usually unhelpful because the idea probably won't fulfill the patentability requirements (or it may be simply that the submitter hasn't bothered to apply for a patent). Trade secrets don't work because of the explicit disclosure by the submitter. So if none of these intellectual property laws apply, is the business obliged to pay the submitter?

The common law principle for the protection of the idea submission asks whether the idea is concrete, novel, and useful,[5] and usually the court will look for some kind of basis for imposing liability on the business. Thus, the court will often suggest that a quasi-contractual

---

4. 30 Cal. 4th 1342 (2003).

5. Sellers v. Am. Broadcasting Co., 668 F.2d 1207 (11th Cir. 1982).

relationship existed, or that there was some kind of confidentiality relationship, or that there was some unique property in the idea.

The cases are very unsatisfactory and a large number of them can be rendered down to the fundamental observation that we've seen in the three areas discussed in this section: courts will focus on the actions of the defendant, and base their decisions on some vague notion of fairness in relation to the use of the submission. Open-ended assessments of equity and fairness are notoriously vague and problematic. For all their numerous failings, the great virtue of the federal regimes of intellectual property is that they all have well-articulated justifications and foundations. Misappropriation and state protections for idea submission lack these justifications, and should be avoided, abandoned or overruled.

## Publicity Rights

There was a time, not long ago, when every airport you went through featured a huge poster of Tiger Woods—chipping out of a bunker, lining up at the tee, putting for the trophy—with a tagline that read something like "Go on. Be a Tiger." You won't see those posters anymore, of course, because for a while it was very common to see a picture of Tiger Woods splashed across the yellow press, in some elevated state of distress, a man teetering on the brink of a disaster, hounded by his demons and our paparazzi.[6] Accenture, the management consultant company that ran the "Be a Tiger" campaign, paid Tiger Woods millions for the privilege of associating its name with his. On the other hand, *US Weekly* paid Tiger nothing for its coverage of his plight. This observation captures, as neatly as any other example, the modern day right of publicity, and its strange reflection, the right of privacy.

---

6. Of course for Tiger, as for so many celebrities, it's hard to tell the difference these days.

## History and Theory

The right of publicity is the area of law that manages the different relationships that public figures have with the press, with the commercial licensing of their persona, and with the need of journalists to report on matters of significance, even if that significance is only our prurient interest in a celebrity falling from grace. Although each state's law is different, generally we can say that the state law right of publicity protects public figures from the unauthorized commercial use of their name, likeness, or other recognizable personal attributes in a way that causes them commercial injury. Sometimes the right comes from common law cases, and other times it's written into a statute. States with businesses that rely on celebrity endorsements—think sports, licensing, or entertainment—tend to have the widest protections, and to have them written into statute. California and New York are usually seen as leading the field here, although Indiana has what is commonly recognized as the broadest law—for example, in that state the publicity rights last for one hundred years after the death of the celebrity. It's not clear why. Perhaps there are lots of important dead celebrities in Indiana.

These days, publicity rights are usually conceived of as a special case of misappropriation theory; that is, the justification is largely based on an intuition that it is wrong for others to take without permission, especially if the taking is used for commercial gain. Alternatively some scholars and courts suggest that we can justify publicity rights as an economic incentive, arguing that celebrities spend money and effort in creating a commercially significant persona from which investment they can gain eventual returns by way of endorsements and payment for appearances. If we allow others to free ride on their fame, so this theory goes, then the celebs won't invest the time and effort to create the persona, and this loss is socially wasteful. Although sometimes used, this justification doesn't bear much scrutiny. Honestly, the Kardashians are going to do anything it takes to become famous, whether or not a given state grants publicity rights—after all the most dangerous place in the world is the space between a Kardashian and a television camera. And it's not like there is a public goods problem with celebrities. They're not a scarce social resource; hell, we're drowning in them. Thus, the economic argument is mostly a stalking horse, presented by courts that are in reality motivated mostly by a moral concern about misappropriation. This is to say, courts get unhappy when defendants use celebrity images without permission, and will use pretty much any justification to find against them.

Historically the law was seen as a feature of personal privacy law stemming from a number of different theories and causes, including rights of solitude, reputational rights such as defamation, rights in confidential information, and the commercial rights of persona. This is significant because there is substantial overlap between publicity rights and privacy rights, and they often intersect. A celebrity is generally entitled to the exceedingly modest protection that privacy laws grant; so, just as for the general public, it's impermissible to wiretap Tiger Woods's phone or to disclose his medical records. However, public figures can't invoke privacy laws for matters that are of public significance, and in the event of scandals such as Woods's the press is given broader reach to investigate and report on what would, for you and me, be a purely private matter.

For all that publicity was once seen as part of privacy, these days publicity rights come from the "if there is a value, someone has a right to that value" camp. And the person who has the right to that value is the person whose face is on the billboard.

## Rights

Like most state law rights, there is no registration process for the right of publicity, and the right is created automatically upon celebrities gaining sufficient fame to warrant protection against the commercial appropriation of their persona. The obvious question then is what level of fame does one need to gain the right? The answer unfortunately is less than obvious. It's clear that it covers well-known entertainers and athletes, and there are numerous examples of people in this category who have (more or less success-fully) sued for infringement of their right of publicity: Tom Cruise, Bette Midler, Clint Eastwood, Nicole Kidman, Tom Waits, Elvis Presley, Groucho Marx, Lindsay Lohan, Bela Lugosi, Muhammad Ali, Arnold Palmer, Jim Brown, Vanna White, and numerous others. One of the other names for the right of publicity is the "right of celebrity,"[7] and it's clear that anyone falling into the fluid-and-dubious category of a "celebrity" will be protected, no matter whether that person is an "A-lister" like Madonna or "D-listers" like the cast of *Jersey Shore*. Almost anyone with some kind of recognizable public persona will be protected, as we can see by noting the significance of publicity rights licensing in making video games. Video game producers will license the likenesses of collegiate athletes, soccer stars, NASCAR drivers, rally-driving stars, and even roller derby players, whose images and personas find their way into the modern crop of sports games such as *Madden NFL*, *Need for Speed*, *FIFA Soccer*, and so on.[8]

---

7. The other commonly used term is the "right of personality."

8. For an insight into the process, see the discussion by the lead designer Norb Rozek from developer Frozen Codebase about their discussions with the Women's Fast Track Derby Association, which owns the publicity rights of the skaters within the league:

"The WFTDA was reasonably receptive to our idea, so we traveled down to Austin, Texas for nationals last September and met about a dozen WFTDA high priestesses at 9 a.m. on the outdoor patio of a Mexican restaurant," explains Rozek, "where, Coronas in one hand and laptops in the other, we pitched them our game proposal."

"We approached them," Rozek emphasized. "And they did not mace us."

More than simply an adaptation of the sport, Frozen Codebase has a full license from the WFTDA, which means real teams and real skaters will be available for play, just like the latest *Madden* football or *FIFA* soccer titles from EA Sports. The company is still in the early stages of development though, and only five teams are in the current version. Many more are promised for the final product.

Zac Shipley, *Frozen Codebase Discusses New WFTDA Roller Derby Video Game*, ISTHMUS, July 17, 2008, http://www.thedailypage.com/daily/article.php?article=23248. The licensing of personas is not without issues, since players in college teams have amateur status and so the players' publicity rights are owned by the college: a fact that has caused a major lawsuit at the time of this writing.

The right of publicity does sometimes extend into the realm of noncelebrities.[9] The application of the law to noncelebrities differs depending on the state, and it remains controversial. The relevant non-celebs are generally limited to people who are public or famous figures but who generally don't get endorsement deals. Politicians, civil rights figures such as Martin Luther King, and even John Dillinger the bank robber have invoked the right of publicity to stop the unauthorized use of their image in various contexts. There is an appreciable difference in the outcome of cases where courts are faced with cases of publicity rights applied to noncelebrities, depending on the underlying theory to which the court subscribes. Consider a case of a politician seeking to stop the unauthorized use of her image on a billboard, by, let's say, the seller of used cars. If the court subscribes to the utilitarian/law-and-economics view of the publicity right, then the politician should lose, because unlike "real" celebrities, politicians didn't invest effort in creating the persona, and theirs is a public office. However, if the court applies misappropriation theory, then this type of use will usually be forbidden because the defendant should not be selling its product by "stealing" attributes of the politician. States differ markedly in their approach to quasi-celebrities, and it's hard to make too many generally applicable statements about how members of this group are or will be treated by the courts.

The final category of potential plaintiffs is that comprised of non-famous people. There is very little case law on this subject, although every now and again a scholar will argue that publicity rights should apply to the ordinary citizen. This argument is almost always derived from the misappropriation theory, on the basis that ordinary folks have as much to lose from the abuse of their image as celebrities. However, in virtually every jurisdiction the argument is a non-starter.

---

9. Which is why we won't use the expression "right of celebrity" here, although many courts do so.

Publicity rights clearly protect the name and likeness of the famous plaintiff, and can extend far beyond these aspects into other features of their commercial persona. Thus, the bourbon-with-a-shot-of-gravel voice of Tom Waits—described by a court as "how you'd sound if you drank a quart of bourbon, smoked a pack of cigarettes and swallowed a pack of razor blades . . . late at night . . . [a]fter not sleeping for three days"—has been protected from a sound-alike imitation in an advertisement, as has the distinctive voice of Bette Midler.[10] Courts have forbidden look-alike actors from impersonating famous celebrities,[11] and, in one storied case, an advertisement featuring a robotic version of Vanna White, the *Wheel of Fortune* letter turner, was held to be an actionable infringement of her publicity rights because the robot was recognizably her "likeness."

Although many states protect rights of publicity in ways that are broadly consistent, one notable area of difference is the treatment of the rights after death. A small number of states protect the rights only during the life of the famous person. Although the reasoning differs slightly, the main reasons for limiting the right include the theory that publicity rights are related to privacy rights—which expire once we die—and the theory that the public deserves to be able to exploit these rights once the person is dead. Most states allow publicity rights to continue after death for periods ranging from twenty to one hundred years. This seems to have something to do with the misappropriation theory: state legislatures (and occasionally judges) seem to believe that publicity rights are some kind of property that survives the death of the celebrity. The period of protection chosen by any given state's legislature or court system is largely random but, weirdly enough it seems to be related to the standard term of copyright protection, which is, as we've seen,

---

10. Waits v. Frito Lay, 978 F.2d 1093 (9th Cir. 1992); Midler v. Ford Motor Co., 849 F.2d 460 (9th Cir. 1988).

11. See e.g. Allen v National Video, Inc., 610 F.Supp. 612 (S.D.N.Y. 1985).

life of the author plus seventy years. Why this should be the appropriate term of celebrity rights is a mystery that surpasses understanding. Indeed why the copyright term should be life-plus-seventy is also a mystery. Some have said that the period for both copyright and publicity rights is connected to the idea that artists or celebrities should be able to provide for themselves and for their children. But honestly, it's arbitrary and path-dependent: some legislator once pulled a number out of a hat, a whole lot of other people said that that number seemed reasonable, and that was the end of the analysis. We've been stuck with these numbers ever since, for no principled reasons other than "We've always done it that way" or "Other states do it that way."

## Defenses

The only significant defense to a publicity right is the First Amendment. It's not hard to see how these sorts of issues come up: recall the example given above about the politician whose image was used on a billboard. There's no freedom of speech issue in the situation where the use is a commercial appropriation by a used car dealer, but a more plausible First Amendment claim can be made of the political use of the politician's image by a political competitor. This type of use will almost always be permitted on the basis that free speech, especially political free speech, is inevitably going to trump personality rights.

But not all cases involving personality rights are so clear-cut as political ads, and courts are often asked to balance competing commercial claims in speech and publicity. In the only publicity rights case ever to reach the Supreme Court, *Zacchini v. Scripps-Howard Broadcasting*,[12] the issue was between a man who made his living being shot out of a cannon and a local television station that filmed

---

12.  433 U.S. 562 (1977).

his act and broadcast it.[13] Mr. Zacchini claimed violation of his publicity rights under Ohio law, and the television station claimed a defense based on the First Amendment. The court agreed with the plaintiff, basing its reasoning on the fact that the station had shown all of Mr. Zacchini's act, destroying his ability to charge admission for it. It was also very significant that the speech which the defendant claimed as protected by the First Amendment was highly commercial.

Various different tests have been used to deal with cases where there are competing commercial claims to speech rights and publicity rights. The Tenth Circuit Court of Appeals, deciding a case under the Oklahoma statute, adopted a "balancing test" that weighs the magnitude of the speech restriction against the state governmental interest in protecting the publicity right.[14] The Missouri Supreme Court's "predominant use" test refuses protection for a defendant merely if the predominant use of the plaintiff's persona is commercial.[15] The California Supreme Court, on the other hand, has taken a leaf out of the copyright jurisprudence for the fair use defense, and grants First Amendment protection for transformative uses: it asks if the defendant has transformed the persona of the plaintiff in some socially valuable, newly expressive way.[16] It's not hard to come up with fact patterns that will have different outcomes depending on which jurisdiction the action is brought in, but then again, each state's publicity rights law differs greatly from each other, so slight variations in their treatment of the relationship to freedom of speech shouldn't come as a huge surprise.

---

13. Yes, I know. Why the Supreme Court decided to take this case, of all possible cases, remains a head-scratcher to pretty much anyone who has ever looked at it.

14. Cardtoons L.C. v. Major League Baseball Players Ass'n, 95 F.3d 959 (10th Cir. 1996).

15. Doe v. TCI Cablevision, 110 S.W. 3d 363 (Mo. 2003).

16. Comedy III Prods., Inc. v. Gary Saderup, Inc., 25 Cal. 4th 387 (2001).

## 〰 Sui Generis Regimes

The strange collection of rights described in the previous sections represents the attempts by state legislators and judges to protect individuals and groups from types of appropriations that seem unfair, whether or not the protections afforded make a whole lot of sense. The rights discussed in this section are the federal equivalent of those state laws. Like state laws against misappropriation, say, or those protecting idea submission, it's hard to understand exactly why the design of boat hulls or semiconductors merit special federal protection, yet this is what has happened. The reason for these unusual protections is twofold: first, there needs to be a lobbying group with enough clout to get a law through Congress, and second, there needs to be a lacuna in the existing intellectual property regimes that means that certain types of creative people feel that they are getting the short end of the stick. The regimes we'll look at here—protections for boat hulls, semiconductor layouts, and fashion designs—all involve variations on these two features.

Federal protection for the design of boat hulls comes about because of *Bonito Boats v. Thunder Craft Boats*,[17] a Supreme Court case that struck down Florida's protection for boat hull designs, ruling that it was preempted by federal patent law.[18] The lobbyists went to work, and in due course the Vessel Hull Design Protection Act was passed by Congress. The act makes up part of Chapter 13 of the federal Copyright Act.[19] Chapter 13 is the chapter that extends to designs generally, but for most practical purposes the chapter provides mainly for the sui generis protection of boat hulls. The protection extends only to designs that are original (not to those with a commonplace shape or simple variations on commonplace shapes), and those that are not dictated solely by utilitarian considerations. The period of

---

17. Bonito Boats, Inc. v. Thunder Craft Boats, Inc., 489 U.S. 141 (1989).

18. We'll look at preemption in the next section.

19. Codified at 17 U.S.C. §§ 1301–32.

protection is only for ten years, and the exclusive rights granted by this law are similar to the rights in patent law—to make, have made, import, sell or use in trade anything that embodies the protected design. Infringement is, of course, the unauthorized practicing of any of the exclusive rights, and like most intellectual property regimes, there are a number of contributory infringement forms. The chapter provides for a number of defenses that make a defendant's life slightly easier: notably a defense for infringing use without knowledge, and infringing acts done in the ordinary course of business.

Equally unusual is the Semiconductor Chip Protection Act (SCPA) of 1984, a response to the rise in economic significance of the U.S. semiconductor chip business during the 1970s and 1980s. The industry became concerned that neither copyright nor patent would protect the large investment necessary to produce the chip designs. Patent protection was unsatisfactory because it would apply only to a small number of especially novel chip designs. Copyright probably wasn't going to apply because the mask work— the pictorial design that is burned into the silicon of the chip—is arguably a utilitarian work, and thus, as we've seen, is precluded from copyright protection. The SCPA was passed and codified into sections 901 through 914 of the Copyright Act. It provides for exclusive rights that are very similar to copyright, and it retains some familiar copyright principles. However, it differs from copyright in some important respects. For example it precludes protection for designs that are staple, commonplace, or familiar to the industry, a limitation that is inspired more by patent's novelty principle than copyright's much weaker originality principle. Also, it provides for a specific defense of reverse engineering if the purpose of the reverse engineering is to understand the concepts underlying the mask work. This is a defense utterly foreign to copyright law, but which provides a kind of balance that allows chip designers time to gain a lead in the market while allowing competitors to inspect the designs for the purposes of improved competition and innovation.

The final sui generis regime worth considering is the Innovative Design Protection and Piracy Prevention Bill, which was before

Congress at the time of this writing.[20] It's not yet law, and may never be; however, lobbyists for fashion designers have for many years introduced various bills seeking to provide sui generis protections for those parts of fashion designs that fall outside copyright and patent protection.[21] The current proposal places a high threshold for protection and would only protect original elements of a piece of clothing, or the original placement of items on an article of clothing, that provide a unique, distinguishable, nontrivial and nonutilitarian variation over prior designs for similar types of articles. The law also has heightened pleading standards and a very short period of protection—three years. Proponents argue that this will stop the unrestrained copying of fashion designs by "knockoff" outlets such as Forever 21 or Zara, actions which many find moral repugnant. Opponents argue that the fashion industry is notably innovative without this additional protection and suggest that this reform will just create a litigation drag on small players. Only time will tell whether the law will pass, and which of the proponents and opponents are correct.

These sui generis regimes shed light on a number of interesting theoretical and practical aspects of intellectual property policy that have been at the heart of this book. First, they demonstrate that intellectual property is often less about theoretical arguments over adequate protections and the level of innovation in society and more about the particular power of a given lobbying group at certain times. Little evidence was provided at the time the protection passed that boat hull designers were particularly susceptible to copying, or that, more saliently, we would have a complete absence of novel boat hull designs should we fail to accord them these special rights. Related to this, we see that groups of people who think

---

20. 111th Congress (2009–10), S.3728.IS.

21. Within fashion, copyright protection only applies to the pictorial designs printed on fabric, and patent is limited to design patents that are only really significant for certain types of shoe designs, and otherwise are used rarely.

of themselves as creative but whose work product happens not to be protected by current intellectual property regimes—think fashion designers—will seek reforms favorable to them on the basis that they, of all creators, are being discriminated against. Perhaps the best way of understanding this is that intellectual property is an ideology. Those arguing for it believe in it without having to justify its value, and those without it feel the absence of it pressing on them as a sore wound. Relying on these principles is a really poor way to make law; but knowing that this is the reality of the process helps us understand how intellectual property law is actually created, and why.

Second, these regimes demonstrate that there is a role for the tailoring of protection within the intellectual property system. Each of these regimes takes the basic principles of copyright and patent and then modifies them to try to balance the special needs of the industry and society. One of the scholarly concerns often expressed about the copyright and patent systems is that, at their core, they are unitary forms of protection that treat all works and inventions the same, without considering that lesser or modified forms of protection might be more socially beneficial. Thus, many have asked why copyright should protect computer software for the same period as a sculpture or book when the life cycle and value of software is so much shorter. Equally, there is evidence that patent protection in its current strong form is probably necessary for the production of modern pharmaceuticals, but is problematic for the computer industry. The sui generis regimes demonstrate that tailoring is possible, even if it is difficult to do.

## ⅕ Intersections

We've explored a large range of intellectual property regimes, both in this and previous chapters. It shouldn't come as a surprise that these regimes intersect in interesting and difficult ways, and in this section we'll cover two ways—preemption and channeling—in which courts and legislatures seek to mediate the relationship between the differing regimes. The first of these, preemption, deals with the relationship between state laws and federal laws, while the second, channeling, covers the relationship among various laws. Into this latter category we'll also fit some observations about how intellectual property owners extend their rights, whether created under federal, state, or common law authority.

## Preemption

Preemption refers generally to the principle enshrined in the Supremacy Clause of the Constitution that a federal law supplants or preempts a state law where the laws are in conflict. Preemption issues can occur, in theory, between any federal and state intellectual property laws; however, as a practical matter the two main preemption battlegrounds are between federal copyright law and state laws relating to misappropriation and publicity rights, and between federal patent law and various state intellectual property laws.

Preemption relating to copyright is straightforward. Section 301 of the Copyright Act explicitly deals with preemption of state rights that are the equivalent of federal copyright laws, and provides that a state law is preempted if the right protected by the state law is equivalent to the exclusive rights granted by copyright, and if the state right relates to a work of authorship that fits within the subject matter of the Copyright Act. Both elements must be satisfied, and so if the state grants a different right, or if the intangible product wouldn't be protected by copyright, then there is no preemption. As an example, a state law that grants rights which are different from the five exclusive copyright rights will not be preempted, nor would a law that protects certain types of unfixed expression, certain types of unexpressed ideas, or works otherwise not covered by the Copyright Act. The test for equivalency in the first limb of the test is very difficult to assess, largely because there is no agreed definition of what we mean by "equivalent rights," but there are other interpretive difficulties with section 301 because its legislative history is sparse and the drafting is problematic. Although it's a slight overstatement, a good rule of thumb is to ask whether the state rights and remedies are qualitatively different from copyright; if so, the state law will not be preempted, and courts have typically upheld state laws that add some additional right or element. Thus, rights of publicity are usually free of preemption difficulties because the persona of a celebrity is usually not fixed and therefore not eligible for copyright protection. This analysis becomes a little more complicated where the relevant attribute of the celebrity persona is fixed in a copyrightable form, as for example where the celebrity's face is in a photo or the defendant is copying the voice of a famous musician who sells musical recordings. The relevant distinction is to ask whether the publicity right claim is merely a copyright infringement claim in different form. So, in *Laws v. Sony Music Entertainment*,[22] a recording artist sued Sony claiming that the use of her voice in a sample used in a recording by Jennifer Lopez and LL Cool J was a misappropriation of her right of publicity under Californian state laws.[23] The court held that the plaintiff's claim was preempted by the Copyright Act because the claim was based on the use of the actual recording, not some other intangible aspect of the singer's persona. This can be distinguished from the *Tom Waits* case mentioned above where the publicity rights claims were not preempted because there was a copying of the celebrity's vocal persona, not a single copyright work.

Other state laws are susceptible to similar types of analysis, and claims in misappropriation are particularly susceptible to invalidation where the plaintiff is seeking to use the misappropriation tort to bring a copyright action in disguise. For example, in *Mayer v. Josiah Wedgewood*[24] the plaintiff claimed misappropriation against

---

22. Laws v. Sony Music Entm't Inc., 448 F.3d 1134 (9th Cir. 2006).

23. CALIF. CIV. CODE § 3344(a).

24. Mayer v. Josiah Wedgewood & Sons, Ltd., 601 F. Supp. 1523 (S.D.N.Y. 1985).

the Wedgewood pottery company for a snowflake design that had, for various reasons, fallen into the public domain and was unprotected by copyright law. The court concluded that the work was exactly the type that sat within copyright's subject matter, and the rights claimed by the plaintiff were no different in nature from the exclusive rights in copyright, notably the reproduction right. Thus the claim was pre-empted by section 301. This can be contrasted with the "hot news" cases where misappropriation wasn't preempted: you can't copyright facts, and so the second limb of section 301 won't apply.

The overlap between patent and state intellectual property laws is another main arena where preemption is an issue. Unlike copyright, there is no specific provision in the Patent Act dealing with preemption, and so courts apply general preemption principles. Most state laws that seek to protect ideas have been found to be preempted by the federal Patent Act. There were a number of early attempts by plaintiffs to use state unfair competition laws to protect material that had failed to meet the patentability standard: in *Sears, Roebuck*[25] and in *Compco*[26] the Supreme Court struck down attempts to use state unfair competition law to protect a lamp and a fluorescent lighting fixture (respectively) that had previously been found unpatentable. The court concluded that the states may not, under some other law such as that forbidding unfair competition, give protection of a kind that clashes with the objectives of the federal patent laws. Another similar preemption case, *Bonito Boats*, found that Florida's attempts to create a special innovation law for the protection of boat hulls was preempted by the patent law—a finding that, in time, led to the remarkable amendment to the Copyright Act by the Vessel Hull Design Protection Act that we discussed in the section above.

Generally, state trade secret laws co-exist happily with federal patent law, although there are two patent policies that provide

---

25. Sears, Roebuck & Co. v. Stiffel Co., 376 U.S. 225 (1964).

26. Compco Corp. v. Day-Brite Lighting, Inc., 376 U.S. 234 (1964).

a potential arena for conflict: the policy promoting disclosure of the invention, and the policy that insufficiently inventive ideas should remain in the public domain. Both policies have been the subject of preemption litigation that eventually concluded that there was no conflict between the laws. Because the secret may never be revealed, it appears that trade secret laws work against the patent policy of promoting disclosure, since one would think that some inventors would choose to use trade secret laws even when they could use patent law. But the Supreme Court in *Kewanee Oil v. Bicron*[27] concluded that concerns about the disclosure policy did not merit a finding of preemption because, inter alia, inventors are unlikely to choose this approach—trade secret protection is much weaker than patent protection, after all—and because of the beneficial effects of allowing trade secret protection for unpatentable inventions and doubtfully patentable inventions. The other implicated patent policy of keeping unpatentable inventions in the public domain is also consistent with trade secret law because a trade secret is never in the public domain until it is released. Thus, it's not the case that the public is deprived of some invention that it otherwise had until the creation of the trade secret law. Even where a trade secret idea falls into the public domain—such as when a trade secret is reverse engineered—courts have held that upholding the obligation of a licensee to keep the idea a secret or pay royalties on it is consistent with the patent law, because the enforcement of this only applies against a single licensee or defendant, and not the world at large.[28]

## Overlaps and Channeling

Preemption isn't the only legal doctrine that governs the interactions between intellectual property regimes, although it's the easiest

---

27. Kewanee Oil Co. v. Bicron Corp., 416 U.S. 470 (1974).

28. Aronson v. Quick Point Pencil Co., 440 U.S. 1096 (1979).

to understand and provides the clearest division between different ones. Outside preemption, the analysis is much more complicated and the best that we can hope for is to understand some general overarching ideas that often arise in cases, but which can hardly be said to be controlling.

First, we need to recognize that there is no general principle that says that only one type of intellectual property can apply to any given thing. It's very common, for example, for a plaintiff to plead and win an intellectual property case based on the dual protections of copyright and trademark, or patent and trademark. As we've seen, copyright and patent law arise out of a different normative justification from trademark law—providing an incentive for production versus reducing consumer confusion—and so different injuries can occur through the infringement of the different types of intellectual property. Take the example of *Nintendo v. Dragon Pacific*, where the defendant sold games cartridges containing the plaintiff's games.[29] Because the games were copyrighted, and the names of them were trademarked, the defendant was liable for $65,000 in statutory damages for copyright infringement and $62,000 for actual damages for trademark infringement (which were then trebled for willful violations). The defendant appealed the award on the basis that this amounted to a "double recovery" for the same violation, but the court disagreed. The harms were quite distinct, said the court: the defendant could have sold the games without labeling them as coming from the plaintiff, which would be a copyright infringement but not a trademark infringement, or it could have sold its own games under the NINTENDO mark, which would be a trademark infringement but not a copyright infringement.

There are simply thousands of examples of multiple protection such as these. The NBC chimes function both as a sound trademark and a copyrighted sound recording. HARRY POTTER is a trademark

---

29.  40 F.3d 1007 (9th Cir. 1994).

applied to all manner of goods and also happens to be a character in a series of copyrighted books. Sildenafil citrate is a patented drug that is marketed under the trademark VIAGRA. And so on.

However, not all multiple protections are appropriate, and occasionally courts and legislatures will invoke an intellectual property "channeling" doctrine that pushes the object into only one form of intellectual property. Preemption is a particularly strong example of this, as it mediates between state and federal systems and denies the state any role in protecting copyrighted works. Another example is the automatic channeling that takes place between trade secret and patent, based on disclosure of the invention. If you want to keep the invention secret, then you cannot obtain a patent, and vice versa.

A similar process of channeling takes place from time to time between federal systems. For example, the functionality doctrine in trademark channels protection into patent law for those features of a mark that provide non-reputational advantages, such as the spring-loaded sign in the *TrafFix* case. The operative concern here is to stop rights-holders from creating a perpetual patent through the backdoor of trademark. This problem also arises sometimes in relation to the interface between copyright and trademark. Thus, in *Dastar v. Twentieth Century Fox* the Supreme Court rejected the attempt of the plaintiff to use a trademark-based reverse passing-off claim to extend copyright protection for a work that was no longer protected.[30] The issue arose when a television series from Fox Studios that had fallen into the public domain was repackaged by another company and marketed without attribution to Fox. The Court concluded that trademark couldn't be used to extend the life of the copyright. Although the Court's analysis was tortured and unclear, the motivation for the channeling seems pretty clearly to have been a desire not to allow a perpetual quasi-copyright through the trademark system.

---

30. Dastar Corp. v. Twentieth Century Fox Film Corp., 539 U.S. 23 (2003).

Numerous other examples exist: attempts within various pieces of legislation to decide whether sculptures should be protected as copyrighted works, designs, or marks; patent office policies that rules for board games should be protected as copyrighted works not as patentable inventions; and the interactions between state publicity rights and the section 2(c) Lanham Act bars on registration of trademarks that identify people. In general however there is no overarching principle that allocates different sorts of intangible objects into one category or the other. For every court that, like Judge Calabresi, proclaims "intellectual property owners should not be permitted to recategorize one form of intellectual property as another,"[31] we find another court that cheerfully permits it.

We can conclude by noting that in most situations, multiple forms of protection will be permitted. Intellectual property rightsholders have large incentives to gain as much protection as possible, and this means that they will—among other strategies—create multiple patents over similar technology, split patents up into continuing and divisional applications, use a suite of trademarks to stop others from using similar marks, and arbitrage protection across multiple forms of intellectual property. Occasionally this will fall afoul of some specific channeling doctrine, but usually not.

The main theme of this book has been about expansion of intellectual property rights, and channeling provides very little in the way of a brake on the one-way ratchet of intellectual property expansion.

---

31. Chosun Int'l, Inc. v. Chrisha Creations, 413 F.3d 325, 327 n.2 (2d Cir. 2005).

# Index